The Summerhill Story

The 1992 Centennial

Frank P. Alcamo

*To Albert & Mary
with enjoyable reading
Frank P. Alcamo*

The A. G. Halldin Publishing Co., Inc.
Indiana, PA
15701-0667

The publication of this book
was funded by the Summerhill Borough Council
Sales and distribution is a project
of the Summerhill Women's Club

Borough Officials: Seated: (left to right): Vince Kitchick, street commissioner; Jill Rosporski; Dennis Cobaugh, mayor. Standing: Dan Penatzer, secretary-treasurer; Chuck Tremel; Jack Bodenschatz, vice president; Ralph Hamilton; Eugene Wess; Woody McCall; Dennis Stofko, solicitor. Absent: Larry Wilburn, president. (Credit: Cindy Rosemas)

ISBN 0-935648-37-2
© 1992 Frank P. Alcamo
    All rights to this book are reserved. No part of this publication may be reproduced, stored in a retrieval system, or transmitted, in any form or any means, electronic, mechanical, photocopying, recording or otherwise, without the prior written permission of Frank P. Alcamo.

LOGO -- The above logo which will be used on all paraphernalia associated with the borough's centennial celebration is the creation of Jean Gallardy and Mike Pearson.

Table of Contents

About the Author v
Acknowledgements vi
Foreword vii

Chapters

1	Overcoming The Wilderness	1
2	Developing New Boundaries And Places	12
3	Conquering A New Frontier By Rail And Water	21
4	The People Who Made The Early Progress	28
5	Summerhill Grows Near The Coal Industry	38
6	Time To Show Independence	47
7	Getting In And Out, Near And Far	70
8	Who's Doing Business Here?	93
9	The New Commercial Look	121
10	The Town's Religious Needs	156
11	Is There A Doctor In Town?	177
12	Do I Have-Ta Go To School?	185
13	Nothing Like An Organized Group	212
14	The Council Beat Goes On	242
15	Providing Community Services	268
16	Potpourri	279
17	This Is Summerhill	315
	Bibliography	x

About The Author

Frank P. Alcamo is the author of two other local histories: The Windber Story (1983) and the South Fork Story (1987). This has been one of his volunteer services since retirement as Windber Area High School principal in 1981. His other services include free income tax return preparations, instructor for Cambria County's other volunteer preparers and speaker for the Internal Revenue Service's outreach program.

Currently, he serves on the board of directors for the Johnstown Area Heritage Association, Cambria County Historical Society, CBW Schools Federal Credit Union, Mid-State Auto Club and AAA Southern Pennsylvania.

Born at 214 Lake Street, South Fork, on May 25, 1920, the only child of Carmelo and Antonia (Trifiro) Alcamo, he graduated from the former South Fork High School in 1938. He earned a bachelor of science degree at Indiana(Pa.) State Teachers College in 1942 and a master of education degree at Pennsylvania State University in 1954.

During World War II, he served as a Lt (j. g.) with the U. S. Naval Reserves. He taught mathematics and science at Wilmore, South Fork-Croyle and Triangle Area High Schools before accepting the administrative position at Windber in 1962.

He and his wife Josephine, a former elementary teacher at South Fork and Windber, reside in Upper Yoder Township, Johnstown, Pa.

Acknowledgements

This publication is a cooperative effort of many: Stella DeLozier who convinced the author to volunteer his services, secured financial backing from Summerhill Borough Council, served as the collector of photographs and information and got the involvement of the women's club to sell and distribute the book.

Jay Harshberger who was the first to share his collection of newspaper clippings, notes and historical documents. He also borrowed scrapbooks from friends outside the area.

Sarah Leishman, curator of the Cambria County Historical Society, who furnished materials from the society's files along with the use of its historical newspapers and library.

Richard Burket, executive director of the Johnstown Area Heritage Association, who assisted with the photographic collection.

Daniel Penatzer and John "Woody" McCall who furnished the available borough council minutes and other governmental information.

My wife Jo who provided advice, support and encouragement and did the proof reading.

Cindy Rosemas who wrote a number of articles for the Portage Dispatch to urge the cooperation of its readers.

Father Ronald Bodenschatz who spent an evening and left three scrapbooks detailing the community's history and the Whitestone Park experience.

J. David Kline and his secretary, Mary Lou Girard, who helped locate the school reports in the Intermediate Unit's archives.

And, the many others, too numerous to list, who helped with the research.

Foreword

This history is written to commemorate the 100th anniversary of Summerhill as a borough. But, this small Pennsylvania borough's history goes back almost 200 years when Thomas and Barbara Croyle came over the mountain from Snake Spring in Bedford County. Their grist mill attracted area farmers from the surrounding wilderness and soon this locale was known as Croyle's Mill.

When Cambria County was established in 1804, the commissioners financed the first county public road from Ebensburg to Croyle's Mill.

When the Commonwealth of Pennsylvania decided to connect its canal systems between Pittsburgh and Philadelphia with a portage railroad over the Allegheny Mountains, this village was renamed Halfway. The route from Johnstown coursed through narrow, twisted valleys and mountains and emerged in the relatively level terrain of the Summerhill area. The journey from here was a continuous climb via a succession of inclines. And, since this area was about midway between Johnstown and Cresson, it was renamed Halfway.

The name Summer Hill was first used by the U. S. Postal Service for its post office located here in 1840.

The Pennsylvania Railroad changed the face of the community by 1854 as it cut through land donated by the Croyles. The right-of-way established a line which divided present day Summerhill into two sections that residents labeled uptown and downtown. A bridge over the tracks and a subway under the road bed later tied the two sections together.

Two highways practically form the borders for the borough. Route 219 is the upper border and Route 53 constitutes the lower boundary.

The entire southwestern part of Pennsylvania was in Cumberland County in 1755. But, by 1771, most of the land was in Bedford County. When the Croyles settled here in 1794, the land was located in Bedford County but, a year later, their claim was recorded in the newly-organized Somerset County. Soon thereafter, 1804, Croyles' property was located in Cambria County as part of Conemaugh Township.

By 1810, Summerhill (then also known as Somerhill) Township was taken from part of Conemaugh Township. The next change occurred in 1858 when Summerhill Township was subdivided and gave up part of its territory to a new township named to honor Thomas and Barbara Croyle.

Thus, Summerhill's history is linked with all these earlier names and territorial subdivisions.

It is only by recalling this past that a better appreciation of this 100th anniversary is possible.

In no way can this work be regarded a complete accounting of these years. Rather, it represents a collection of documentations found in borough, school and county records, local newspaers, earlier historical writings, and information shared by numerous individuals.

It is hoped this history will become a valued volume that preserves this local heritage.

Summerhill

If by any chance on some nice bright day
You journey 'mid Pennsylvania's hills so green
Do check your map and wend your way
To Summerhill -- a welcome there -- so serene.

It's a little hamlet, but yet a very big one
You'll breathe its spirit in the freshening air
Its heart will reach out to meet -- to greet you
Its hope and worries very soon you'll want to share

Now what makes this town a different place?
It's the people, a special kind of folk -- how true
The nicest people in the world, the homey kind you love
You'll belong to them always, and they'll belong to you.

    --Written by Agnes Doyle, a New York resident
    1961.

Bibliography

Books

AAA Western Tour Book. Washington, D. C: American Automobile Association, 1939.

Alcamo, Frank P., **The South Fork Story: The First 100 Years.** Indiana, Pa: The A. G. Halldin Publishing Co., 1987.

Alcamo, Frank P., **The Windber Story: A 20th Century Model Pennsylvania Coal Town.** N. p.: n. p., 1983.

Alexander, Edwin P., **On The Mainline: The Pennsylvania Railroad In The 19th Century.** New York: Clarkson N. Potter, Inc., 1971.

Baumgardner, Mahlon and Hoenstine, Floyd, **The Allegheny Old Portage Railroad 1834-1854.** Ebensburg: n. p., 1952.

Biographical And Portrait Cyclopedia Of Cambria County. Philadelphia: Union Publishing Co., 1896.

Caldwell, J. A., **Illustrated And Historical Combination Atlas Of Cambria County From Surveys Of J. A. Caldwell.** Philadelphia: Atlas Publishing Co., 1890.

Cambria County Historical Society, **Sesquicentennial Cambria County 1804-1954.** Johnstown: The Johnstown Tribune Publishing Co., 1954

Cambria County Medical Association, **Medical Comment In Commemoration Of The 80th Anniversary Of The Cambria County Medical Society 1852-1932.** Johnstown: William H. Raab and Son, Inc., 1932.

Chapman, Thomas J., **The Valley Of The Conemaugh.** Altoona, Pa.: McCrum & Dern, Printers, 1865.

Croyle, Wallace, **My Search For The Truth.** N. p.: n. p.

Degen, Paula and Carl, **Johnstown Flood Of 1889: The Tragedy Of The Conemaugh.** Eastern National Park & Monument Assoc., 1984.

Donehoo, George P., **Pennsylvanika -- A History, Volume IV.** New York: Lewis Historical Publishing Co., 1926.

Espenshade, A. Howay, **Pennsylvania Place Names.** Harrisburg, Pa: Evangelical Press, 1925.

Gable, John E., **History Of Cambria County, Volumes I & II.** Indianapolis: Historical Publishing Co., 1926.

Hay, George, **The Medical Comment, Cambria County Medical Society 1852-1952.** Johnstown: William H. Raab and Son, Inc., 1952.

Inventory Of The County Archives Of Pennsylvania, Cambria County, Board of County Commissioners. Ebensburg: Archives Publishing Co. of Pa., Inc., 1950.

Johnstown Branch American Association of University Women, **Women Of Cambria County.** Indiana, Pa: The A. G. Halldin Pub. Co., 1988.

Official Automobile Blue Book 1918, Volume 3. New York: Automobile Blue Book Publishing Co., 1918.

Portage Area Historical Society, **Portrait Of A Town: Portage, Pennsylvania 1890-1990**. Indiana, Pa: The A. G. Halldin Publishing Co., 1990

Preuss, Arthur, **A Dictionary Of Secret And Other Societies**. St. Louis, Mo: B. Herder Book Co., 1924.

Rohrbeck, Benson W., **Cambria's Trolleys**. West Chester, Pa: Ben Rohrbeck Traction Publications, 1976.

Schmidt, Alvin J., **Fraternal Organizations**. Westport, Conn: Greenwood Press, 1980.

Smith, Helene and Swetnam, George, **A Guidebook To Historic Western Pennsylvania**. Pittsburgh, Pa: University of Pittsburgh Press, 1991.

Storey, Henry Wilson, **History Of Cambria County With Genealogical Memoirs, Volumes I, II & III**. New York: Lewis Publishing Co., 1907.

Walkinshaw, Lewis Clark, **Annals of Southwestern Pennsylvania, Volumes III & IV**. New York: Lewis Historical Publishing Co., 1939.

Weber, Denise Dusza, **Delano's Domain: A History Of Warren Delano's Mining Towns Of Vintondale, Wehrum And Claghorn, Volume I 1789-1930**. Indiana, Pa: The A. G. Halldin Publishing Co., 1991.

Wickersham, J. P., **Pennsylvania Report Of The Superintendent Of Public Instruction**. Harrisburg, Pa: Commonwealth of PA, 1879.

Newspapers

Cambria Dispatch -- Portage, Pennsylvania
Cambria Freeman -- Ebensburg, Pennsylvania
Cambria Herald -- Ebensburg, Pennsylvania
Democrat And Sentinel -- Ebensburg, Pennsylvania
Johnstown Democrat -- Johnstown, Pennsylvania
Johnstown Tribune-Democrat -- Johnstown, Pennsylvania
Johnstown Weekly Tribune -- Johnstown, Pennsylvania
Portage Dispatch -- Portage, Pennsylvania

Other References

Ambroe, Maude, **Early Times In Forest Hills School District**, Dunlo, Pa. **Cambria County Deed Books**, Recorder of Deeds, Courthouse, Ebensburg, Pa.

Cambria County Inventory Of Historical Sites, Cambria County Planning Commission, Court House Annex, Ebensburg, 1975-76.

Conemaugh Country, The History & Genealogy Of Cambria County, Volume 1, No. 2, September 1981, Southwest PA Genealogical Services, Laughlintown, Pa.

Davis, W. R., **Pioneer Trails**. Pamphlet published by Cambria County Historical Society, Ebensburg, Pa.

Demographic Data 1984, Cambria County Planning Commission, Ebensburg, Pa.

History Of Parish Of St. Augustine, St. Augustine, PA., New Guide Publishing Co., Inc., 1922.

History Of Summerhill 1810-1966. Summerhill Women's Club project published in mimeographed form.

Leiden, Mrs. Robert, **Joseph Long 1808-1882: His Ancestors And Descendents.**

Mitchell, Lawrence C., **A Historical Geography Of Cambria County, Pennsylvania.** Master of Arts Thesis in Geography, Michigan State University, 1965.

McCormick, John, **History Of Cambria County,** unpublished paper, 1902

McCormick, John, **Souvenir Of Reunion And History Of St. Bartholomev's Church, Wilmore, PA.** Johnstown: Johnstown Tribune Publishing Co., 1909.

McCormick, John, **Summerhill And Ehrenfeld.** History published in Johnstown Daily Tribune, August 30, 1906.

Pennsylvania County Data Book, 1987.

Pennsylvania Railroad Guide of 1855.

Pennsylvania Railroad List of Stations and Sidings 1945.

Pennsylvania's Roads Before The Automobile, Historic Pennsylvania Leaflet No. 33, Pennsylvania Historical & Museum Commission, Harrisburg, Pa., 1972.

Pringle Hill Cemetery & Association, Summerhill and Croyle Townships by Pringle Hill Cemetery Association, 1983.

School Reports to County Superintendent of Schools.

Simendinger, C. W., Tax Collector's Cash Book, 1922-24.

St. James Church 75th Anniversary Program Book, South Fork, 1981.

St. James Golden Jubilee Program Book, South Fork, 1956.

St. John Evangelical Lutheran Chruch, Summerhill. History compiled by Wallace and Margaret Croyle, Alice McGough and Fern Myers, 1987

St. John's Catholic Church Golden Jubilee, 1903-1953, Summerhill, Pa.,

St. John The Baptist Church, St. John's Church, Summerhill, Pa., 1978.

Stock, Patrick M., **A Study of the History of Cambria County and the Early Development of its Resources and Industry**. Indiana University of Pennsylvania term paper, May 1990.

Summerhill Assessement Records, 1895-1955, Ebensburg Courthouse

Summerhill Borough Comprehensive Plan, Cambria County Planning Commission, Ebensburg, Pa., 1979.

Summerhill Borough Council Minutes.

Wirfel, Marjorie A. and Wess, Rick R., **New Germany Memories,** Immaculate Conception Bicentennial Association, 1976.

Chapter 1

Overcoming The Wilderness

Summerhill, located in the mountains of Cambria County, Pennsylvania, was part of the Allegheny Wilderness -- an area of dense forest inhabited by wild animals and some hostile Indians who traveled the land to hunt and fish.

There were not many settlements because of the rugged terrain and the very cold winters.

Swedes who settled along the Delaware River in 1638 probably were the first Europeans to make their homes in any part of what is now called Pennsylvania. A settlement was made on Tinicum Island in 1643. Tinicum is now a state park.

Charles II of England signed the charter, in 1681, granting Pennsylvania to William Penn. Penn organized Pennsylvania into three counties: Philadelphia, Bucks and Chester.

The French began the occupation of western Pennsylvania in 1733. Great land purchases were made in 1736 and the famous "Walking Purchase" in 1737. The "Walking Purchase" caused much resentment among the Indians. Trouble began to brew.

Then, in 1744, the French and English got into a dispute about the ownership of the land west of the Alleghenies. Louis XV of France claimed the land belonged to France because of LaSalle's explorations as early as 1679. George II of England denied the claim. So, in 1753, the French went to Pittsburgh and erected Fort Duquesne.

Since friendly relations were being strained with the Indians, a conference of the Six Nations (Mohawks, Oneidas, Senecas, Tuscaroras, Onondagas and Cayugas) was held in Albany, New York, in 1754.

The conference resulted in another act which angered the Indians. Thomas and Richard Penn, heirs of William Penn, secured a deed in return for 400 pounds. After the Indians returned home and had a chance to consider the agreement, they realized that all their lands west of the Alleghenies had been sold.

This created more dissatisfaction and discontent among the Indians. They turned to the French for help. The French promised to get the land back for the Indians.

The Indians went on the warpath. An attempt was made to negotiate a fairer purchase but, by and large, the Indians weren't completely satisfied and continued to attack settlers.

These hostilities preceded the great war between France and England (Seven Years War of 1756-1763) in which France relinquished its claims east of the Mississippi to England.

A number of Indian tribes, under the leadership of Pontiac, started an independent war along the whole frontier. They were temporarily in full possession of the land except for a few fortified places like Fort Pitt.

Colonel Henry Bouquet was ordered to rescue the garrison at Fort Pitt. His troops defeated the Indians at Bushy Run, about 20 miles from Fort Pitt, in 1763.

White supremacy was re-established in western Pennsylvania.

The last land purchase was transacted in 1768 at Fort Stanwix, New York, in which all the land south of the Kittanning Trail in western Pennsylvania was secured for $10,000. This purchase included land now known as Cambria County.

The Commonwealth of Pennsylvania opened this territory to settlers April 3, 1769.

Southwestern Pennsylvania was settled, for the main part, from 1769 to 1774.

The Kittanning Trail

The Kittanning Trail was the primary highway to the West until 1758. It was used, from 1717 to 1730, by numerous Shawnees in their exodus from the Juniata Valley to the Allegheny Valley. The trail was an extension of the Old Allegheny Path which ran from Philadelphia to Frankstown (about two miles west of Hollidaysburg on Route 22).

At Frankstown, the route followed a course to Hollidaysburg where it moved in a northwesterly direction. At the Blair-Cambria county line, the highway passed through the Kittanning Gap, south of Coupon and near Ashville. Here, it took to the waters of Clearfield Creek and headed west to Chest Springs. Then, the path returned to land, leading to Loretto, cutting left towards Eckenrode Mill and crossing Chest Creek, above Carrolltown. At Shazen, the course turned west and crossed the West Branch of the Susquehanna River, about two miles south of Cherry Tree. From here, it was a direct route to Kittanning.

It was at Kittanning that Colonel Armstrong won a major victory over the Delaware Indians in 1756.

Historians have written that the French and Indians returned to Kittanning after attacking Fort Granville, near Lewistown. They are said to have brought as captives the four Girty boys, their mother, stepfather and stepbrother John Turner. The stepfather was burned at the stake. The mother and the children were assigned to different tribes.

It is evident that the Kittanning Trail skirted most of Cambria County as it cut through the northern portion into Clearfield County.

The Old Forbes Road

Another avenue from the Atlantic Seaboard to the west was along the Old Forbes Road, constructed in 1758 by the British during the French and Indian War.

This route did not go through Cambria County; rather, it went through the adjacent counties of Bedford, Somerset and Westmoreland.

Therefore, settlers who left southeastern Pennsylvania on their western explorations met the mountains around Hollidaysburg and opted to bear either north on the Kittanning Trail or south on the Old Forbes Road.

The westward expansion was somewhat hindered by this forbidding range of mountains. It appeared that the eastern and western waters would never be joined by a convenient, safe passageway.

Activity along the Forbes Road brought Robert MacRay to the Bedford Area about the middle of the 18th Century. He established a trading post there. The Raystown Branch of the Juniata River was named in his honor.

Garrett Pendergass was also another early trader in the Bedford Area. He built a trading post near the river. But, within several years, he was caught up by hostile Indians who drove him and other settlers to Carlisle or to Virginia.

A fort was built at Raystown. It was orginally named Fort Raystown but later renamed in honor of the Duke of Bedford.

After the British took Fort Duquesne, Fort Bedford remained an outpost on the frontier, serving as a refuge from the Indians for settlers who followed the Army.

Fort Bedford played a part in the settlement of southeastern Cambria County.

A Branch of the Kittanning Trail

There was a branch of the Kittanning Trail that ran southwesterly to the Little Conemaugh River into the Indian settlement of Con-ne-mach (today's Johnstown).

John McCormick in his 1902 history of St. Bartholomew's Church of Wilmore relates that this branch wound up the ridge past Loretto, then south to the eastern side of Munster, down the ridge through Portage Township where it crossed the Little Conemaugh River at two places, "thence ascending the hill to avoid the swamp and laurel on the flat near the river diagonally across the depression in the hill on which stands the church of St. Bartholomew". From here, McCormick intimated the journey continued to Johnstown at the point where the Little Conemaugh and Stonycreek Rivers merge to form the Conemaugh River.

This part of the route would place the travelers through the Summerhill Area in the waters running near Route 53 and through Ehrenfeld and South Fork.

It was this path, according to McCormick, that "undoubtedly served as a bridle-path for the pioneers of this region".

This trail can be seen on Reading Howell's map of 1792.

The Conemaugh Path

Another major Indian trail was the Conemaugh Path which ran from Bedford to Johnstown and continued westward along the Conemaugh River. This route completely bypassed the Summerhill Area as it wound through Richland and Upper Yoder into Johnstown.

Early Traders

It is apparent that traders were the first whites to venture into what is now Cambria County.

John Hart who was licensed in 1744 to trade with the Indians used the Kittanning Path to meet the tribes. On the high ground, near Carrolltown, where the path crossed the Continental Divide, Hart set up a campsite which is commemorated today as Hart's Sleeping Place.

Jonas Davenport is reported in 1731 encountering "three Shawneese towns, 45 families and 200 men with their chief Okawela on Connemach Creek."

James LeTort's log of 1731 indicated he traded with 20 families and 60 braves of Delaware Indians at the junction of the Little Conemaugh and Stonycreek Rivers (today's Point).

Thomas J. Chapman's 1865 book, The Valley of the Conemaugh, mentions that Conrad Weiser, an Indian agent, and his companion George Croghan passed through the Conemaugh Valley in 1748; Christopher Gist crossed the Allegheny Mountains in 1750; and Christian Frderick Post, the messenger of the Governor of Pennsylvania to the Indians on the Ohio, passed through in 1758.

Land Warrants and Patents

Upon the opening of the land office at Lancaster, April 3, 1769, applications for warrants started coming in from settlers and speculators.

Warrants were issued when a person wanted to settle on a certain tract of land. He was required to pay a sum of money and produce two copies of a survey, one for himself and one for the State. Thereafter, the warrantee was required to settle on the land, clear five acres within two years, build a house and raise grain each year for five years. If he satisfied these requirements, he then was granted a Patent for the land. Relatively few warrants led to ownership.

Another method of possession was to choose 400 acres of unoccupied land. This was known as squatter's rights. The squatter could build a house, live there five years and clear five of the 400 acres. After which, he could go to the Commonwealth, pay $150 and receive a deed for 400 acres.

These procedures created some problems because the settler who chose to secure a Warrant for 400 acres could be displaced by a squatter who would come along and "squat" on his 400 acres, build a house, stay five years and apply for the Patent. This resulted in ejectment suits where the squatter usually got 150 acres and the warrantee 250 acres.

It is this situation which makes researching early deeds very difficult and time-consuming. Then, too, deeds were first recorded in Cambria County in 1804; others were first recorded in one of the three original counties which encompassed what became Cambria County in the early 19th Century.

Most early records for Cambria were housed in Carlisle. They were lost when the Carlisle Courthouse burned.

It's interesting to note that the Summerhill Women's Club history project (1810-1966) reveals that an old deed is recorded at Ebensburg (1872) that a tract of land in Summerhill was purchased from William and Mary Murray; Elisha Plummer and Mary Ann, his wife; and Samuel Croyle, executor of Thomas Croyle.

This tract of 438 acres was warranted in the name of Benjamin Williams September 11,1794 and patented to William Clark December 22, 1797.

Another warrant of local interest was one in 1769 issued to Charles Campbell of Westmoreland County for 249 acres. This included all of the downtown Johnstown area below the Haynes Street Bridge.

A second warrant, four days later, certified a claim for a section of Cambria City to.James Dougherty.

Other warrants were issued to Peter Snyder (1776) for Hornerstown; Benedict Dorsey (1776), Woodvale; Martin Riley (1787), Osborne Section; and Thomas Afflick (1788), Minersville.

In 1800, Thomas Croyle bought 438 acres from William Clark for $460 on the north side of the Little Conemaugh River.

Settlement of the Allegheny

The settlement of the Allegheny (1769-1799) took three patterns, according to the 1990 Cambria County Historical Society folder on the pioneer trails in rural Cambria County, researched by Walter R. Davis.

One pattern was "Up to the Conemaugh" from Bedford, made up of old Pennsylvania German and Scotch-Irish stock. They settled in the southern part of Cambria County, including the Mainline Area from Johnstown through South Fork, Summerhill, Wilmore and to Cresson.

The other two patterns Davis tagged as "Over the Front" from Frankstown on the Juniata. This pattern was subdivided into a Blair's Gap (old U. S. 22) and a Kittanning Point (Horseshoe Curve) route.

The Blair's Gap division brought "freshly-immigrated" Welsh Protestant, around the Ebensburg Area. The Kittanning division brought the Irish and German Catholics of the northern part of the county.

Nevertheless, there was no big rush to claim land. Travel on foot or horseback was arduous. Worrying about Indian attacks caused much concern. It was difficult maneuvering through the dense forests and rough terrain.

Croyle Land Claim

The March 22, 1895 edition of the Johnstown Weekly Tribune relates what a Mr. Croyle told Squire B. F. Slick of Conemaugh Township in 1852 in Croyle's old cooper shop of Summerhill:

"In 1794, Thomas and Barbara Croyle took their wallets on their backs and set out on foot westward from Hagerstown, Maryland, to seek their fortune. They found often only ill broken footpaths to guide them on their journey, and sometimes not even those. The loneliness was broken once in passing through what was known as the Switzer settlement in Bedford County."

"Arriving at the site of the present town of Summerhill, then but a barren laurel valley, they encamped for several days. Finding all kinds of game plenty and a soil that appeared rich enough to produce abundantly if properly cultivated, the old pioneer proposed to his wife that they settle down there and make that their home."

Slick continues to tell that the Croyles built a log cabin and "set to work to clear out the laurel." Then, in the Spring of 1795, they "set out on foot to Hagerstown, Maryland, and returned each with a pig in a sack. By Autumn they had seven porkers."

"During the winter of 1795, they killed 94 deer, 3 bears and 16 wild turkeys besides a great deal of other game." These were stored in their attic, "jerked" or dried.

Legend has it that the Croyles on three different occasions went to Fort Bedford for protection from Indian raids. Each time Indians had burned their cabin and destroyed their property. So, they built a stone house with windows on only two sides. The south side and one facing the hill and creek had no windows. The other two sides faced level land and could be easily protected.

A plague prepared by the Cambria County Historical Society substantiates this claim. Listed as an Allegheny Wilderness Pioneer Site, the plaque reads:

The Croyle House -- a 1991 photograph.

Side view of the Croyle House -- a 1991 photograph.

> 1794-1808
> Croyle's Mill
> Thomas and Barbara Croyle came here from Bedford in 1794. They lost two log houses to fire and Indians before completing this, their "stone" house in 1801. Its unique "fortlike" structure allowed windows only on good lanes of rifle fire.

Another Version

Wallace Croyle of Summerhill R. D. 1, in his recent book **My Search For The Truth** gives a different version:

"While out trying to clear land so they could plant other food, they kept the wild meat in the eaves to smoke and dry for winter food and when they came back, their house had burned to the ground from the fire they left in the fireplace. They built another log house and the same thing happened to it. In the meantime they were building a mill to grind their grain; so they built a stone house in 1808 and it is still in use today."

The 1991 edition of **A Guidebook to Historic Western Pennsylvania**, published by the University of Pittsburgh Press, lists the Croyle House as one of the only four centenary stone houses remaining in the county at the time of the U. S. bicentennial survey. The guide notes that the house was built in 1804 with an addition in 1835. This publication also states that the log house was burned by Indians and replaced by the currrent stone structure.

The Adams Family

Another Indian tale tells about the Adams Family. The story claims they were the first settlers in the region. They came west from Berks County about 1769 and settled in the present Richland Area. Reportedly, Rachel was killed by Delaware Indians. Samuel and an Indian apparently killed each other on Sandy Run. Historians generally agree the attacks took place around 1777. The Adams family was either going to Fort Bedford or were coming back from the Fort when the killings occurred.

Solomon Run, Rachel's Run and Rachel's Hill and Adams Township bear their names.

Other Early Settlers

Other literature offers confusing stories concerning the earliest settlers.

Some writers credit Abiah Taylor as the first settler because he acquired land in East Carroll Township -- west of Chest Creek -- around 1773. However, this is four years after the reputed arrival of the Adams Family.

Another claim is that the first structure built by a white settler was in the Loretto Area about 1768 -- the McGuire Hunting Camp. This claim also states that twenty years later Captain Michael McGuire owned 1400 acres, known as McGuire's Settlement, near Loretto.

The 1790 U. S. Census listed the McGuires as the only family west of the Allegheny.

One conclusion we can draw from all these claims is that it took two decades after the Fort Stanwix Treaty to make this area safe for settlers and to attract the most adventurous and enterprising ones.

The pace accelerated in the last decade of the 18th Century.

Frankstown Road

The Galbraith or Frankstown Road opened as the first public road to the county. It crossed what is now Jackson Township, went near Mundy's Corner to the top of Laurel Mountain and crossed the road leading from Route 22 to Vintondale.

The Frankstown Road to the Little Conemaugh River at the Pennsylvania Railroad station in Johnstown opened about 1792. Originally, this road went through Dale Borough until the road down the hill from Daisytown was opened. The road subsequently went through Coopersdale and , after it crossed the hill, it joined the Galbraith Road leading to Pittsburgh.

Storm Grist Mill

John Storm built a grist mill on Clearfield Creek in 1792. This is considered the first grist mill in Cambria County. The mill operated for many decades; later as Siebert's Mill. The location is now known as Sybertown in Gallitzin Township.

Philadelphia Influence

During this decade, the Philadelphia influence became prominent.

General McConnell invested in an extensive tract of land (1794) in Chest Township.

Dr. Benjamin Rush secured a patent (1795) for the land which makes up Ebensburg.

Conrad Luther, who reportedly deserted the British at Lancaster and joined the Continental Army, located on a farm near Carrolltown (1796).

John Cable Family

The earliest family to settle north of the Little Conemaugh River was John Martin Cable at Elk Pasture, between Summerhill and Wilmore. This tract, it is believed, was surveyed to Samuel Griffin in 1773 and contained a cabin built by a man named Knott.

Hannah Cable was said to have been born here in 1783. She is recorded as having died in Indiana County (1830) as Hannah Cable Coleman. Her birthplace is the former Victor Beyer farm, not far east of Summerhill.

Two of Cable's daughters, Mary and Christina, married George and Philip Pringle. They located (1795) in the area known as Pringle Hill, about 1 1/2 miles from Summerhill.

Father Gallitzin

And, Father Demetrius Augustine Gallitzin offered Mass for the first time in Loretto on Christmas Eve of 1799. This marked the establishment of the first Catholic parish between the Appalachians and the Mississippi.

Johnstown Settlers

It should be noted here that the warrants previously mentioned in this chapter for the Johnstown Area covered the years from 1769 to 1788.

John Horner was another early pioneer who owned most of the land that now includes the 7th and 17th wards of the city and Dale Borough. Horner built the second grist mill in the county -- on Solomon Run about 1793.

Joseph Johns got title to the Campbell tract (most of downtown Johnstown below Haynes Street Bridge) in 1793. He built a log cabin the following year at the present intersection of Vine and Levergood Streets and started farming on about 30 acres. Later, this tract was used to lay out "Conemaugh Old Town".

Additional warrants were recorded at this time. Jacob Stutzman and Robert Adams (1795) for Kernville and James Flack (1797) for Conemaugh Borough.

Abraham Hildebrand constructed a grist mill on the Little Conemaugh River about 1797.

Beulah and Ebensburg

Morgan John Rhys and his faithful climbed the mountain in the summer of 1797 and settled in the Ebensburg woods to lay out Beulah, a town one mile square with 395 acres reserved for public buildings, schools, a library, a seminary and 200 more acres for a religious society.

This location was promoted as the site of the county seat. It was named as the first polling place and the first federal post office in the county.

Beulah lost out to Ebensburg due to the pioneering efforts of Rees Lloyd whose Welsh colonists walked from Philadelphia in the Fall of 1796 and chose their site on the Conemaugh headwaters. They spent the winter in hemlock shacks and in the spring they built Ebenezer Chapel, followed by grist and saw mills which began operations in 1799.

Ebensburg, as we all know, became the county seat and is located in an area with three US highways -- 22, 422 and 219 .

The Development Pattern

The wilderness was slowly being conquered. There were signs of significant progress around the Kittanning Trail in the northern section of the county, permanent settlements in the Ebensburg Area and a flurry of land transactions around Johnstown.

Within an area of several miles along the Little Conemaugh River, the Summerhill section was developing with the Cables, Pringles and Croyles.

Chapter 2

Developing New Boundaries And Places

The evolution of Cambria County came about through a succession of legislative acts subdividing the boundaries to accomodate increasing population.

William Penn began with three counties in 1682 -- Bucks, Chester and Philadelphia.

Chronologically, the subdivisions leading up to Cambria County were:

    1729 -- Lancaster County from part of Chester
    1750 -- Cumberland from part of Lancaster
    1771 -- Bedford from part of Cumberland
    1787 -- Huntingdon from part of Bedford
    1795 -- Somerset from part of Bedford
    1804 -- Cambria from parts of Huntingdon, Somerset and Bedford

When Bedford County was part of Cumberland County (1750-1771), settlers had to travel to Carlisle to transact county business. As the Cambria population grew, more residents complained about the long, inconvenient travel to Carlisle. Then, the cries were also heard when Bedford and Somerset were the seats of the area.

Cambria County

Even though Cambria County was established in 1804, it was kept under the jurisdiction of Somerset County until 1807 because of the sparse population in Cambria at that time. The Court of Common Pleas held its first Ebensburg session March 7, 1808.

From the onset, Cambria County was nicknamed "the mountain county" because it was made up of the Allegheny Plateau between Laurel Hill and the summit of the Allegheny Mountains. It is the only county in the State with a Welsh name -- "the land of the Cymry or Cumbri", a word usually interpreted as meaning "compatriots".

Cambria County started with three townships -- Allegheny, Cambria and Conemaugh.

Allegheny Township included all of the northern third of the county; Cambria Township, the center section; and Conemaugh Township, the southern part.

Cambria County is bounded by Somerset County on the south; Westmoreland and Indiana Counties on the west; Clearfield County on the north; and Blair and Bedford counties on the east.

Its area is 692 square miles.

The elevation at the Conrail bridge in Johnstown is 1,180 feet, according to the survey made by Sylvester Welch, chief engineer of the Pennsylvania Canal and the Allegheny Portage Railroad.

The elevation at Summerhill is 1,530 feet.

McCormick's Description

John McCormick in an unpublished history of the county explains that it is divided into two drainage areas by the Dividing Ridge beginning near Cresson "thence westward to Winterset on the E. & C. Branch Railroad which crosses it nineteen times and is so exactly on the Divide six times that the drainage from the north side of the line flows into Chesapeake Bay and from the southern site the water flows to the Gulf of Mexico."

In his treatise about glacial erosion of the county, McCormick claims "the surface of Cambria County shows marks of glacial erosion up to an elevation of 2,000 feet, and the channels of the principal streams, modified by the appearance of localities in which the original glacier channels cut through leaving the present river channels give us a striking proof of the extent of this erosion."

"For instance, we can trace the action of the Little Conemaugh and the North Branch glaciers to where they united at the present town of Wilmore, to be somewhat impeded by the glacial flow down from the region of New Germany almost transversely causing an erosion of the channel of the Little Conemaugh at Summerhill to a depth of at least 70 feet lower than it is now as was proven by the building of the three arch stone bridge over Sipe's milldam in 1888, to find a solid foundation for which an excavation of 35 feet in depth revealed nothing harder than blue mud, so that piles about 35 feet in length had to be driven down to find a solid foundation which does not appear to be as firm, after all, as it should be, as the addition to the original two track bridge also of two tracks now shows a difference in the transverse level of the two sections which show a crack indicating a settling apart, and as a measure tending to security, the Pennsylvania Railroad Company a few years ago had holes drilled through the two bridges, and great iron rods with nuts and threads on both ends placed through the holes and tightened as tight as possible, and below the foundations of the southern piers had great excavations made and filled with solid concrete pillars as supports to the piers."

(This has to be the longest sentence the author of this book has ever recopied.)

McCormick claims the Lickdale clay near the bridge of the road to New Germany shows many rounded pebbles and stone.

Below Summerhill, he notes the glacier "at first apparently made a considerable bend around and past Devils Hollow finally cutting through the neck of the bend where the channel of the river is now located."

When Cambria County was created March 26, 1804, it became the 41st county in the state. Today, there are 67 counties.

Population of the new county (1804) was estimated at 50 families.

County Mapping of 1816

A legislative act of 1816 required maps for each county. Walter B. Hudson and John Morrison made the Cambria County map and reported the following:

-- Ebensburg had a population of 150 people; Munster, 80; and Johnstown, 60.

-- the county is covered with a thick heavy growth of excellent timber.

-- the altitude of the county is almost as high as the summit of the Allegheny; it has the nature and appearance of mountain lands.

-- there are many fine tracts entirely clear of stone.

-- the quarries near Ebensburg offer soft, grey granite which is interspersed with glistening particles of a metallic appearance.

-- Farmers raise Fall grain but not as good as that east of the mountains.

-- potatoes, turnips and all kinds of Spring grain (except corn) do extremely well.

-- the county is considered excellent for grazing.

-- principal timber is wild cherry, poplar, chestnut, ash oak, sugar maple, cucumber, pince and hickory.

-- birch, hemlock and laurel abound in the marshy lands.

-- minerals include iron, stone coal and marl (soil consisting of clay, sand and calcium carbonate used as a fertilizer and for making cement or bricks).

-- the Conemaugh River is navigable for boats three or four months in the Spring; channels are free of obstructions.

-- all the streams have sufficient fall for mills, etc. and do not fail so much in dry seasons as most of the western waters.

-- Poplar Run could easily be connected with Bobb's Creek since the heads interlock with those of the Conemaugh. This would be the shortest route from Harrisburg to Pittsburgh.

Hudson and Morrison also believed that Conemaugh River could easily be connected to either Clearfield or Chest Creeks between Ebensburg and Munster and that this route would be shorter and better than any connections with the higher branches of the Allegheny River.

One must remember that these suggestions were made long before the Allegheny Portage Railroad plan.

Cambria County Population

Cambria County's population peaked in 1940 with a total census figure of 213,459. During the past 50 years, the county has lost 70,664 people -- a drop of 33% since 1940. The largest decline from one decade to another just occurred in 1990 with a loss of 20,234 people since 1980.

Cambria County Population

Year	Population
1810	2,117
1820	3,287
1830	7,076
1840	11,256
1850	17,773
1860	29,155
1870	36,369
1880	46,811
1890	66,375
1900	104,847
1910	166,131
1920	197,839
1930	203,146
1940	213,459
1950	209,541
1960	201,988
1970	186,785
1980	183,263
1990	163,029

Source: U.S. Census

The Naming of Summerhill

As the county developed, the three original townships were further subdivided until there were a total of 30 in number. Today, 27 townships remain.

Summerhill went from being part of Conemaugh Township from 1804 to 1810, to Summerhill Township from 1810 to 1858, and Croyle Township from 1858 to the present day.

When Summerhill Township was formed, February 7, 1810, it was the first new township in the county. It was originally spelled "Somerhill", probably in honor of Joseph and David Somers who have been credited as two important landowners in this locality, according to Espenshade's **Pennsylvania Place Names**.

Summerhill Borough, according to this source, took its name from old Summerhill Township. However, borough records show the borough was first known as Summer Hill. The change to Summerhill was first noted on the 1926 tax receipts.

Chapman's Description

Thomas J. Chapman in his **Valley of the Conemaugh** told about a large number of thriving towns and villages situated upon the Conemaugh River with Johnstown as the largest at the confluence of Stonycreek and the Conemaugh (1865).

"Above Johnstown, on this stream, are Conemaugh, Summerhill and Wilmore."

"There is much early history connected with valley of the Conemaugh", wrote Chapman. "No great efforts to form settlements within its boundaries were made until a comparatively recent date."

Chapman reported towns for the southern part of the county as Johnstown and surrounding boroughs of Summerhill, Wilmore, Foot-of-Four, Summit, Cresson, Gallitzin, Perkinsville, Scalp Level, Geistown and Parkstown.

Perkinsville was a small village on the canal about three miles west of Johnstown. Parkstown was on the Old Frankstown Road, about two miles east of Johnstown.

Of these towns, Chapman described Summerhill, Wilmore, Foot-of-Four and Summitville as relics of the Allegheny Portage Railroad "which in its time ran through them, and which gave origin to their existence."

About Summerhill, Chapman wrote "Summerhill, which should have been termed Winter Hollow, is located in a narrow valley between hills through which the Portage Railroad ran. The Pennsylvania Railroad runs close by the old village and sustains its vitality. It contains two or three hundred inhabitants."

Summerhill's Population

Summerhill's population was in the 800s from 1940 to 1960. During the 1970s and 1980s, the population stabilized in the lower 700 range. The latest census shows 614 inhabitants. The declining population relates to the loss of many coal, steel and railroading jobs.

```
       Summerhill Borough Population

         1930              785
         1940              861
         1950              849
         1960              863
         1970              726
         1980              725
         1990              614
              Source: U.S. Census
```

Summerhill Area of 1820

Early Summerhill Township was a more extensive area than today's township. Jackson, Washington, Blacklick, Munster, Croyle and Portage Townships took territories from the township's original boundaries.

Therefore, a tax list for 1820 contains many property owners not part of today's Summerhill Area. However, the names of Croyle, Pringle, Dimond, Long, McGough, Plumer and Skally (spellings from the list) are there. Missing is Somers or Sumers.

The following, assumed to be within present day Summerhill Area, indicate the holdings and land use in 1820:

	Acres	Cleared	Horses	Cows
Thomas Croyl	530	21	5	8
John Dimond	200	30	1	2
Sara Dimond	-	-	-	1
Paul George	300	-	1	1
Philip George	400	10	2	-
Joseph Long	196	12	2	1

Thomas McGough	332	20	-	2
Ester McGough	-	-	1	2
John Plumer	100	15	2	1
Richard Plumer	-	-	1	-
William Plumer	100	50	2	3
George Pringle	204	37 1/2	2	2
George Pringle Jr.	94	33	1	-
Philip Pringle	-	-	2	2
William Pringle	-	-	1	-
Hugh Skally	330	20	-	-
John Skally	300	53	7	3
Michael Skally	250	20	3	2
Michael Skally Jr.	100	-	-	-
Philip Skally	302	30	3	5
Philip Skally Jr.	100	3	-	-

This tax list also offers an insight about early life styles:

Samual Bolsby	bookbinder
William Burk	stonemason
Patrick Camel	shoemaker
Thomas Croyl	gristmill, sawmill
Paul George	gristmill, sawmill
Joseph Lilly	tavern
Michael Litsinger	sawmill, stonemason
Joseph Long	tailor
John Mikzell	tavern
Lewis Morack	carpenter
William McMin	schoolmaster
Barnet Ripple	blacksmith, tavern
Jacob Sala	bookbinder, apothecary
Jonathan Shoup	apothecary
John Skally	distillery
William Smith	D. D.
Jacob Troxel	tavern
Barnet Willmore	bookbinder

Four taverns and a distillery tells us how these early settlers relaxed. But, why three bookbinders? And, not one barber?

Unseated Land Warrants

The list indicates a lot of unseated land warranted to other parties.

Warranted to George Pringle were 332 acres taxed to Robert Patterson and 223 acres listed for John Proctor.

Unseated land warranted to Rev. Rees Lloyd of Ebensburg fame include

John Everman, 439 acres 120 perches; John Musser, 439 acres 64 perches; John Shaffer, 402 acres; James Wilson, 368 acres; Daniel Stevenson, 457 acres 134 perches; and Amon Warrel, 450 acres.

All this points to the fact that the Summerhill Area and most of Cambria County was made up of individual farming locations with much of land still in its virgin state. Those who did venture into these mountains found life very primitive and difficult. But, these people had lot of faith. They did not reject hard work. They were determined to succeed.

Pennsylvania's East-West Route

Perhaps, the most important event in the development of the Summerhill Area and its neighbors along the Little Conemaugh Valley were the deliberations of how Pennsylvania would beat its competitors for an east-west route.

Pittsburgh had become a city in 1816 with a population of 10,000 people. Wherever possible, navigation was by water. The early highways were the waterways. Unless there was level, unobstructed terrain, land travel in the hills and mountain ridges were too time-consuming, uncomfortable and dangerous.

Situated at the head of navigation on the Ohio River, Pittsburgh was the key portal to the westward expansion and western riches.

The three main eastern seaports were at New York, Baltimore and Philadelphia. Each tried to prove it was closer to Pittsburgh.

Baltimore was the leader in this battle with a national road to the west through Maryland in 1822.

New York countered with the Erie Canal in 1825.

Pennsylvania was using a stagecoach route from Philadelphia through the Allegheny Mountains to Pittsburgh which took up to three weeks. The wagon road through the Alleghenies was known as the Huntingdon, Cambria and Indiana Turnpike. It crossed at Cresson and struggled through the rugged terrain around Ebensburg, Blairsville and New Alexandria. This route was running a good third in the three-way race.

Looking for a way to overcome the lead of its rivals, Pennsylvania realized it had to make use of its rivers. The Conemaugh River, beginning at the Point in Johnstown, was already a public highway, since 1787. The Stonycreek River was declared a public highway in 1820.

Pennsylvania's Canal System

In 1824, the Pennsylvania Legislature authorized a board of commissioners to propose a canal system from Harrisburg to Pittsburgh. Two of the three commissioners agreed that there should be a continuous waterway between these two cities via the Juniata-Conemaugh route.

This disagreement temporarily stalled further planning. At the same time, supporters of railroads intervened and, in 1825, the Pennsylvania Senate appointed a commission to investigate the possibility of a railroad link between these two cities.

The canal idea prevailed because railroading, at this time, had not developed to the point where it could recruit the necessary support.

On February 25, 1826, an act authorized the construction of the Pennsylvania Canal at state expense via the Juniata-Conemaugh route.

In the meanwhile, travel continued by any route possible. By November 1829, the first boatload from Philadelphia reached Pittsburgh because the canal was complete from Pittsburgh to Blairsville. Blairsville was located on the Northern Turnpike, the early overland route connecting Huntingdon and Pittsburgh. Canal boats traveled east from Pittsburgh and stopped at Blairsville where the cargos were transferred to wagon trains.

By 1830, it was decided that a railroad was the best way of crossing the Alleghenies and on March 21, 1831 Governor Wolf approved the construction of a 37-mile railroad system from Johnstown to Hollidaysburg.

The Pennsylvania Canal System was completed by March 18, 1834 at a total cost of $16,500,000.

This brought new life into the Summerhill Area as well as Johnstown. Johnstown was described no longer "a town with elderberry bushes growing in its streets." It had about 200 people, 30 houses, two taverns and five stores and one mill.

Summerhill had much less. Croyle's Mill was the main attraction along with the settlement of Pringle Hill. But, the presence of the railroad would foster a new development of the area.

Chapter 3

Conquering A New Frontier By Rail And Water

The Pennsylvania Canal System solved the state's dilemma by combining rail and water travel across the state. To do so, engineers had to conquer the frontier of the Allegheny Mountains.

From Philadelphia, passengers and freight moved by steam train to the Susquehanna River at Columbia. From here, boats followed the Susquehanna and Juniata Rivers to Hollidaysburg. Elevations at Hollidaysburg and Johnstown differ only by several hundred feet but the range of mountains between them ascend to a height of 2,341 feet.

Allegheny Portage Railroad

Engineers came up with a daring and unique plan -- a portage (carrying or transporting of boats and supplies overland between navigable waters) via a series of 10 inclined planes, powered by stationary engines. This portion of the system became known as the Allegheny Portage Railroad (APRR).

The canal boats were again placed in the water at the Johnstown canal basin and pulled along the Conemaugh, Kiskiminetas and Allegheny Rivers to Pittsburgh.

Thus, the completed Pennsylvania Canal System extended 395 miles somewhat directly across the state. The journey from Philadelphia to Pittsburgh could be made in little over seven days.

The AAPR was one of the most remarkable engineering feats of its time. Not only did it solve the problem of crossing the rugged Alleghenies but it also served to open a new frontier.

The 10 inclined planes were numbered eastward from Johnstown. Each plane was like a giant slide conveying the road's load up or down the different elevations. The planes varied in length from 1,480 to 3,117 feet. Overall, they covered about 4.4 miles of the APRR; the other 32 miles were on the levels between the planes.

Length & Lifting Power of the Inclined Planes

Plane No.		Length (in feet)	Lifting Power (in feet)
1	Before Staple Bend Tunnel	1,608	150
2	at Portage	1,760	133

3	Between Portage & Lilly	1,480	133
4	at Lilly	2,195	188
5	West slope of Summit	2,629	195
6	East slope of Summit	2,714	267
7	Short distance from 6	2,655	260
8	Short distance from 7	3,117	306
9	near bottom on mountain	2,721	190
10	around area of Duncansville	2,296	178

The Allegheny Portage Railroad made the trip over the mountain in easy stages. Horses pulled the railroad cars on the levels to the foot of each inclined plane. Stationary steam engines hauled the cars to the next level. Horses again pulled the cars to the next inclined plane where the procedure was repeated. A similar succession lowered the cars on the eastern slope from the summit (the highest point) to the canal basin at Hollidaysburg.

Staple Bend Tunnel

From Johnstown, the distance to the foot of Plane No. 1 was 4.13 miles. At the head of the plane, Staple Bend Tunnel cut through the rocky mountain. Staple Bend, 901 feet long, is the first railroad tunnel built in the United States. It was abandoned in 1854 when the Pennsylvania Railroad completed its line. The tunnel and right-of-way passed into the possession of Bethlehem Steel Corporation. The steel company buried a 48-inch waterline through the middle of the tunnel to carry water from Wilmore Reservoir.

Currently, the National Park Service is negotiating to purchase the tunnel and the right-of-way and allow Bethlehem an easement for the waterline. The Park Service has plans to construct a picnic area and trail to the tunnel as another tourist attraction of the area.

Nicklin's Journey Over the Allegheny Portage

Philip N. Nicklin of Philadelphia wrote about his 1835 trip from Johnstown for a book he entitled **A Pleasant Perigrination Through The Prettiest Parts of Pennsylvania.**

He described his travel along the level passing through Summerhill as a "very interesting part of the route, not only on account of the wilderness and beauty of the scenery, but also of the excitement mingled with vague apprehension."

At the foot of plane no. 1, Nicklin said the horses were unhitched and the cars pulled up the 1,608-foot plane and through Staple Bend Tunnel. At the end of the tunnel, the cars were attached to a steam tug which carried them through Summerhill to Portage. This stretch, he said, "is one of the most interesting portions of the Portage Rail Road, from the beauty of its location and the ingenuity of its contruction ... passes through some of the wildest scenery in the state; the axe, the chisel and the spade having cut its way through the forest, rock and mountain."

It took one hour to travel the 14 miles of this level.

Beginnings of Wilmore

With the beginning of the railroad's construction in 1831, laborers settled in small groups along the route. Bernard Wilmore laid out the town of Jefferson in 1831, but, the next year when the post office opened, the name was changed to Wilmore.

Many of the railroad laborers were Irish Catholics. St. Bartholomew's Catholic Church was established in Wilmore to provide for their religious needs.

The railroad created other changes in the area.

Every day there was one regular passenger train each way. One usually left Johnstown between 6 and 7 o'clock in the morning and arrived at Hollidaysburg between one and two o'clock. The westbound train left about the same hour and arrived at Johnstown before two o'clock. Therefore, two trains ran through Summerhill each day.

Wood was the fuel for the locomotives. The small ones could carry a quarter of a cord enough for a seven-mile run. The larger locomotives, later on, consumed five to seven cords of wood in a good day'work.

Timbering - The First Industry

This created what was perhaps the first industry of the new frontier -- timbering.

Farmers delivered wood along the railroad line at $1.25 a cord. The wood was usually sold to an inspector who traveled along the road. The wood was stacked along the route for pickup. In this way, early settlers now had another incentive to clear their lands and were able to pick up some money at the same time. Summerhill stood in a strategic location. Being midway between Staple Bend Tunnel and the second plane, with Croyle's sawmill, was an advantage.

Wallace Croyle addressed this favorite position in his family history.

The sawmill furnished lumber during the construction of the Allegheny Portage Railroad and , in 1833, the State of Pennsylvania contracted with Thomas Croyle to remove the sawmill "in order to enable the contractor to procure a sufficient foundation for the slope wall."

Another contract was awarded to build a wood shed and water station at the mill site for a refueling stop of the railroad's locomotives. Allen Rose was paid $20 to bore and lay 650 feet of wooden pipes to the water station; George Murry, $336.24 to build the water station and the wood shed.

Halfway House

The Superintendent of Motive Power, John Snodgrass, referred to this water station as the Halfway House. A railroad record indicated that, in 1839, a Superintendent Moorhead noted that a "lateral road" had to be constructed around the shed "for the accomodation of the motive power in furnishing wood."

Wallace Croyle proclaims that "evidently Summerhill, the town now located at the original Croyle site first developed into a community during the period when the Allegheny Portage Railroad stopped at its halfway house on the long level."

Wallace wrote that George Murray built a hotel and store where builders of the Old Portage could stay and get supplies. This building was also known as Halfway House. It is believed to have been located near the present site of the Forest Hills Ambulance building.

Another source indicates the Halfway House was the first inn on the old stage road, now route 53.

Another reference claims that the Halfway House was given its name because it was half way between Cresson and Johnstown, along the early stagecoach route.

Historian Henry Storey believed that South Fork was known as Halfway House when James Burns emigrated from Ireland in 1850. Burns had a job as subdivision boss for railroad construction about four years.

The Johnstown Weekly Tribune of February 22, 1929 referred to Halfway House as a one-story log house along the old Portage Railroad that was used as a general store and eating house for persons using the boats.

George Murray on December 12, 1859 sold the Halfway House to his brother William for $600, according to a deed recorded in Cambria County Courthouse.

William Murray left Summerhill in 1866 and that probably was the end of Halfway House because other houses took its place.

The next significant part of Summerhill's history occurred after 1836. The traffic on the Portage Railroad had increased to the extent that the Legislature directed the canal commissioners to find a route over the mountains which would avoid the inclined planes.

Traffic was curtailed for five months in order to make repairs that flood waters created in June 1838, between Hollidaysburg and Huntingdon.

After the repairs, freight cars were hauled at night for the first time.

Between 1843 and 1848, wire rope replaced the hemp used to haul cars up the planes. Locomotives gradually replaced all horses except those used between plane nos. 8 and 9 on the eastern slope.

The last passenger to leave Johnstown for Pittsburgh reportedly left the city in August, 1851. Freight boats remained a little longer -- until 1860.

Canal System Problems

The canal system had many problems. The biggest was ice which closed the canal from early December until the second week of March. Muskrats and beavers riddled the canal walls. Spring floods damaged the works and during dry spells the water level was too low for proper navigation. A severe winter caused a lot of damage to the rail lines. The system of changes from land to water caused delay and inconvenience.

The cause of the delays were the inclined planes but action to eliminate them was withheld until after the Pennsylvania Railroad started its line from Harrisburg to Pittsburgh in 1847.

The Legislature, even though it was in competition with the Pennsylvania Railroad, authorized work on the Allegheny Portage. By 1853, the use of planes no. 1, 2 and 3 were discontinued.

The New Portage Railroad

The line was now known as the New Portage Railroad. It followed the route of the Old Portage from Johnstown to Conemaugh. It crossed the Little Conemaugh River between Conemaugh and Franklin. About two miles east of Wilmore it left the old roadbed and cut to the south around plane no. 2, near Portage.

About a half-mile west of Benscreek, the road cut back to the old roadbed, detoured around plane no. 3 at Benscreek and almost paralleled the Pennsylvania Railroad track to Cassandra, passed unter the PRR tracks and continued through Lilly and Cresson.

At the foot of plane no. 3, the New Portage left the bed of the Old Portage and did not rejoin the former roadbed until plane no. 8

Instead of crossing the mountain at the Summit, the New Portage swerved northward and cut through the mountain near Gallitzin -- the Gallitzin Tunnel. This tunnel, completed in 1853, is 3,700 feet long, pierces the Alleghenies 3,000 feet above sea level and still is used by the PRR for westbound traffic.

Descending the eastern slope, the New Portage skirted the gulches and gullies and crossed the Old Portage at plane no. 8, snaked down the mountain and ran into the Old Portage bed at Duncansville.

The new distance from Johnstown to Hollidaysburg was 41 miles -- about five miles longer than the old route. However, a train could travel the distance in four to five hours compared to 10 to 12 hours on the old route.

The New Portage route, free of inclined planes, was opened in 1855. It cost the State over $2 million.

Difficulties of Early Travel

To appreciate the difficulties of early travel, this account as printed in the 1896 Cyclopedia helps to offer more understanding:

"In 1847, Emanuel Young started for the west by stage. Near Stoyestown, the stage got stuck in a snow drift. Passengers shoveled their way out and got to Stoyestown for supper. Passengers were tired and let the the stage go on. The landlord advised Young to go to Johnstown and from there to Pittsburg by boat. The landlord brought him to Johnstown by sled but when they arrived in Johnstown found the canal frozen and the boats could not run for two or three weeks; so Young went to work for Thomas Shay at a slaughtery near the corner of Bedford Street."

The Pennsylvania Railroad

December 1854, the Pennsylvania Railroad completed its line from Philadelphia to Pittsburgh. The New Portage continued operations in 1856 and until August 1 of 1857.

During 1856, and until abandoned, the PRR and the New Portage operated under an agreement that both used the same tracks part of the way and parallel tracks at other points.

The two railroads used the same eastward trackage to South Fork bridge. Here the roads diverged. The PRR crossed to the south side of the Little Conemaugh River enroute towards Summerhill. The New Portage kept on the north side of the Little Conemaugh along the Fifficktown-Ehrenfeld hillside.

The State offered the New Portage for sale three times in 1857. There were no offers. Finally, the Pennsylvania Railroad bought the system at a public auction in June of 1857 for $7.5 million.

During this period Summerhill was surrounded by two different railroad systems passing through town.

The Pennsylvania continued to grow. During the Civil War period, the road was double-tracked through Summerhill. The third and fourth tracks were added shortly before 1900.

The Horseshoe Curve

Another spectacular engineering feat was completed by the PRR with the opening of the Horseshoe Curve, February 15, 1854. Extensive construction is presently underway here by the National Park Service for a multimillion dollar visitors center as part of the America's Industrial Heritage Project involving a nine-county region in southwestern Pennsylvania.

Other County Developments

Besides all the railroading activities, there were other important developments within the new county's territory.

Joseph Long settled in New Germany in 1818. The community he founded has retained strong ties to Summerhill, sharing many long-standing family names.

Ebensburg incorporated as the first county borough in 1825; Loretto followed in 1845.

By the time the Pennsylvania Railroad completed its line between Philadelphia and Pittsburgh, the county's population was accelerating at an increasing pace because thousands of immigrants were passing through on their westward move to find a new life.

More townships were created. By 1847, there were eight: Summerhill, Clearfield, Susquehanna, Jackson, Washington, Richland, White and Carroll.

During the 1850s, the beginnings of Cambria Iron Company in Johnstown transformed the region into an important industrial site. Cambria Iron, by the 1870s, went on to become the leading steel producer in the country. A decade later, Cambria Iron was the largest iron and steel employer in the United States, rivaled in size only by the country's large textile mills.

Coal became more directly associated to Summerhill's growth. Small operators were getting involved like Matthew and Michael Myers, west of Lilly; Charles Murray, in the neighborhood of Vinco; west of the Summit and at the foot of plane no. 5.

Near the Johnstown railroad station, the Rhey Furnace mine began operations about 1853. And in the same year, Cambria Iron went big with their Rolling Mill mine on Yoder Hill -- an operation which lasted from 1853 to 1931.

Cambria County was now positioned to offer a choice of five major industries -- agriculture, timbering, iron making, coal mining and railroading. Workers were actively recruited wherever possible, even foreign countries.

Croyle Township was formed in 1858 from another section of Summerhill Township. The move placed Summerhill, New Germany and Pringle Hill under the jurisdiction of Croyle Township supervisors. There was no South Fork, or Fifficktown at the offset. They came later when its coal deposits were developed and mined.

Chapter 4

The People Who Made The Early Progress

The Croyle Family

Thomas Croyle was born in 1760 in Bedford County; his wife, the former Barbara Garn, 1769 in Amsterdam, Holland. A 25-year-old Thomas and his 16-year-old bride exchanged marriage vows in Hagerstown, Maryland.

Thomas learned the blacksmith trade from his father and along with his brother, George, operated a blacksmith shop on Mile Level of Forbes Road.

Thomas and another brother, Charles, were members of the Bedford County Militia during the Revolutionary War. They were released in 1789.

Charles accompanied Thomas and his family (wife Barbara and son Samuel) north to the little Conemaugh River at Summerhill in 1795. They were among the first settlers here.

They liked the area and decided to make it their home for life. Charles, 75, died in 1836; Barbara, 86, 1855; Thomas, 98, 1858; and son Samuel, 74, 1867. Collectively, these four family members logged a combined 236 years in Summerhill.

Thomas' death coincided with the date the new township was named in their honor.

The Croyles first project in this new land was to build a log cabin. It was destroyed by fire. They rebuilt only to meet the same fate. Undaunted, they tried a third time with a stone house which is still standing and utilized after more than 180 years. This house, at 305 Main Street, continues to be a topic of historical anecdotes.

Another task was to dam the Little Conemaugh River and construct a grist mill to grind their grain. Farmers brought their grain too. The mill became the center of activity for this growing community. It became known as Croyle's Mill.

Its importance was underscored when a dirt road was laid in 1806 from Ebensburg to Croyle's Mill as the first public work undertaken by Cambria County government.

The mill had a long life and continued operations well into the 20th Century. (More details are given in a later chapter.)

In 1820, the Croyles built a small log church and donated 2 1/2 acres of land for religious purposes of any denomination. St. John's Lutheran Church stands at this location today, complete with burial grounds where the Croyles and other members of their families are buried.

When the Pennsylvania Railroad established their right-of-way through Summerhill, the Croyles donated 200 feet for the good of the community.

John McCormick in his history of Summerhill (**Johnstown Daily Tribune, August 30, 1906**) notes that Barbara Croyle was known as Granny Croyle because she was a mid-wife and "skillful in the use of herbs as medicines for the cure of nearly all ailments of the early settlers."

Thomas Croyle, according to McCormick, gained ownership of many tracts of land -- some surveyed on a warrant from the Land Office and others purchased from executors of John Rohrer of Lancaster and parcels surveyed in the name of Daniel Whitmore. He also attained a tract warranted in the name of Benjamin Williams and patented in the name of William Clark.

McCormick states that there were nearly 200 acres in Thomas Croyle's name by 1866.

Even though Thomas' name was used in legal transactions, McCormick points out that Barbara was the real business manager of the family. He said the reason was that Thomas was an "easy-going, good-natured man." Barbara took over financial management when her husband lost $600 on a bond for a political friend.

"She bears the reputation of having been a very useful member of society in the neighborhood --kind, hospitable and neighborly -- and it is said that no deserving neighbor ever applied to her for a loan without receiving aid when in her powers to extend it."

A check of deeds recorded at the Cambria County Courthouse shows 62 property transfers in the name of Barbara Croyle. There are numerous transfers to Tarance McGarr, August 15, 1837 and one to the German Reform and Lutheran congregation (September 16, 1838) for $2.50 with John Pringle and John Boyl as trustees and Frederick Croyle, treasurer.

Other deeds include properties in Summerhill, Summerhill Township, Croyle Township and Richland Township. She sold properties to Jacob Stineman Jr., Isaac Paul, William Murray, Richard J. Hughes, South Fork Coal & Iron Company, Summerhill Township School District, Pennsylvania Railroad, South Fork Water Company, J. C. Luke, South Fork Borough, Phoenix Powder manufacturing Company of New York and South Fork Cemetery.

Thomas and Barbara Croyle had two sons -- Samuel and Frederick -- and five daughters -- Margaret, Sarah, Mary, Elizabeth and Esther.

Samuel, the oldest of the children, helped his father at the grist mill and the saw mill. He served as justice of the peace in Croyle Township.

Samuel met his death on the railroad. On a business trip to Summerhill, he was crossing the PRR tracks as a stock train was approaching. He waited but when the locomotive arrived near him, the flag beam fell and struck him. In spite of attention from Doctors Fish and Lowman, he died within hours. He was survived by his wife, the former Susana Weaver, and eight of 10 children.

Frederick (1795-1847) was widowed twice, married three times and died at the age of 52 years. His death was blamed on the scarlet fever epidemic.

Frederick owned 386 acres in Croyle Township. Since he left no will, the Court appointed his son Joseph as administrator and brother-in-law Jacob Stineman as guardian for his other three sons.

Joseph Croyle (1824-1894) was a prosperous farmer about 1 1/2 miles southwest of Summerhill. He started one of the first coal mines in Croyle Township, near South Fork. For a time, he was a partner in the coal mining business with the Stinemans as one of five stockholders and directors of South Fork Coal & Iron Company. He also worked as mine superintendent for six years besides leasing a mine on his land to the company.

His father's third wife (Joseph's stepmother) was Margaret Stineman, a sister of Jacob Stineman Jr.

Margaret Croyle married William Reynolds. They moved to Illinois and had eight children. Sarah married James McAbee.

Elizabeth became the wife of James Patterson. A daughter of the Pattersons married John Wentroth, one of Summerhill's earliest innkeepers.

Esther married George Murray who was Summerhill's first postmaster.

Through the generations, Croyles have left their marks upon the region's history.

Among them is William Henry Croyle (1857-1945) who was the Argyle Coal Company blacksmith at South Fork for 52 years, a Summerhill school director and member of the Lutheran Church Council for over 50 years.

Wendell Croyle (1848-1928) worked as foreman in some of the Stineman mines and lived in South Fork for all his married life with his wife, the former Jennie Rager.

Clyde (Web) Croyle (1886-1983) worked in area coal mines and painted houses during the mining "slack periods".

Wallace Croyle (1915-) who researched the family history and published "My Search For The Truth" has recorded much of the information about the Croyle family.

One can spend days and months tracing the roots planted by Thomas and Barbara Croyle and be overwhelmed with the number of descendants and their life stories.

From the Croyles and other early families, close ties were welded with neighboring South Fork and nearby townships.

As noted, the Croyles intermarried with the Stinemans -- another family which played a principle role in the development of Summerhill Borough.

The Stineman Family

The Stineman family began with Christian Stineman, a tailor, who settled in Bedford County. Here, Jacob Stineman Sr. was born. Jacob moved first to Conemaugh Township and then Richland Township to make his home. This area later became Adams Township, a neighbor of Croyle Township.

Jacob Stineman Sr. was another pioneer of southern Pennsylvania who located here before Cambria County was organized. On the bank of South Fork Creek, he also built a cabin, cleared and farmed land, built and operated a mill.

He married Elizabeth Ling of Bedford. They had 13 children.

One of the children was Jacob Jr. who married Mary Croyle, a daughter of Thomas and Barbara Croyle.

Jacob and Mary (Croyle) Stineman Jr. resided in Adams Township, too. They had six children. Two of them grew up to play major roles in the development of coal and real estate throughout the region, including Summerhill.

Another child, Margaret, married Frederick Croyle, a son of Thomas & Barbara Croyle.

Thus, Margaret became a daughter-in-law of Thomas and Barbara Croyle; Jacob, a son-in-law of the Croyles.

George B. Stineman (1837-1906), one of Jacob and Mary Stineman's sons, started as a school teacher and Civil War veteran. After the war, he engaged in lumbering with his brother, Jacob C., in South Fork.

The Johnstown Flood of 1889 wiped out their lumbering business. George B. returned to the farm but after five years returned to South Fork for a long career as businessman, realtor, coal operator, bank official, school director and borough treasurer. He was also the town's first burgess and first postmaster.

George B. Stineman's real estate business included about 60 Summerhill transactions from 1889 to 1922. He sold land to buyers with names like:

Bengaugh	Green	Murphy
Betz	Grove	Nelson
Bimle	Guyer	Paul
Blatch	Hildebrand	Plummer
Blomberg	Houp	Schmidt
Bodenshatz	Hugentoger	Schneid
Bracken	Kahoe	Sherbine
Brosch	Kime	Shilkowski
Brummert	Kukla	Simendinger
Byers	Long	Urban
Dugan	Mangus	Weiss
Gallardy	Mathieson	Wess
Gangway	McConnell	Wirfel
George	McGough	

In addition, George B. Stineman was active in real estate partnerships doing business in Summerhill Borough. Details follow in a succeeding chapter.

Jacob C. Stineman (1843-1913) also began as a teacher and Civil War veteran. But, in 1868, he started work as a coal miner and quickly advanced to foreman, superintendent and coal operator.

He served as a director for Stineman Coal & Coke, Stineman Coal Mining Company and South Fork Fire Brick Company. He was a board member of First National Bank, the water and electric companies. In addition, he was a successful politician; first as county sheriff and later State Senator.

Jacob sold little real estate in his name in Summerhill. On record were two deals with Peter M. Brown and William W. Paul in 1866 and one with John Giffith in 1868. Jacob's real estate activities were concentrated in South Fork while his brother, George B., took care of most of Summerhill's transactions.

The Pringle Family

The Croyles came from the south to crack the wilderness at Summerhill in 1794. Two years later, Philip Pringle approached from the east, Huntingdon County, to break ground several miles from the Croyles.

This was the beginning of Pringle Hill.

A son, William, received the most newspaper attention because he lived to a "ripe old age". He was born August 14, 1797 and died March 20, 1895, at the age of 97 years.

The Johnstown Weekly Tribune, in a story noting his death, said that when Philip Pringle moved here the county "was a howling wilderness, it being a frequent occurrence for the members of the family to come home from a day's hunt with a bear or a deer."

An earlier story, August 17, 1894, told about a family reunion for what was to be the last birthday celebration for William Pringle.

The reporter wrote that William "can distinctly remember instances while he was yet a boy roaming through the woods when the Red Man of America crossed his path, but before he grew to manhood, the Indians had left for more western lands."

William married Elizabeth Bolewine of Somerset County, when he was 20 years old. They had 11 children and lived two years in Indiana County, two years in Somerset County before returning to his father's Pringle Hill farm.

Elizabeth, 64, passed away in 1862.

William was also the subject of a biographical sketch in Caldwell's 1890 Atlas. Here, the editors reported that William had 38 grandchildren and seven great-grandchildren. "He saw the old Portage Road built and saw it go down, and saw the great Pennsylvania Central built." The writeup contended William was a famous hunter, "having killed more than 200 deer, and bear without number."

This publication showed property owners on the map of Croyle Township included C. A. Pringle, J. W. Pringle, W. Pringle, I. W. Pringle and S. Pringle.

Neighboring landowners were M. Settlemyer, Joseph S. Stull, James Vickroy, T. Griffith and Francis Bailey.

Union Publishing Company's Cyclopedia of 1896 has an account of William's son, Alexander B., who was born in 1829. Alexander stayed on the farm until 1861 and then was a freight conductor on the PRR between Altoona and Pittsburgh for three years, left to fight in the Civil War and returned to the railroad until 1873.

At this time of his life, he settled on a farm in Summit Hill Township and, in 1884, retired to Conemaugh Borough.

Two sons were doctors -- Allison A. and William N. -- and two were engineers for the PRR.

Researching family histories has become a very popular activity, especially for those who have retired and begin thinking about their roots. Through this process, lot of early history is being uncovered.

Such an example is provided from the obituary of Elizabeth, daughter of George and Catherine (Paul) Pringle, who died at the age of 90 years.

She was born on Pringle Hill in 1823. Her marriage was to John Wonders who was a boatman on the Leech Line of the Pennsylvania Canal. After the canal was abandoned, Wonders moved to New Paris where they lived for 34 years. They relocated to Cambria County in 1893.

Elizabeth was buried at Pringle Hill Cemetery. Her services were conducted in Pringle Hill EUB Church by Rev. Franklin E. Hetrick, pastor of South Fork EUB Church.

Another example concerns the death of Delilah (Pringle) Arnold who died at the New Castle, Pa., home of her daughter. Delilah was a daughter of Joseph and Lucinda (Ake) Pringle.

This time, 1916, Rev. Arthur Ritchie, pastor of Summerhill United Brethren Church, performed burial rites.

Among her survivors were a brother, C. A. Pringle; a daughter, Gertrude Seaman; and a son, Walter, all of Summerhill. Her body was viewed in her brother's home in Summerhill.

As these examples show close ties of Pringle Hill with Summerhill, one wonders if Summerhill had expanded beyond its original boundaries, would Pringle Hill been incorporated as part of the borough?

History of Pringle Hill

The history of Pringle Hill evolves around its cemetery, according to Mrs. Henrietta (Arnold) Harding who penned these recollections in 1960:

Martin Pringle donated the first acre of the cemetery, followed by another acre from the Berghane family. Neighbors followed suit and, in short order, there was a cemetery of seven acres.

Preachers, traveling mostly on horse back, visited the area and stayed with cooperating families. They held services every night. On Sundays, they conducted three services. In winter, worshippers attended at the Wilmore or Summerhill churches.

As the community enlarged, a meeting was held at Joseph W. Pringle's house to make plans for the construction of a church next to the cemetery. The construction was placed in the hands of The Dopps, local carpenters, and other volunteers.

The stove, bell and organ were purchased with money contributed by parishioners. The altar bible and windows were donated by individual members. Reverend Gross, the minister at Wilmore and Summerhill, added Pringle Hill to his charge.

With their own church, revival meetings were held and, within a year, the size of the congregation was doubled.

The first death occurred within a year. The casket was made in Summerhill by a Mr. Cooper. And, since Joseph Pringle owned a Big Spring Wagon, he picked up the casket and delivered it to the deceased's residence. The women of the congregation prepared the body for burial. There were no funeral directors at this time. A wake was held. Neighbors brought baskets of food and stayed throughout the night with the deceased.

As the members of the congregation passed on and others moved from the area, the church was finally abandoned. The cemetery, however, remains. It is a well-maintained and ideally located in this beautiful farm country with its paved roads crossing through the farms with modernized homes and new, contemporary dwellings.

Visitation of the graves poses no problems since there are good paved roads in the area.

The Long Family

Joseph Long (1808-1882) came to America with his parents and three brothers in 1812. The family disembarked at Philadelphia where the elder Long got caught up in the westward movement. He bought a horse and cart, packed their belongings and struck out to the unknown. They ended up in Somerset County, but only stayed two years and moved to the little settlement at Johnstown.

Their primary concern was to find a Catholic Church. The only one, at the time, was located in Loretto -- the first Catholic Church in western Pennsylvania, built by Father Demetrius Gallitzin in 1799. Another problem was the lack of a road to Loretto from Johnstown. So, in six months, the Longs were on the move again.

This time, their mission was to locate so that the Loretto church was accessible. They found a suitable spot in what is now known as New Germany.

Loretto was only 12 miles away and there was a road to get there.

The 1922 Golden Jubilee of Mr. and Mrs. John T. Long. Standing: Daughters Amelia and Nettie, Jacob Hoover and Simon Robine (Credit: Jack Bodenschatz)

As more Catholics settled in the county, more churches were constructed and the Longs were able to choose between Ebensburg and Wilmore, sometimes Carrolltown.

Joseph Long married Barbara Schwab (1807-1887), a native of Baden, Germany, in 1833. Father Gallitzin performed the marriage ceremony.

The newly-weds settled on the Long homestead, about two miles from New Germany cemetery. The language spoken by the family was German. Even though the Longs were from Switzerland, they spoke German.

The construction of the Allegheny Portage Railroad brought many Irish-Catholics into the area. St. Bartholomew's Church was built at Wilmore in 1840 to accomodate their needs. The Longs and other settlers from New Germany became parishioners of this new church.

During the ensuing decade, New Germany members increased to the point that they could support a parish of their own. So, in the Spring of 1854, Father Clement Staub was assigned as their pastor. A log church was dedicated by the end of that year.

John T. Long

Joseph and Barbara Long parented three sons and four daughters. Their son, John T. Long (1848-1929), emerged as the family member who not only would tie New Germany with Summerhill but become Summerhill's most successful businessman and community leader.

John learned to be a carpenter and for his journeywork labored throughout Ohio and Illinois, including a stay in Chicago during the Great Chicago Fire of 1871.

Upon his return to Cambria County, he married Mary Strittmatter, daughter of Andrew Strittmatter of Carroll Township, and went housekeeping in Summerhill to pursue the business of contracting and building. The year was 1872.

They had two daughters: Amelia and Brunetta.

By 1877, John T. Long built a planing mill operated by water power. Nine years later, he enlarged the mill, converted to steam power and began to manufacture all kinds of building materials. By 1896, his plant was worth about $10,000; he was doing from $30,000 to $50,000 work per year.

John gained a reputation as a church and road builder. He was Summerhill Borough's first burgess and served four successive terms as justice of the peace.

New Germany

New Germany and Summerhill share many ties. The two communities share a priest for their individual Catholic churches. Many families have strong ancestoral bonds which have been expanded by intermarriages. New Germany Grove, across the road from the Immaculate Conception Church, serves both communities for picnics, festivals and other special functions. The dinner opening Summerhill's 100th anniversary celebration is scheduled at the Grove.

For mail delivery purposes, New Germany carries an R. D. #1, Summerhill address. Comparing recent voter lists, the following surnames appear on both the Summerhill Borough and Croyle Township precinct no. 1 lists: Beyer, Bodenschatz, Bopp, Brown, Croyle, Leventry, Long, Madison, McCall, Meier, Miller Motchenbaugh, Penatzer, Rosenberger, Schrift, Shope, Shrift, Smith, Susko, Tully, Wess, White, Wilson and Wirfel.

New Germany is located about two miles north of Summerhill and five miles south of Ebensburg. Since New Germany has no official boundary lines, where does it begin? Where does it end? Ebensburg Road (Legislative Route 11025) passes through it on its way to Ebensburg. The section from Summerhill to New Germany has some of the most beautiful, new and remodeled homes of the area. The owners are primarily descendants and relatives of New Germany and Summerhill families.

Another unique feature of New Germany is its history in lumbering. It has to be somewhat of a center for the processing of wood and sale of furniture through the C & C Lumber Company, Lewis Long Lumber Company, New Germany Wood Products and Smith Furniture.

Other current businesses include County Tire Warehouse, Wess Energy Saving Systems and Wess Hair Salon.

The serenity of this community was shaken recently when it was learned that a $500 million steel mini-mill and cogeneration plant was being considered in the New Germany Area. The proposal has been on hold since the great outcry from the New Germany residents and, also, that no agreement could be reached with Penelec to purchase electricity from the cogeneration plant.

Chapter 5

Summerhill Grows Near The Coal Industry

The Allegheny Portage Railroad put Summerhill on the map in the early 1830s. The Postoffice Department established the "Summer Hill" office, July 29, 1840. Pennsylvania Railroad gave Summerhill, in the 1850s, further prominence by building a station and including the town as a regular stop for passenger trains, both eastward and westward.

During these decades, the establishment of the New Germany and Pringle Hill sections helped enhance Summerhill's regional importance. But, the greatest catalytic action was yet to come -- the coal industry in the adjoining hills of its western border.

It is evident that when the early pioneers came to this area they were looking for flat lands. This explains the chosen sites of Pringle Hill, Summerhill, New Germany, Wilmore and the surrounding farmlands. The formidable range of mountains and gorges, along the Little Conemaugh, probably drove them into these clearings.

But, when the route for the Portage Railroad was being cut, coal deposits were uncovered; they were somewhat ignored. Wood was plentiful and didn't require the investment of money to cut and transport. Wood was easy to burn, an adequate supply was available "in the back yard" and the burning smell seemed to be a normal part of rural living. Above all, the trees had to be removed to make room for farm lands and cabins.

Early Coal Developers

George and William Murray were the first around Summerhill to extract the coal for blacksmithing purposes. Samuel S. Paul, with the help of John K. Shryock of Wilmore, started the first coal mine in this area, halfway between Summerhill and South Fork -- referred to as Sunshine. In the same vicinity, Shryock and Nicholas S. George prospected on the south bank of the Little Conemaugh River and located the E, or Lemon seam, which had little use at the time.

The railroad was substituting coal for wood in the 1870s. A need developed for good burning coal. More prospecting uncovered what they needed, the B, or Miller, seam of coal.

South Fork Coal & Iron Company was chartered in 1869; Joseph Croyle was president; George B. Stineman, director; Jacob C. Stineman, superintendent. The opening was on the hillside along present Route 53, about 1 1/2 miles west of Summerhill. A long chute-like tipple was constructed from the mine to the mainline tracks, where PRR fueled its engines on their runs through this section.

Euclid Mine, near the railroad tower at South Fork, began about 1875. The owner was J. C. Luke, who had established a medical practice in Summerhill.

Two years earlier, Joseph Croyle leased a mine on his 240-acre farm and, in 1880, the Stinemans began mining on the Bealtown Hill, high above the banks of South Fork Creek.

The Argyle mines came into being the next year opposite the railroad signal tower in South Fork. The tipple extended over a spur line, parallel to the mainline. A coaling station furnished coal for the railroad's steam engines.

Ehrenfeld became part of the boom in 1883.

There was a scramble for building lots to house the daily arrival of coal miners. And, since lot of these operations were within walking distance from Summerhill, the little town was able to provide some housing.

The spin-off helped Summerhill because of its commercial development. At first, Summerhill was the only place there were stores. Railroad hand cars were frequently dispatched from South Fork Station to buy provisions at Summerhill and transport them back to South Fork.

The valley was never the same. Areas that early settlers ignored were now valuable real estate. Population exploded. Builders were busy. Merchants were scurrying for choice locations. Even, some merchants relocated from Summerhill. Investors in Philadelphia suddenly took notice and participated. Hotels were in great demand. Railroad sidings were being constructed. Coal trains became a daily event as they were assembled and sent on their way to eastern markets.

The pace disrupted the quiet and uncomplicated ways of the past. The area had become a player in America's industrial revolution!

Ehrenfeld's Impact on Summerhill

Ehrenfeld's impact was more direct on Summerhill because its location was contiguous.

Philip Hartman was sent, in 1883, by John C. Scott & Sons to open a mine. The firm reorganized into the Webster Coal and Coke Company. The community was named Webster Mines. A town of 124 houses was laid out; the homes were rented to the miners. The development grew to 246 homes by 1906.

Again, there were those who made homes in sections adjoining Ehrenfeld -- Fifficktown and Summerhill --because of the short walking distance to the mine.

Webster Land & Improvement Company was organized in 1892 for "purchasing, holding, leasing and selling real estate in Ehrenfed." Stockholders were: William B., John C. and Charles H. Scott of Philadelphia, 332 shares each; Philip Hartman and James A. Maquire, Ehrenfeld, two shares each. The company was capitalized at 1,000 shares at $50 per share -- a total of $50,000.

The Scotts were involved with Summerhill Borough. Tax assessement records of the borough show that in 1895-96, taxes for 40 acres of land -- Dibert Tract -- were levied against J. C. Scott & Sons. This tract was titled to Griffith, Scott and Stineman in 1897.

Early Summerhill Land Transactions

Ten years earlier, 1887, a tract of borough land had been vested in the names of Thomas Griffith, John Brown and George B. Stineman by William Murray. It was named the Griffith, Brown and Stineman tract.

When Thomas Griffith died, his interest was equally divided among John T. Griffith, Dr. Abner Griffith, Webster Griffith and Annie E. Lyte.

Upon John T. Griffith's death, his interest was sold to Dr. Abner Griffith, Webster Griffith and Annie E. Lyte.

Meanwhile, John Brown, in 1893, by voluntary assignment for the benefit of creditors, transferred his share to J. B. Green, then a physician in Summerhill.

Dr. Green sold his interest, in 1896, to Webster Land & Improvement Company.

Complicating? There is more!

Webster Land & Improvement, two years later, sold their holdings to George B. Stineman, Webster Griffith and Annie E. Lyte.

Dr. Abner Griffith had died; his entitlement went to Webster Griffith and Annie Lyte.

Coal rights throughout these deals remained with Webster Land & Improvement Company.

Griffith, Stineman & Lyte partnership divided the land into lots. One of the first deals, March 20, 1889, was a sale of lots 90 and 91 to George Weiss of Summerhill. These lots were situated along Spring Street, bounded by Second Avenue and Ebensburg Road. Lots 92 and 93 were sold by the same group, the same day to Katie Weiss of Summerhill.

In 1921, ownership transferred to Humphrey and Katherine Humphreys. Humphrey passed away and when Katherine died, in 1934, there was no will. Survivors shared the estate. The Court had to deal with 40 individuals scattered locally in Summerhill, Brownstown, Wilmore, Croyle Township, Johnstown, Conemaugh, South Fork, Derry, New Kensington and Nanty Glo. Others were living in Ohio and Minnesota.

Katherine Humphreys' property was purchased by Homer and Genevieve Hershberger. Homer died in 1947; the property went to Genevieve by right of survivorship. October, 1958, a deed from Genevieve was executed to show the sale of the property to Calvin J. and Betty Jane Harshberger, present owners.

The deed noted that the lots were on the plan of Griffith, Brown & Stineman or Griffith, Stineman & Lyte.

This accounting, courtesy of Jay Harshberger, illustrates how properties have passed through many hands in the borough's history. It also gives a sampling of George B. Stineman's role as a real estate agent in Summerhill's early days.

It has often been said, "Changes are inevitable. Today's happenings are tomorrow's history."

Stineman continued his real estate partnership for many years. Summerhill Borough's tax records recorded this group as Stineman-Griffith; tracing was possible through these records. The amount of land taxed follows:

1897-1900	39 acres
1901-1904	34 acres
1905	33 acres
1906-1910	19 acres
1911-1932	11 acres
1933-1954	10 7/8 acres
1955	9 5/8 acres

One can conclude that 1906 was the best year for their land sales; 14 acres were sold. The next best year was 1911 with the sale of eight acres. These figures indicate that it took the Stineman-Griffith partnership 35 years to sell 28 of their 39 acres.

Commercial Establishments of 1890

Caldwell's Atlas of Cambria County gives a view of this portion of the Conemaugh Valley in 1890.

Business directories show Wilmore with a meat market, hotel, clothing store, grocery and shoemaker. G. D. Pringle is listed as a carpenter, contractor and builder. Robertson and Sherbine dealt in general merchandise and sales of farm equipment, wagons, buggies, phosphates, coal and real estate.

South Fork cataloged George B. Stineman general store, Brown, George & Company general store, South Fork Supply Company, a meat-grocery store, Crouse Hotel and J. C. Murphy as carpenter, contractor and builder. Dr. J. C. Luke moved from Summerhill to be South Fork's physician-surgeon and manager of Euclid Coal Company.

Summerhill's Directory of 1890

Summerhill had a more extensive lineup:
* John D. Wentroth -- Summer Hill House
* Peter Brown -- Railroad House, shoemaker
* A. Carpenter -- Carpenter House
* P. F. Lewis -- general merchandise, country produce, and agent for American, Inman, Red Star and Guion Steamship Lines
* John N. Brown -- general merchandise, planing mill and sawmill
* C. A. Dimond -- general merchandise, meat market
* Daniel A. Sipe -- feed and flour manufacturing
* D. G. Seaman -- blacksmith
* J. T. Long -- architect, contractor and builder, dealer and manufacturer of wood products
* William McClarren -- masonry contractor and builder
* William T. McConnell -- surveyor and engineer
* Dr. J. A. Hendricks -- physician and surgeon

Where Wilmore and South Fork each supported four general retail outlets, Summerhill was positioned with three. But, Summerhill offered three hotels compared to one at South Fork and another at Wilmore. The only blacksmith registered in Summerhill. The only place steamship tickets could be purchased was from P. F. Lewis in Summerhill.

With the mills of John Brown and John Long, Summerhill qualified as the area's lumbering center. Also, Summerhill was regarded the trading hub.

John Brown was characterized as one of the enterprising citizens, leading merchant, justice of the peace and "in charge of PRR's business at its station." His saw and planing mills were located along Ebensburg Road, just off Main Street.

John T. Long's planing mill occupied the area enclosed by Croyle, Mill and Laurel Streets.

Summerhill's Map of 1890

The Pennsylvania Railroad's two tracks divided the town into two sections. The section to the south of the railroad was almost completely built-up with residential and business properties. The northern section displayed development along Jackson Street up to a line with Quarry Alley. About six other properties were scattered above this line.

The area encompassing First and Second Avenues was marked off for lots and titled as the Brown Addition.

C. A. Dimond's slaughter house was located along Mill Street. Dr. Hendrick occupied a house near the intersection of Portage and Main Streets.

Griffith, Brown and Stineman holdings included a large area beyond the

Summerhill of 1890 (Caldwell's Atlas of 1890)

eastern bank of Laurel Run.

The railroad depot area consisted of two frame buildings parallel to the tracks in an open-square type of setting.

Facing the depot were C. A. Dimond's store and the Carpenter House. To the east, across Main Street, was the Summerhill House. Further east, across Laurel Run, stood the Railroad House, next to the railroad shop building.

The tracks divided Main Street into two sections. John Brown's store was on the northern side, about the present location of the GBU building.

D. G. Seaman's blacksmith shop sat on Jackson Street and a block below on Main Street was the school building.

The location of P. F. Lewis was not identified on Caldwell's map but was listed in the directory.

There were three properties on the western side of Jackson Street, facing Second Avenue, that stood alone with no other immediate neighbors. They were the properties of G. Hettle, W. McClarren and W. T. McConnell. McClarren was the masonry contractor; McConnell, surveyor and engineer.

The names of Griffith, Brown and Stineman appeared at the stone quarry. It is unclear if this meant they owned the quarry, the land around it, or both.

D. A. Sipe's mill was shown over a stream which cut off from the Little Conemaugh River, ran under the mill and returned to the river.

St. John's Lutheran Church was identified at its present location, along with its adjacent cemetery.

After crossing a bridge over the Little Conemaugh, Portage Street is charted with another bridge crossing Laurel Run and continuing under the railroad overpass on the way to Wilmore.

The only roads identified on this map are Portage, Main, Jackson, Market Streets and First and Second Avenues. Perhaps, the reason the others were not labeled is because they were still unnamed. This exercise would take place when the town became a borough.

Over the years, citizens made it a custom to refer to the section of town, south of the railroad tracks, as downtown and, north of the tracks, uptown.

Listed Property Owners

Using this connotation, the following families lived or owned sites in the downtown area in 1890: C. Myers, J. McCandle, W.H. Dimond, M. Stock, E.W Hull, C.A. Dimond, J.M. Skelly, D.A. Sipe, S. Myers, J.D. Dimond, D.A. Bertwell, I. Plummer, M. Tully, P. Farrell, P. Brown, Mrs. Kurtz, P. McCall, J.W. Plummer, J.T. Long, J. D. Wentroth, Dr. Hendrick, G. Gable, Mrs. Stineman, J.D. Plummer, A. Carpenter, Mrs. J Reynolds, J. Secher, J. Kick, T. Seman, H. Quinn, William Gitman, J. Brown and M. Lamb.

Of these C. Myers is shown six times; J.D. Wentroth, six times; C.A. Dimond, D.A. Sipe and M. Tully, two times each.

The uptown property owners included H. Davis, J. Sluser, J. Long, Mrs. Weinzert, Griffith-Brown-Stineman, Mrs. S.S. Hare, Mrs. Croyle, John Brown, J.W. Plummer, W.H. Brown, J.D. Wentroth, A. Werner, P. Karnes, N. S. George, D. G. Seaman, H J. Rorabugh, W.I. Nipps, R. Mathison, J. Reynolds, T. J. Seaman, G.E. Betz, H. Humper, J.F. Sequaskon, J. Map, R. Wellin, G. Hettle, W. McClarren and W.T. McConnell. Mrs. S.S. Hare and D.G. Seaman are listed three times; Mrs. Croyle and John Brown, twice.

(Spellings are as they appear on Caldwell's map.)

J. T. Long Residence (Caldwell's Atlas of 1890)

J. T. Long Planing Mill (Caldwell's Atlas 1890)

45

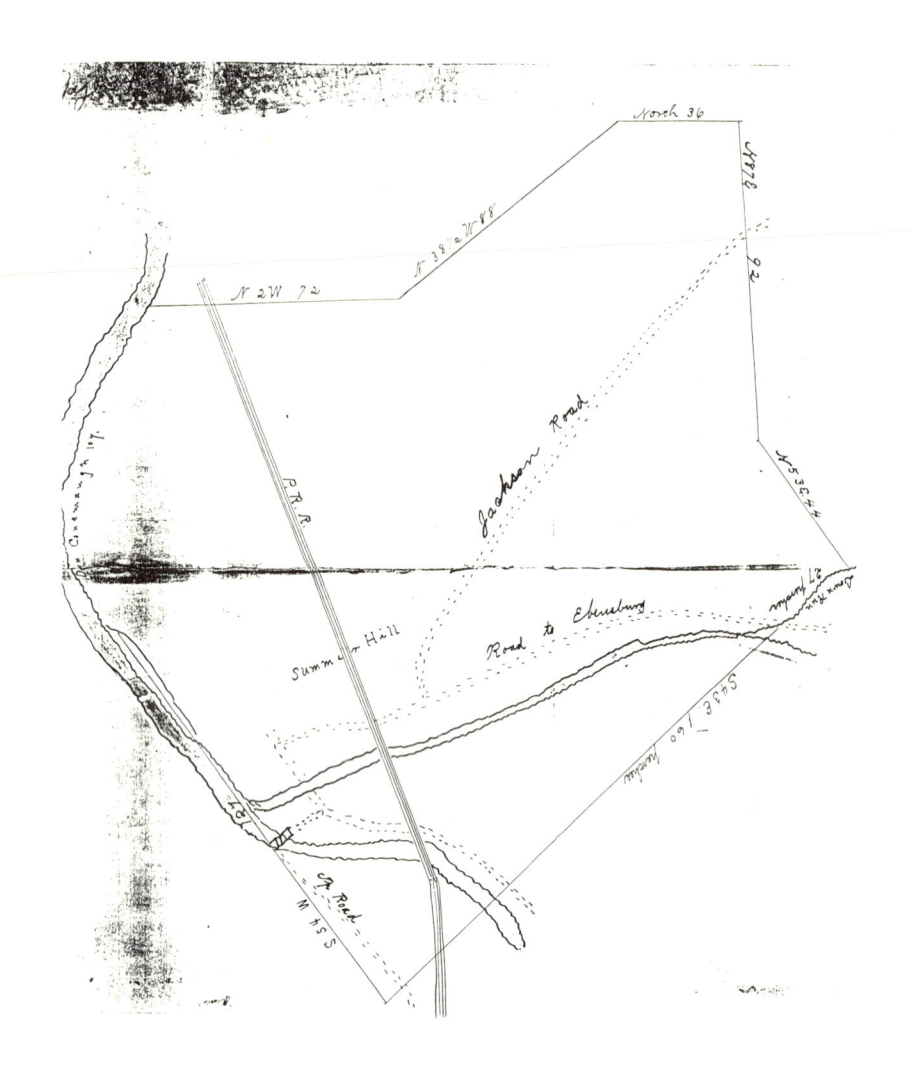

Original map filed with Cambria County Courthouse for the Summerhill Charter in 1892.

Chapter 6

Time To Show Independence

The year is 1892. Leading citizens realize it is time for Summerhill to declare its independence from township governance. Wilmore has been doing it since 1859; South Fork since 1887. In addition, there is Ebensburg, Loretto, Carrolltown, Chest Springs, Franklin, East Conemaugh, Gallitzin, Tunnelhill, Lilly, Ashville, Portage, Morrellville and Dale enjoying the status.

Besides, the 1880 census estimates Summerhill's population at 343 people and Wilmore, 310.

Johnstown is now a city, taking in the former boroughs of Prospect, Cambria, Conemaugh, Millville, Coopersdale, Woodvale and Grubbtown.

Summerhill Borough's Official Boundaries

The Summerhill charter is affirmed by Cambria County Court on September 6, 1892. The official boundaries are:

"Beginning at the northeast corner of the bridge on the township road leading to South Fork, thence North 2 degrees West 72 perches, thence North 38 1/2 degrees West 88 perches, thence North 36 perches to stones, thence North 87 degrees East 92 perches to stones, thence North 53 degrees East 44 perches to Isaac Paul at the branch of Laurel Run, thence down said run by its various courses 27 perches across Ebensburg Road, thence South 43 degrees East 160 perches, thence South 54 degrees West 127 perches to the lower end of D. A. Sipes' tail race, thence down the north branch of the Conemaugh River by its various courses 107 perches to the place of beginning."

This all adds up to 0.8 square mile which is larger than South Fork (.05), Ehrenfeld (0.4) or Wilmore (0.3).

The Town's Petitioners

62 townspeople sign the petition: Henry and C. BERSCHNEIDER: George and George E. BETZ; James BODENSCHATZ; A. 0., C. D., John, Peter and William H. BROWN; C. W. CHAPPELL; W. H. CROYLE; H. W. DAVIS: C. A. and Stephen DIMOND; G. DUNMIRE; Charles and George GABLE; John GALLAROLZ; W. E. GEORGE; Michael GESSLER; William GILMARS; Dr. J. B. GREEN; Dr. J. A. HENDRICKS; George HETTLE; H. D. HOOVER; E. W. HULL; John and William KICK; Philip KEARNS; Francis KURTZ; Michael LEACH; John LARRY; P. F. LEWIS; J. T. LONG; Charles MANGLE; Robert MATHIESON; Patrick McCALL; J. F. McGOUGH; William McCLARREN; Willian T. McCONNELL; Sylveste

MOSS; William J. Niffs; Isaac T. PEARCE; James D., David P. and J. W. PLUMMER; Henry QUINN; H. J. RORABAUGH; D.G. and Thomas J. SEAMAN; Peter SCHRIFT; M. SHERBINE; John M. and Joseph H Skelly; Joseph S. STULL; Michael TULLY; Mrs. M . B. WADSWORTH; John D. and George J. WENTROTH; Anthony WERNER; and Isaac WIKE. (All spellings as they appear on courthouse document.)

First Elected Officers

People vote at the office of J. T. Long, September 29, 1892, from 7 A.M. to 7 P. M. J. G. McGough gives notice of the election and its purpose. Michael Tully is the judge of elections. J. W. Kerns and W. H. Brown are the inspectors of election.

The Court appoints Joseph Brown as auditor to receive and file nomination certificates, nomination papers of the candidates and be responsible for printing and distributing the ballots.

George Betz, Anthony Werner, Dr. J. B. Green, J. D. Wentroth, J. W. Plummer and D. Gardner Seaman are the successful candidates for borough council. John T. Long wins the burgess position.

These elected councilmen meet October 8, 1892 to take the following oath:
"I do swear that I will support the constitution of the United States, the constitution of the Commonwealth of Pennsylvania and that I will fill the office of councilman for the Borough of Summerhill with fidelity and to the best of my ability."

Two days later, they hold a meeting and elect J. W. Plummer, secretary; Dr. J. B. Green, treasurer. Dr. Green offers to furnish the "necessary books".

The First Regular Election

The next council meeting did not occur until four months later because the regular election of borough officials falls on February 21, 1893. Those elected in 1892 could only serve until this election. So, the Summerhill people vote again.

This time, the winners are Dr. J. B. Green and George Betz, three-year terms; Anthony Werner and Charles Mangus, two years; and William McClarren and Clem Bersnider, one year. (The spelling of names are as they appear in official council minutes).

At the organizational meeting of February 25, 1893, McClarren is elected secretary; Werner, treasurer.

The new council names Conrad Bersnider as street commissioner and Joseph H. Skelly as constable. In May, Dr. Green assumes the office of president. Meetings are established for the last Saturday of each month.

The Council's Deliberations By Years
1893

P. F. Lewis takes his oath as Burgess and appoints a committee -- Green, McClarren and Betz -- to recommend a site for the council room and the borough jail.

It must be noted that Summerhill Borough Council operates under the commission form of government where council members share equal power, the burgess is in charge of the police department and the council functions through various committees or departments.

The deliberations during the next 13 meetings in 1893 provide some interesting details!

* Payment for the printing of ordinances and stationery waits until there is enough money in the treasury.

* Peter Kiney is permitted to pay $6 in advance "for the privelege of selling meat."

* The treasurer is directed to collect license money from Ebensburg.

* A lock is purchased from J. D. Wentroth for $60.

* William T. McConnell is hired "to divide several tracts of land in and adjoining the borough (spelling Burrow in the officials minutes) and survey streets and alleys."

* Dr. Green and George Betz secure specifications from J. T. Long for council chambers and the jail. Council approves them and notices are posted that bids are due by May 15.

* At the May 15th meeting, John Wright is awarded the jail bid for $270.56. Council reconsiders J. T. Long's bid of $295 at a special June meeting and awards the contract to him for $295 "less one door and frame."

* John Gaglardi (spelling in the minute book) receives $13.50 to construct the jail foundation.

* Real estate taxes are set at 4 mills.

* Attorney M. D. Kittell is paid for services to incorporate the borough.

* A. 0. Brown is appointed High Constable in April. E. W. Hull is named for the same position in July.

* The street commissioner and his men are employed at $1.50 per day, "provided they be worth it."

* The scale for the use of a team of horses is $3 for an ten-hour day.

* Councilmen Mangus, Bersnider and Betz investigate C. A. Dimond's slaughter house and premises to determine if "he maintains a nuisance." Council declares a nuisance in August.

* Mangus and Betz serve as a committee to buy a stove. J. D. Plummer donates one.

* Treasurer Anthony Werner receives $4.19 for making a trip to Ebensburg to collect license money.

* William McClarren, secretary, is paid $14.40 as his salary up to August 26.

* Dr. Green advances his own money to pay borough expenses and collects whenever the treasury is able. Noted in the official minutes: (1) $3 for "hand cupps" and (2) $3.15 for building a fence and board walk around the jail. In August, he receives a payment of $94.38 to reimburse him for the lumber purchased for board walks. In September, the minutes note that Dr. Green laid the board walk in front of J. T. Long's and "that he receive interest on his money till the bill is paid."

* A parcel of land is purchased from John D. and Mary Ann Wentroth for $75. This land was originally warranted in the name of Benjamin Williams and the title, through sundry deeds and conveyances, became vested in Jacob Stineman. Stineman sold the land, in 1866, to Elizabeth Paterson. Mary Ann Wentroth acquired the property as an heir of Elizabeth Paterson. Now, the land was the property of the borough.

* A committee of Green, Betz, Werner, Mangus and Bersnider were charged with the responsibility "go over streets to see where work is needed worst." It has to be remembered streets were not paved at this time.

* After serving six months, P. F. Lewis resigns as Burgess. No reason is given.

* Many small payments (small at today's standards) during 1893, such as: (1) Anthony Werner -- $6.50 and $7.81 for hardware and $2.25 for a keg of nails; (2) D.A. McGough -- $2.10 to record a deed; (3) John D. Wentroth -- $1 for 1/2 day of hauling; (4) D. G. Seaman -- 70¢ for blacksmithing; (5) John Long -- 35¢ for 2 1/2 hours of labor; and (6) E. W. Hull -- 67¢ for lists and board for a prisoner.

1894

* There are nine regular and four special council meetings.
* The treasurer's compensation is set at 4% of collections.
* The secretary receives a six-dollar balance of his salary to bring his annual total to $20.40.
* Frank Kurtz, W. H. Dimond and Will George replace Werner, McClarren and Berschneider (previously indicated as Bersnider) as councilmen.
* William Plummer is the new street commissioner.
* Reorganization in March places Frank Kurtz in the president's chair. John Kerns is secretary and James D. Plummer, the treasurer.
* George B. Skelly sells the borough 1 1/2 tons of coal for $1.50.
* William Davis is selected as borough solicitor at a retainer fee of $50 a year.
* The tax rate remains at 4 mills.
* William McConnell rents the council room for one dollar a month.
* Ordinance No. 1 passes and allows taxpayers to work out their borough taxes, up to August 1, 1894. Thereafter, unpaid taxes are collected by the

street commissioner who is required to have a $500 bond.

* Council authorizes the purchase of lumber from Isreal Rorabaugh for the year. Later in the year, however, they allow Will Brown to sell the borough lumber at 50¢, if it is agreeable to the Burgess.

* Viewers for the borough are paid $2 a day.

* A motion proclaims that "any person or persons jumping off or on freight trains for pleasure be arrested."

* Instructions direct that there be "a survey of streets that at present do not belong to the borough and a petition made to the court."

* Councilmen Betz, Mangus and Dimond agree to "examine and look after the bridge (on Portage Street) and if they think it is necessary to call a special meeting." At such a meeting, in July, masons are hired at $2.50 a day to erect abutments. Ten barrels of cement at $1.25 per barrel are ordered. James H. Skelly is paid 20¢ an hour for four days of masonry work. A handrail is installed for the public's safety.

* Board walks take up much of the councilmen's attention. A project authorizes the construction of a plank walk "at Mrs. Wadsworth's alley and run to Will George's," and another "be laid from J. D. Plummer's alley to Mrs. Kurtz's property." A 4-foot walk is approved from the school to Will George's property. And, another motion furnishes lumber to Paul Wirfel to complete a 2-foot walk from Will George's place to his.

* Perhaps, the most unusual item of business relates to the street commissioner. Council authorizes the commissioner be paid $44.50 in full, up to September 1, 1894, but that $4.50 be deducted "for a fine imposed upon him by the burgess for fighting in the borough and that the burgess be paid 50¢ out of that."

* Dr. Green continues to be reimbursed for his expenditures, such as 80¢ for a hammer, prothonotary fees of $3.75, and payment of cement and freight.

* Market and Madison Streets create another important concern. The street commissioner is directed to have a survey made of Market Street and the burgess post notices that the street will begin at the corner of James D. Plummer, run along the properties of J. D. Wentroth, Mrs. Francis Kurtz, Mrs. Reynolds, J. D. Wentroth and M. C. Dimond to Church Street and the PRR on the right. Along Church Street, M. C. Dimond on the left and the church property on the right, Market Street will run through J. T. Long's property, cross Mill Street, go through M. C. Dimond's lot and stop at Portage Street.

* Madison Street's survey would begin at Jackson Street, go through Mrs. Sarah Hare and Pennsylvania Railroad properties and meet the road to Ehrenfeld.

* John D. Plummer was ordered to move five panels of fencing which blocks the alley and prevents the passage of a team and wagon.

1895

* Charles Mangus, W. H. Dimond and Will George are replaced by P. C. Yahner, Peter Schrift and George Hettle as councilman. Yahner, however, only serves four months and resigns.
* It is agreed that councilmen be paid for attending regular meetings - 50¢ a night.
* Dr. Green returns to the presidency. James D. Plummer remains as treasurer.
* John T. McGough is the chief of police. He serves until August when his seat is declared vacant and E. W. Hull is named to fill it.
* John T. Long is the new street commissioner. John Kearns (note change in spelling) is still secretary; his pay is now $12 per year.
* Burgess Skelly requests a law book for the use of the borough. He also presides at a meeting in June because the president is absent.
* The first Board of Health is named: Dr. J. A. Hendricks, five years; E. W. Hull, four years; H. J. Rorabaugh, three years; P. P. Sipe, two years; and H. E. Meckley, one year.
* Croyle Street is cut from M. C. Dimond's to the old Portage Road. By council action, all parties owning land were directed to give clear titles, without charge. The borough pays for the preparation of deeds.
* Another project involves the erection of a 5-foot vertical fence from Wentroth Avenue to one side of Portage Road, at borough expense.
* Attorney William Davis was paid to April 1, 1895 and notified his services would no longer be needed.
* The borough pays Mrs. Sarah Hare $15 for a right-of-way of Madison Street.
* Approval is given to build a coal and tool shed at the rear of the jail or council chamber.
* A road scrapper is added to the borough's road equipment.
* The street commissioner is to hire painters at $1.30 per day to paint the bridge at or near Kick's.
* The estate of Conrad Myers is given credit for 1894 taxes in exchange for sand used by the borough.
* The Summerhill business directory for 1895 includes some new names, according to the assessor's records:

>Peter Brown--shoemaker
>C. A. Dimond--butcher
>Dr. J. B. Green--physician
>John Griffith--saloon keeper
>Frank Kurtz--hotel keeper
>J. T. Long--contractor
>Patrick McCall--grocer
>James D. Plummer--grocer

                Max Reich--barber
            Anthony Werner--merchant
           J. D. Wentroth--hotel keeper

* Sipe's Mill is measured at 49 acres and an assessed valuation of $3,200.
* 140 individuals, 12 horses and 34 cattle are certified for county tax purposes.

1896

* February of 1896 brings a big change in the council's membership. Dr. J. B. Green ends his tenure which extends from the date of incorporation. Likewise, George Betz retires. He, too, was one of the first councilmen.
* Continuing from the 1895 body are Frank Kurtz, Peter Schrift and George Hettle. New members are C. A. Dimond, Pat McCall, Paul Wirfel and Henry Berschneider.
* Pat McCall is president. J. W. Kearns and J. D. Plummer continue as secretary and treasurer, respectively.
* Taxes remain at 4 mills.
* In April, Pat McCall is named street commissioner, only to resign the following month. Perhaps, this constituted a conflict as president.
* An ordinance, patterned after one in South Fork, was approved to give right-of-way through several streets to the Johnstown Telephone Company.
* J. T. Long is paid for fence along Mill Street -- 192 feet at 11¢ per foot.
* Wooden walks are authorized on Jackson and Market Streets.
* The burgess, James H. Skelly, is authorized to contact the borough solicitor about a suit against the Pennsylvania Railroad Company for obstruction of Market Street.

1897

Frank Kurtz is voted president for the year. J. W. Kearns continues as secretary, but J. T. Long replaces J. D. Plummer, who just completed three consecutive years as treasurer.

* M. D. Kittell is the new solicitor. John B. Slausser is hired as the new street commissioner at $1.50 an hour.
* A stone crossing is placed from Mrs. Hare's stable to Union Hall. Walks are made for Madison and Mill Streets.
* George Hettle and Paul Wirfel give up their council seats. H. J. Rorabaugh serves until October. George E. Betz returns as councilman after an absence of a year.
* Johnstown and Bell Telephone Companies furnish 50¢ a year for each pole they have in the borough.

1898

* In January, the Johnstown Weekly Tribune reports Summerhill has 111 houses and 150 lots, valued at $75,730. And, there are 27 male dogs and one female! Other taxable properties include 14 horses/mules and 29 cows.

* The newspaper, February 18, reported the following results of the town's elections:

* Council (2 to be elected) -- J. T. Pearce, Rep. (34); Ed D. Myers, Rep. (30); **Michael Tully, Dem. (62);** and **P. Yahner, Dem. (59).**

* School Director (3 to be elected) -- W. H. Croyle, Rep. (36); **John Galardy, Rep. (53);** Peter Sipe, Rep. (32); James D. Plummer, Dem. (41); **Frank Kurtz, Dem. (56);** and **John McGough, Dem. (58).**

* Assessor -- Milton Sherbine, Rep. (37) and **Clem Berschneider, Dem. (55).**

* Auditor -- Jacob Angus, Rep. (36) and **Charles Long, Dem. (57).**

* Judge of Elections -- Philip Pringle, Rep. (39) and **William H. Dimond, Dem. (59).**

* Inspector -- W. L. Hull, Rep. (34) and **Daniel Kearn, Dem. (56).**

* In August, the number of taxable individuals were reported as 163 and the value of all real estate at $89,960. No stages, omnibusses, hacks nor cabs were listed for taxation.

* Ebensburg Court approves liquor licenses for John Griffith on Main Street; Francis Kurtz, Carpenter House; and P. C. Yahner, Summerhill House.

* Frank Kurtz completes his term as councilman, a position he has held since 1894, and is elected as a school director.

* P. C. Yahner is back as councilman and Michael Tully is the new member.

* C. A. Dimond is now president of the council; Kearns is retained as secretary. W. H. Dimond is the new street commissioner. J. T. Long stays as treasurer. E. W. Hull serves as burgess.

* The school board is granted permission to vacate a part of the alley behind the school and replace it with an alley running along the lot of William Gillman to Jackson Street. The new alley must be at least 12 feet wide and provide enough room for the passage of a team of horses and a wagon.

* Twelve-inch terra cotta pipe is installed at W. H. Croyle's and Wentroth Street, back of Dr. Barnett's property.

1899

* The president, secretary and treasurer do not change.

* P. C. Yahner attends his last meeting in April; Henry Berschneider, in February. They are replaced by Ed Kehoe and P. J. McGough. However, McGough only serves from April through July.

* Secretary Kearns also is given the job of street commissioner.

* The tax millage is still 4 mills.
* Those with wire fences along the streets are told to remove them within 30 days.
* Council decides it will buy several street lamps. Anyone who wants a street lamp must take the responsibility of lighting it. The borough will furnish the oil.
* Council members who miss regular meetings without "sufficient cause", will be fined 50¢ for each absence.
* A wall is to be constructed along Market Street in front of the Evangelical Lutheran Church, at or in front of a corner post before the church and along Market Street toward the PRR line "as far as the street commissioner may see proper." The wall must be "3 feet at or near the grave yard and the terminus 2 feet."
* A hitching post is to be removed near the Griffith Wash House.
* Pennsylvania Railroad is urged to install gates on both sides of the track crossing.
* An ordinance is drafted about cows, sheep, hogs and pigs.

1900

* C. A. Dimond is in his third year as president. J. W. Kearns who has been secretary since 1894 is replaced with Charles Kime. Peter Sipe is the new treasurer. J. B. Schlosser takes over the duties of street commissioner. The new burgess is Aaron Sherbine.
* The new secretary does not record names of the councilmen who attend meetings until the October minutes. It appears that Dimond, Rorabaugh and, perhaps, McGough give up their council membership in August.
* The October 10 meeting shows only three in attendance -- Michael Tully, M. A. Sherbine and G. D. Seaman. The following session, on October 25, shows H. Humphreys is added to this trio. The November meeting lists Tully, Seaman, Humphreys and Adam Bimel. The next two sessions, before newly-elected members are seated, the attendants are Seaman, Kehoe, Bimel, Sherbine and Tully.
* It must have been a year of turmoil because Burgess Sherbine resigns in June, Schlosser gives up his street commissioner's position and Charles Kime resigns as secretary. William T. McConnell fills two positions -- secretary and street commissioner. Very little business is transacted.
* The tax rate is left unchanged. William H. Sechler is hired as a new solicitor. A safe is purchased from J. T. Long for $40 and Central District & Printing Telegraph Company is permitted to install poles for telegraph and telephone transmissions. It is decided to try a car load of gravel for the borough's walks.

1901

* Reorganization seats Frank Kurtz, Dan Kearns and Oliver Shrift as new council members. The rest of the board includes Ed Kehoe, Adam Bimel and Milton A. Sherbine. E. W. Hull is the burgess.

* There's no record of an election for president. McConnell is still secretary at a salary of $15 a year. Frank Kurtz is voted treasurer but several days later he declines. James D. Plummer accepts the position. He had been the borough's treasurer during 1894-95-96.

* E. W. Hull resigns his second position, tax collector, and opts to serve only as burgess. George J. Wentroth is elected tax collector. Lewis White is the new street commissioner at $1.75 a day. Sylvester Plummer is hired as chief of police at a monthly salary of $50. However, the salary is reduced later to $30 a month. Plummer resigns. He is replaced by Henry Wise who accepts the $30 rate.

* The solicitor's (W. H. Sechler) salary comes under scrutiny, too. Council votes to pay $35 this year and, if the solicitor does not accept, they'll pay $40 -- which is a cut of $10.

* An unpopular move, the first tax increase is imposed -- up one mill from 4 to 5.

* A meeting of property owners was held to determine if they will "take water or not." The burgess is to meet with the water company manager to see if they will offer six water plugs for the borough at no charge. If not, the burgess is to find out if the water company will "put them in cheaper than the others."

* An oil lamp is approved in front of the council room. The town's policeman is charged with its cleaning and lighting.

* George Bodenschatz sells the borough 1,388 feet of hemlock for $18.

1902

* At reorganization, it appears like the lineup for a race with nine councilmen listed for the meeting. By late May, this number drops to seven. In June, Michael Smith attends his last meeting. Now, and until reorganization next year, there are six members -- Milton Sherbine, C. 0. Dimond, P. C, Yahner, G. Y. Betz, Frank Kurtz and Daniel Kearns.

* Sherbine is chosen for president. Plummer retains the treasurer's post. Secretary McConnell died and a resolution was adopted in February to eulogize him. John Kearns is recruited to accept his old job as secretary.

* As usual, there is a new street commissioner. This time it is Sylvester Plummer.

* The solicitor also is changed. Thomas J. Itell gets the job.

* A request is made to Pennsylvania Railroad to eliminate the railroad crossing and build a subway under the tracks for pedestrians and an overhead bridge for teams at "the east end of the cut, west of the station."

* Market Street is again being surveyed. This time council decides to hire an engineer to do the job.

* Sidewalks are addressed again. It is agreed to "use all old boards to repair board walks and tear up all walks that are level and put in cinders in its place the walks to be torn up in places that are level and not dangerous and the walks to be torn up only to repair walks that are dangerous and necessary." Clear?

* Board walks past Gallardy and the one leading to Burk's Hotel are to be "torn away or repaired, whichever is best."

* By Fall of 1902, there was a problem about tax collector. Early in August, J. G. McGough was elected. Later in the month, G. Y. Betz was named.

* Next month, John Kearns resigns as secretary. Peter Betz is called upon to serve as secretary pro-tem.

* Sewerage became a major project in October. First, an ordinance was passed prohibiting the discharge of sewerage into Laurel Run. Next, A. L. Anderson was paid $2,498.37 for installing the sewer lines on Wentroth Avenue and Croyle Street.

* The burgess was directed to "continue cleaning streets and putting lines in filthy places in alleys." Authority was given to buy 20-inch pipe for Main Street from G. D. Seaman's blacksmith shop to the Little Conemaugh River. D. A. Sipes' Grist Mill was urged to empty their sewer pipe to Sipe's tailrace (the channel through which water flows after going over a water wheel). To finance these jobs, sewer bonds were purchased.

* Small pox was a health problem and the lawmakers ordered a door-to-door check to determine if there were any cases. Reports to the burgess were required every three days.

1903

* Property owners were not required to pay a $5 tap-in fee for sewage disposal.

* A Board of Trade was established. Wallace Plummer, J. T. Long, Anthony Werner, E. W. Hull and Irving Sipe agreed to serve.

* The year was marked by a total replacement of councilmen. Sworn into office were Thomas E. Kime, James G. Rattigan, Isiah Myers, Henry Davis and P. J. McGough.

* Thomas Kime was selected president. Charles Kime took over as secretary and J. D. Plummer stayed as treasurer.

* A new street commissioner? You bet, he was John Schlosser.

* C. A. Pringle became burgess upon the resignation of John F. McGough. William Davis was named to replace Itell as solicitor.

* In July, George Betz resigns as tax collector, but council refuses to accept it. However, two months later, John B. Schlooser is given the job, in addition to working as street commissioner.

* A new Board of Health includes Michael Tully, five years; John Schlosser, four years; Pat McCall, three years; Joseph H. Skelly, two years and Ben Grove, one year.

* James Baughman becomes a special policeman. He is paid one dollar for every arrest.

* The burgess is directed to notify Wallace Plummer to repair his store's cellar door.

* W. R. Kirby appears for the first time as a vendor to the borough for picks, shovels and handles.

* Conemaugh Valley Street Railway Company receives approval for a right-of-way, provided the work begins within 18 months and the line is completed within three years.

* Sidewalk work never ends. This time, it is repairs on Jackson Street from the street crossing at the north end of D. G. Seaman's lot to the corner of George E. Betz's property. A second repair is the walk in front of Mrs. Wadsworth's house.

1904

* Council actions slow down. Sidewalk work consists of removing boards near J. T. Long's Mill and laying slate and the "best quality of lumber." Repairs also are ordered on the walk by Dimond's. And, orders were approved to lay a "string walk" up to Fred Wess, using 1,000 feet of two-inch planks.

* For the horses, two hitching posts were to be placed at the blacksmith shop.

* Officers for the year were Thomas E. Kime, president; G. I. Sipe, clerk; J. D. Plummer, treasurer; B. Schlosser, street commissioner; and William Davis, solicitor.

1905

* If John B. Schlosser is the same B. Schlosser who has been street commissioner for the past two years, he is setting a new record for this position by serving the third consecutive term. This position apparently was the most coveted. Each year, there was a new appointee.

* There is no change in solicitor nor clerk. There's no record of an election of officers except that P. J. McGough is signing the minutes as council president.

* James D. Plummer retains duties of treasurer. His compensation, the first time noted, is 3% -- of what? There is no explanation. It's surmised his pay is based on the amount of money he handles.

* A problem is noted with Cambria County Water Supply Company. It appears that they cut or broke off the tops of the fire plugs. Council wants the solicitor to file a suit.

* The only mention of sidewalks for the year is to repair the one in front of George Myers.

1906

* This is the year of a big tax increase -- from 5 mills since 1901 to 8 mills for 1906 -- a 60% boost.
* There's a new council, too. Five members dropped out last year. The only holdovers are Joseph H. Skelly and H. W. Davis. But, Davis resigns early in the year. New members are George Kurtz, John A. Rorabaugh, John F. McGough, John M. Bodenschatz and William Hettle.
* Skelly is the president. The secretary, treasurer, solicitor and street commissioner are reelected. M. Sherbine is the burgess. H. C. Stinebeiser polices the borough for $5 a month.
* A sewer line is laid from Dierling Alley to the Ebensburg Road, crossing land belonging to St. John's Church.
* Lumber is purchased for street crossings at St. John's Church, Clark's Corner, Lutheran Church, Post Office, between the Griffith and Long properties and from George Myers corner to George Kurtz. Plank also is laid along the band hall to the corner of J. M. Clark's.
* The question of building and repairing sidewalks takes a new approach. The solicitor is asked to draft an ordinance that property owners will build their own walks and, in addition, keep cattle off the streets and not have dogs roam freely.
* A. J. Oaks is given a copy of a franchise for electric lights.
* Johnstown-Ebensburg-Northern Railway Company sends a representative to discuss a street car franchise.
* Summit Water Company, by ordinance, is given permission to run lines through the town if they deliver five car loads of limestone screenings to the borough, free of charge.
* Joseph Stinebiser is given police authority from November 15 to March of 1907.
* A new Board of Health includes Dr. Stotts, Dr. Jones, Joseph Stinebiser, all for one-year terms; Joseph Geisler and John Schlosser, two years; and George Kurtz and Ed Wicks, three years.

1907

* John Maffet is the only new councilman. All officers are reelected. Lyman Harr is the new policeman.
* There is a new payment schedule for the borough clerk -- $1 a meeting.
* A. J. Oaks' electric plant franchise is reconsidered for 40 years, instead of ten. J. T. Long offers his proposal for an electric light plant.
* Taxes go up again. This time from 8 to 9 mills.
* The borough engineer is going to prepare a map of the town.

* John L. Elder is hired to survey streets for future sewer lines. His bid is accepted to dig for the lines on Main and Jackson Streets at 54¢ a foot. The borough orders 3,500 bricks for catch basins.

* The council goes on record to borrow $1,000 at 6% from Ebensburg First National Bank to help pay for the sewer work.

* An engineer is employed to "take the levels of all streets and fix the grade of all sidewalks." Property owners are notified to build their own sidewalks, within 30 days. Walks are to be constructed with brick or concrete and completed within 60 days.

* The Lutheran Church offers to give the borough about 32 feet of ground northeast of the church to "eliminate the sharp turn." In return, the borough agrees to build a stone wall and lay a sidewalk.

* A stone crossing is sanctioned from George Meyers corner to George Kurtz, from the postoffice to the subway, from Curt Askey to the church corner, from John Clark's corner to Crosser corner, and from Bloomberg to McCall's corner.

1908

* The Summerhill Electric Light, Heat & Power Company ordinance is passed upon the third reading.

* Gone from council are Maffet, Skelly and Hettle and now it's Joseph M. Stull (president), John M. Bodenschatz, George Kurtz, John A. Rorabuagh, James Kane, Martin Bloomberg and Calvin Wonders.

* Joseph Geisler is the new street commissioner and police officer; Peter Betz, clerk; and Charles Greer of Johnstown, solicitor. Plummer is still the treasurer.

* Another Board of Health is named: Dr. C. B. Jones, president; Ed Wicks, secretary; and J. B. Schlosser, Joseph Geisler and C. A. Pringle, members.

* W. R. Kirby, Joseph Brown and C. A. Pringle are paid $2 each for auditing the borough accounts.

* Even though the real estate tax remains at 9 mills, a new tax is levied -- 50¢ per year for a male dog; $1.00, for females. And, all dogs "that run at large are to be muzzled every year from June 20 to September 20."

* Cattle must be "penned in" from 8 P. M. to 6 A. M. Failure to do so will result in a one dollar fine.

* Johnstown & Gallitzin Railway street car line is approved if the company runs its line over Croyle, Market and Main Streets. In addition, the company is to furnish electric lights over these streets and macadamize the spaces between the rails and a foot outside of each rail.

1909

* A resolution is offered by Wilmore Rural Telephone Company. No other information is given in the minutes.
* John M. Bodenschatz, John A. Rorabaugh and Calvin Wonders end their terms. James Kane resigned at the end of 1908. Carryover councilmen are Kurtz, Stull and Bloomberg. Welcomed abroad are Jacob Meier, Edward Claycomb (president), John B. Smith and John Mulvehill. J. T. Long is the new burgess; M. A. Sherbine gives up the office to become justice of the peace.
* The secretary and treasurer do not change, but the street commissioner's job goes to Michael Tully.
* Calvin Wonders, Austin Mervine and Conrad Meyers are appointed to the Board of Health to fill vacancies.
* The street commissioner now is paid 20¢ an hour; his laborers, 15¢ an hour. John Richardson gets $10 a month for policing duties. Auditors have been increased to $3.
* A one-horse team commands 25¢ an hour; two-horse teams, 40¢ an hour. (A horse, according to this scale, is worth more than a laborer and at least equal to or more than the street commissioner? Perhaps, it only proves people accorded horses great respect for their labors.)
* Taxes are increased again -- from 9 to 10 mills.
* The bridge across Laurel Run is repaired, between Emma Sherbine's store and the livery stable.
* At last, a hanging lamp is purchased for the council room from C. E. Claycomb for $4.50. It must of been a fancy one since $4.50 represented 30 hours of work for a laborer!

1910

* Martin Bloomberg ends his council service. P. C. Yahner serves again and is named president. Anthony Werner takes over as treasurer, ending the ten-year reign of James D. Plummer. There's no change of clerk or street commissioner.
* Council is still struggling with street car companies. Johnstown & Altoona Railway's resolution is extended to August 1, 1911, if the company begins construction before October 1, 1910.
* It is agreed to extend Madison Street to Main Street and join Jackson with Madison. The minutes also note that Jackson Street will be straightened and the names of Market and Madison Street will be changed to Main Street.
* By the end of summer, more resignations. Michael Tully gives up being street commissioner; C. A. Pringle is appointed. Peter Betz resigns as secretary; W. H. Meier is elected.
* Several land deals are completed: One is to pay John H. and Mary A.

Wentroth $200 for an unspecified tract of land.

* A second deal grants $100 to Fred Dierling for a lot, move a building three feet from the street, relocate the stable to another lot, and exchange a piece of ground on the corner of Union Hall for another lot belonging to Dierling. There's also an exchange of properties with D. G. Seaman. A third transaction trades a strip of ground along the new Main Street, owned by PRR, for another parcel at the northern entrance to the subway, owned by the borough.

1911

* This is the first year in a long time there was no change of councilmen. The year's body is identical to last year's. Even the officers and appointments remain the same.

* Taxes are raised to 12 mills.

* The sewer system is still under construction.

* Old Portage Road is improved from the county bridge to Malonek's property.

* E. T. Penrose is given "the privilege to erect, construct, operate and maintain over, upon and along, the highways of the Borough of Summerhill, electric lines for the transmission and distribution of electric current to be supplied for purposes of light, heat and power." He is granted 18 months to begin construction.

* Dogs get council's attention, again. A resolution decrees that dogs must be muzzled or tied from the date of "this notice until the council sees fit to repeal this resolution."

The First Twenty Years

The preceding accounts, from 1892 to 1911, were possible because Summerhill Borough Council minutes were available for this period and because meticulous details were written by the secretaries. It is very unusual to find early minutes written with such particulars.

These writings have recorded facts that could never be found in print anywhere. They are a treasure of information about the history of the borough's earliest days.

How else could one write and show the constant changes of council members and borough officials, especially the street commissioner.

The continual problem of keeping up wooden sidewalks and street crossings emphasizes how the town, for many years, only had money for this purpose. And, how Dr. J. B. Green advanced his funds to pay for early expenses.

Although twenty years passed, streets were still unpaved. A number remained to be built or even named. Alleys, which probably were established by property owners, were referred to by their names, such as so-and-so's alley. Intersections were identified by the name of the nearest property holder.

These minutes also reveal the existence of many places never mentioned in newspapers or other print materials of the day -- Burk's Hotel, Seaman's Blacksmith Shop, Union Hall, Dimond's Slaughter House, Griffith Wash House, Emma Sherbine's Store and others.

And, too, many notations in the official council minutes provide names of early residents and property owners which shows the continuing turnover of population and business establishments.

If one were to make a statement about the town's early leaders, how many names would be mentioned? The number approaches 50 for the first 20 years.

General view of Summerhill around 1910. (Credit: Lillian M. Pisarski.)

Jackson Street around 1910. (Credit: Anna C. Jordan and Dorothy Rolla.)

Main Street around 1910. (Credit: Lillian M. Pisarski)

PAINTERS ABOUT 1913. (Left to right): Walter "Happy" Hull; Mr. Cook, owner of hotel; William Rosenberger, bartender; Webb Croyle. (Credit: Louis Rosenberger)

(Credit: Lillian M. Pisarski)

(Credit: Joseph Claycomb)

(Credit: Jack Bodenschatz)

(Credit: Anna C. Jordan)

Town Fathers (1892-1911)

A chronological listing of the first town fathers looks like this:

J. D. Wentroth	Oct 1892 to Nov 1892
Dr. J. B. Green	Oct 1892 to Feb 1896
Anthony Werner	Oct 1892 to Feb 1894
D. G. Seaman	Oct 1892 to Feb 1893
	Apr 1900 to Jan 1901
George Betz	Oct 1892 to Feb 1896
	Mar 1897 to Oct 1899
J. W. Plummer	Oct 1892 to Feb 1893
Charles Mangus	Mar 1893 to Jan 1895
William McClarren	Mar 1893 to Feb 1894
Clem Berschneider	Mar 1893 to Feb 1894
Frank Kurtz	Mar 1894 to Oct 1894
	Feb 1901 to Feb 1903
W. H. Dimond	Apr 1894 to Oct 1894
Will George	Apr 1894 to Jun 1894
P. C. Yahner	Feb 1895 to Apr 1895
	Feb 1898 to Apr 1899
	May 1902 to Feb 1903
	Apr 1910 to **
Peter Schrift	Feb 1895 to Nov 1898
George Hettle	Jun 1895 to May 1897
Pat McCall	Feb 1896 to Dec 1896
C. A. Dimond	Feb 1896 to Aug 1900
Paul Wirfel	Feb 1896 to Jun 1897
Henry Berschneider	Feb 1896 to Feb 1899
	Mar 1902 to May 1902
H. J. Rorabaugh	Feb 1897 to Sep 1897
	Mar 1902 to Aug 1900
Michael Tully	Feb 1898 to Jan 1901
Ed Kehoe	Feb 1899 to Mar 1902
P. J. McGough	Apr 1899 to Aug 1900
	Mar 1903 to Jul 1905
M. A. Sherbine	Apr 1900 to Feb 1903
H. Humphreys	Apr 1900 to Apr 1902
Adam Bimel	May 1900 to Apr 1902
Dan Kearns	Feb 1901 to Feb 1903
Oliver Shrift	Feb 1901 to Mar 1902
Michael Smith	Mar 1902 to Jun 1902
C. O. Dimond	May 1902 to Feb 1903
G. Y. Betz	May 1902 to Feb 1903
Thomas E. Kime	Mar 1903 to Feb 1905

Isiah Myers	Mar 1903 to May 1905
Henry Davis	Mar 1903 to Apr 1906
James D. Rattigan	Mar 1903 to Apr 1905
Fred Wess	Mar 1904 to Jul 1905
Joseph H. Skelly	Mar 1905 to Mar 1907
George Kurtz	Mar 1906 to **
John A. Rorabaugh	Mar 1906 to Mar 1909
John M. Bodenschatz	Mar 1906 to Mar 1909
John F. McGough	Mar 1906 to Feb 1907
William Hettle	Mar 1906 to Mar 1907
Harry W. Davis	Mar 1906 to Apr 1906
John Maffet	Mar 1907 to Feb 1908
Joseph S. Stull	Mar 1908 to **
James Kane	Mar 1908 to Dec 1908
Martin Bloomberg	Mar 1908 to Feb 1910
Calvin Wonders	Apr 1908 to Mar 1909
Jacob Meier	Dec 1908 to **
C. Edward Claycomb	Mar 1909 to **
John B. Smith	Mar 1909 to **
John Mulvehill	Apr 1909 to **

** indicates still in office as of June 1911, the end of available records.

From this list, the following served three years or more: Dr. J. B. Green, George Betz, P. C. Yahner, Peter Schrift, C. A. Dimond, H. J. Rorabaugh, Henry Berschneider, P. J. McGough, Ed Kehoe, Henry Davis, George Kurtz, John A. Rorabaugh, John M. Bodenschatz and Joseph S. Stull.

Summerhill of 1910

What kind of community was Summerhill in 1910?

A review of tax assessment records indicate it was a miners and laborers town. Of 187 listed occupations, 59 were laborers and 55 were miners. Railroading could only claim 17 residents.

A total of 30 businessmen were represented by 2 clerks, 2 butchers, 4 merchants, 6 teamsters, a barber, 3 hotel men, 2 millers, a store manager, a contractor, a shoemaker, 2 liverymen, a plaster and a tinner. There were also 14 carpenters.

The teamsters were J. W. Hugentoger, Milton A. Sherbine, Lonza Forest, Jacent Gelman, Joseph Geisler and Vincent Gaboni.

Classified as merchants were C. E. Claycomb, Church Street; W. R. Kirby, Jackson Street, and Charles Plummer, Main Street. Butchers were Selestine Betz and Hugh Brummert. Anthony Werner was the tinner; Max Reich, barber; John A. Rorabaugh, sawyer; Gotlep Pick, shoemaker, and A. L. and W. H. Poling, liverymen.

John Gallardy and Joseph H. Skelly were taxed as masons. W. H. Croyle, Oscar Mervine, Daniel Siberts and D. G. Seaman were registered as blacksmiths.

Peter Betz was listed as a teacher and Benjamin L. Clark as a principal.

Representing railroaders were John G. Betz and H. J. Rorabaugh, firemen; Rudolph Stinebiser, Charles Doyle, Laurie Leach and John Simendinger, brakemen; W. B. Dimond, flagman; George Erwin, car inspector; Ambrose McCall and Thomas Seaman, engineers; and S. S. Robine and William Wran, agents.

Assessed as ministers were J. T. Fox on Jackson Street and Clemence M. Stratman, Main Street. Obviously, the Lutheran and Catholic, respectively.

The doctor was C. B. Jones.

Summerhill Railroad Station about 1910. (Credit: Lillian M. Pisarski)

At the PRR Depot. On the porch (l. to r.): Adam Bimle, Simon Robine, James Lynch. Near track: Francis (Socky) George. (Credit: Mabel Duffy)

Mr. and Mrs. Charles Bender near the switch tower -- grandparents of Anna C. Jordan.

Railroad Jump Bridge to Ehrenfeld. (Credit: Anna C. Jordan)

Famous K-4 Passenger Train (c. 1950)

PRR Decapod (c. 1950)

Early photo of PRR overpass in Summerhill. (Credit: Mary M. Gabany)

Early photo of PRR overpass over Route 53. (Credit: Lillian M. Pisarski)

Conrail freight traveling through Summerhill in 1991.

Trailer train going east through Summerhill in 1991.

Chapter 7

Getting In And Out, Near And Far

The Canal-Rail System

The Allegheny Portage Railroad, in the 1830s, put Summerhill on the map as one of the towns along the Pennsylvania Canal System, between the state's two largest cities of Pittsburgh and Philadelphia. It provided economic vitality and growth.

Along its route there was much activity. Moving pass Summerhill were heavy boxcars, diminutive passenger coaches, small and long sectionalized canal boats. Wood and coal stations fueled the engines. State agents directed passengers, controlled freight movement and collected tolls. Blacksmiths, blowers, strikers, machinists and finishers were employed to forge or repair engine and track parts to keep the entire line moving smoothly.

The canal-portage rail line served its purpose until 1855. For 21 years, the Portage transported the heavy wave of immigrants from the Atlantic seacoast to points west. It hauled as much as 250,000 tons of freight annually.

The Pennsylvania Railroad

The Pennsylvania Railroad, in the 1850s, opened Summerhill to the world with its interlocking divisions and connections with all points in the United States.

Four passenger trains ran through everyday in 1853. Two traveling west arrived in Johnstown at 1:22 a. m. and 3:37 p. m. Two others left Johnstown for the east at 1:10 a. m. and 12.55 p. m.

A railroad map of 1855 showed nine stations between Altoona and Johnstown -- Kittaning Point, Gallitzin, Cresson, Lilly, Portage, Wilmore, SUMMERHILL, Viaduct and Conemaugh.

Summerhill was 27.4 rail miles west of Altoona and 10.9 rail miles east of Johnstown. Pittsburgh to Summerhill was 89.3 miles; Philadelphia was 158.6 miles away.

By 1875, three more station stops were added between Altoona and Johnstown -- Sonman, South Fork and Mineral Point.

Station	Distance From Altoona
Gallitzin	11.8 miles
Cresson	14.4 miles
Lilly	17.3 miles
Sonman	18.3 miles
Portage	21.4 miles
Wilmore	23.9 miles
SUMMERHILL	26.2 miles
South Fork	28.1 miles
Viaduct	30.1 miles
Mineral Point	31.1 miles
Conemaugh	35.0 miles
Johnstown	37.6 miles

A train trip from Johnstown to Summerhill required four stops before arriving in the borough. From Summerhill to Altoona appeared twice as long because of eight station stops.

The construction of the Pennsylvania line brought more people to Summerhill and its neighbors. The company even established work camps along the way. Summerhill shared in the emerging hotel-rooming house business.

During the Civil War, the road was double-tracked. The third track was laid shortly before 1900. The South Fork bridge was widened in 1900 to add the fourth track. This four-track system was used for over 70 years. During the past decade, one of the two eastbound has been eliminated and returned the mainline to a three-track system.

For 80 years the Pennsy had a monopoly in passenger and freight haulage. While it ran adjacent to most towns, it cut through the center of Summerhill. It was Summerhill's biggest landowner. In addition to the right-of-way, it occupied tracts for passenger, freight and express buildings, signal tower, water tank and utility sheds.

Town's Romance With Trains

The passing trains were like a moving picture for Summerhill residents. People daily looked for coal trains, strings of boxcars with corporate names, transportation of livestock, construction materials, farm equipment, iron ore and an assortment of other goods. Some checked their watches to see if the passenger trains were running on time. And, there were those who looked for private labels on special coaches.

Railroad watching was Summerhill's most popular pasttime. The chugging steam locomotives, with belching, black clouds of smoke, pounded up the grade on eastbound tracks. Those traveling west seemed to glide effortlessly on the down grade.

There was a friendliness with train crews. Waves of greeting were exchanged with engineers, firemen, brakemen, conductors and passengers. A special treat was when a member of the crew lived in Summerhill!

And, there was a special romance with Pennsylvania locomotives, especially the K-4 and the freight cabooses. Cabooses are no longer used in today's railroading.

Historic Attraction of the K-4

The K-4 is now regarded a historic attraction and the official state steam locomotive.

Retired from service in 1956, a group of train enthusiasts have restored the K-4 #1361 and housed it at the Railroaders Memorial Museum in Altoona. The museum also displays locomotive, car, shop and station artifacts, artwork and photographs, and scale models. It is also home to "The Loretto", private railroad car of steel magnate Charles Schwab.

A 150-ton behemoth of the Pacific 4-6-2 wheel arrangement, the K-4 pulled famed trains like the all-pullman Broadway Limited, the Spirit of St. Louis, the Manhattan Limited, the General, the Admiral, the Pittsburgher, the Red Arrow and the Congressional Limited. It also pulled commuters, known in these parts as locals or mail trains, and sometimes were pressed into freight service.

National Park Service Projects

A $13 million, five-year project by the National Park Service started with groundbreaking for a $5 million visitors center at the Horseshoe Curve in 1990. The project includes a replica of an engine house which once powered Incline #6.

The Horseshoe Curve, considered the greatest engineering feat of all time, was designed as a means of conquering the steep Allegheny Mountains through slightly graded railroad tracks shaped in a semi-circle allowing trains to climb the hill at a gradual pace. It has been a popular tourist attraction for more than 135 years.

The Lemon House, at the Summit, once was a tavern and eatery in the mid-1800s along the Allegheny Portage Railroad. It now serves as park vistor center where tourists can enjoy slide programs, exhibits and artifacts on the railroad and canal systems.

1864 PRR Passenger Schedule

The following schedule of PRR train service appeared in the June 15, 1864 edition of the Ebensburg Democrat and Sentinel:

Mail train traveling west

Altoona	7:15 p. m.
Kittanning	7:30 p. m.
Gallitzin	7:50 p. m.
Cresson	7:58 p. m.
Lilly's	8:05 p. m.
Portage	8:16 p. m.
Wilmore	8:25 p. m.
Summerhill	8:31 p. m.
Mineral Point	8:42 p. m.
Conemaugh	8:55 p. m.
Johnstown	9:01 p. m.

Note: It took one hour and 46 minutes for this mail train to make the run from Altoona to Johnstown. Summerhill to Johnstown took half-an-hour.

Through Express traveling east

Johnstown	9:30 a. m.
Conemaugh	9:35 a. m.
Mineral Point	9:49 a. m.
Summerhill	10:00 a. m.
Wilmore	10:10 a. m.
Portage	10:18 a. m.
Lilly's	10:29 a. m.
Cresson	10:39 a. m.
Gallitzin	10:49 a. m.
Kittanning	11:10 a. m.
Altoona	11:25 a. m.

Summerhill Branch

Summerhill Branch appears in a listing of stations and sidings in a 1945 publication of Pennsylvania Railroad Company.

The branch consisted of a station with a telephone office and sidings to Pennsylvania Coal & Coke Corporation's mines #3 and #8; Hand Coal Company's Priscilla mine #1 and Argyle Coal Company's mine #4. These spurs followed the former roadbed of the Allegheny Portage Railroad.

Simon Robine, a Lilly native, was assigned at South Fork in 1900. He became Summerhill's station agent in 1905 and served in this capacity for many years.

James Lynch worked as clerk at Summerhill and Wilmore stations for many years prior to his death in 1934 at the age of 60.

The photo on page 70 shows Adam Bimel (track foreman), Simon Robine and James Lynch standing on a wooden side porch of the Summerhill Station. A fourth person, standing below the porch along the railroad tracks, has been identified as Sockey George.

Joe Bimle was a well-known railroad foreman in later Summerhill railroading history.

A 1930 Johnstown Tribune story announced the retirement of Elizabeth A. Pringle as a telegraph operator after 41 years of service for the Pennsylvania Railroad.

An 1863 native of Wilmore, she started with the railroad in 1886 and worked as an operator at many offices on the Pittsburgh Division. She ended her career at the block station in Pitcairn. Her residence at retirement was at Forest Hills, Wilkinsburg.

Passenger Train Stops At Summerhill

In earlier heydays, 14 passenger trains stopped daily at Summerhill.

Father Ronald Bodenschatz recalls the following train connections about 1936:

Westbound -- 6:12 a. m., 8:10 a. m. and 3:50 p. m.

Eastbound -- 10:30 a. m., 1:00 p. m. and 7:00 p. m.

Father Bodenschatz and about ten other Summerhill youths boarded the 8:10 a. m. train to the Johnstown Station where they had two more miles for classes at Johnstown Catholic High School. The street car ride from the Johnstown Station to the school cost 5¢. They were dismissed early to make the evening train home.

About the 1940s, passenger train stops had dropped to two eastbound and two westbound. The last passenger to pick up or discharge riders in Summerhill was in the Fall of 1941. However, at this time, there were still 26 passenger trains running through Summerhill.

As more and more travelers turned to the automobile for transportation, Pennsylvania Railroad passenger service continued to decline. By 1952, there was a choice of nine eastbound and nine westbound trains at Johnstown. By 1956, the number had declined to six daily runs with stops only at Altoona, Latrobe, Greensburg and Pittsburgh.

All the Summerhill railroad buildings were gone by 1950. Most of the road's mainline stations were also eliminated.

The Johnstown Station was scheduled for demolition but it was saved because of the planned use as a welcoming center for America's Industrial Heritage Project. This project is focusing on transportation and the iron, steel and coal industries of the scenic Allegheny Highlands. It is designed to promote designated points in a nine-county area and increase tourism in this section of the state.

The railroad has undergone a series of operational changes. In 1976, the freight division changed to Conrail; the passenger became Amtrak.

What remains in Summerhill is the signal tower and a new overhead bridge. The sounds of diesels pulling freight and passengers have replaced the steam locomotives with their belching, black smoke. The community is much cleaner but railroad services and employment are things of the past.

Summerhill's Streetcar

Early plans for a streetcar line from Johnstown called for one to follow the Little Conemaugh River, through South Fork, Summerhill and Portage, and ending at Altoona.

Summerhill Council was first approached in 1903 by a company named Conemaugh Valley Street Railway. Again, in 1908, there was Johnstown & Gallitzin Railway. This company changed its name to Johnstown & Altoona Railway and was granted an extension to August 1, 1911, if construction got underway by October 1, 1910.

Meanwhile, the Southern Cambria Railway Company, after three years of construction, completed a line from Johnstown to South Fork. The first run was made January 11, 1910.

This renewed interest to extend streetcar services beyond South Fork. The Johnstown & Altoona company had failed to attract enough investors. A new company was proposed.

South Fork-Portage Railway Company was chartered on September 20, 1912 for 999 years. Capital stock was for 960 shares at $50 a share -- a total of $48,000.

John J. Huebuer (president), Andrew J. Strayer, Arthur C. Simler and 0. P. Thomas, all of Johnstown, each subscribed for 50 shares. Other investors were Charles N. Crouse, South Fork, 50 shares; Charles H. Morgan, Altoona, 50 shares; and Charles W. Shryock, Wilmore, 20 shares.

Plans specified an electrical power operation of five miles from South Fork to Wilmore.

The charter described the route as follows:

> "Beginning at the intersection of Grant and Main Streets in South Fork -- easterly on Maple for about 898 feet to the easterly boundary line of the borough -- thence easterly for 6,700 feet on and over lands of Jacob Stineman, the heirs of George B. Stineman, Joseph Crompton, George Gates, Eugene A. Garvey trustee, all in Croyle Township, thence on and over a bridge to be erected to cross the Little Conemaugh, thence to Summerhill Borough on and over land of Minnie M. Diamond for 227 feet to a point on old Portage Road or Portage Road to the borough boundary and Croyle Township -- East 2,035 feet on one side of old

Portage Road or highway in Croyle Township -- West of the deep cut of the old line of Pennsylvania Railroad thence East 2,100 feet and over property of Pennsylvania Railroad to a point on old Portage Road or highway to the boundary line of the townships of Croyle and Summerhill, East on one side of old Portage Road or highway for 6,471 feet to the westerly line of Wilmore Borough -- back to beginning."

Construction began in the Spring of 1913 with a single track from South Fork. Two heavy steel, center-door interurban combination cars were ordered from Niles Car Company.

Contracts were awarded for a 300-KW substation at Portage and for roadbed work and trackage.

The company ran out of money and couldn't attract more investors. Construction ended about a mile east of Summerhill at the old Portage Railroad cut. Grading was completed to Portage and a bridge was constructed at Wilmore.

The result was three miles of rail without turnouts.

It was impossible to operate two cars without turnouts. There was no way to get one car past the other.

So, one car stood at the Summerhill end of the track until the line was abandoned. It was never used. The other car shuttled daily, back and forth, on an hourly schedule.

Popular Publications, May 1948, said, "The ponderous interurban, with its whistle, arc headlight and impressive pilot was little short of ridiculous on this three-mile interurban pike."

Because of the center doors, a two-man crew was necessary. The road could never meet operating expenses. It went into receivership and was reorganized as Penn Central Railway in 1918.

Like the Southern Cambria, from Johnstown to South Fork, the Penn Central had its troubles with the hilly route. Coming into South Fork, the right-of-way passed down a heavy grade onto Maple Street. On several occasions, the car glided down Maple Street and knocked down power poles and threw South Fork into darkness.

On another occasion, the Summerhill car ran off the tracks, clipped off the front of a South Fork store and barber shop, ran across Grant, Main and Lake Streets and ended at the branch railing crossing of the Pennsylvania Railroad. A PRR derrick lifted the car on one of its tracks, carried it up to the old Portage cut and placed it back on its own runway.

The end came in 1928 when South Fork Council blocked entry into South Fork with a large bumper at the borough line.

Gone was the investors' money and the dreams that this road would extend through Portage, Lilly and Gallitzin.

Anyway, streetcars had their day. The Southern Cambria suspended operations in 1928, too.

Old Iron Bridge in Summerhill. (Credit: Jack Bodenschatz)

Evolution of Highways

Even during the years railroad and trolley travel were common, the horse was still used to pull wagons and buggies. They delivered groceries, hauled road materials, took families on pleasure rides, worked the fields, served as the primary means of local travel and chores.

The horse brought the Croyle family from Bedford to Summerhill in 1794, and served an important role for over a century. The motor car, in the 1920s, started to take its place. But, the animal is still remembered. Automobile engines are rated in horsepower. Merry-go-rounds use models for amusement rides. Riding stables and race tracks still flourish.

The changeover from horse to the "horseless carriage" was not without reluctance. Automobiles had greater difficulty maneuvering muddy roads. On many occasions, horses had to be used to pull many a motor vehicle from the mud.

Poor roads and the lack of them made the automobile an unwise investment -- too expensive and too unreliable.

Before the auto would replace the horse, many good roads had to be built. The cost of such roads posed a major task for municipalities like Summerhill.

For over 40 years, the borough struggled to keep its local streets and alleys passable. During heavy rains, they were muddy and sometimes virtually impassable. During dry spells, they were too dusty and dirty. Cinders, stones and gravel were not permanent enough. Bricks laid by hand or concrete spread by laborers were not affordable.

The answer came through a cheaper process known as macadamizing. This process utilized small broken stones rolled in successive layers on a dry earth roadbed and bound by tar or asphalt.

Today, all of Summerhill's streets and alleys are paved in this manner. It is a source of pride for the community and its leaders.

Once out of reach for the average family, the automobile has become a necessity. One car garages are being replaced with larger units to house two or more vehicles per household.

The auto revolutionized the character of American life. Busses transport large groups. Trailer trucks and piggy-back combinations haul loads which were once the exclusive business of the railroads. Pennsylvania now owns 41,000 miles of state highways. This does not include county and locally-owned highways.

Parking has surfaced as a new need. Many buildings have been demolished to make room for parking lots, not only in cities but small towns as well.

The Main Street business districts of most communities have been replaced by regional malls where there is a collection of all types of stores and unlimited, unmetered parking.

The number of motor vehicles have increased to such an extent that a major problem throughout the country is the lack of sufficient four-lane highways to link local communities with major markets and, also, provide an incentive to attract new industries.

Summerhill finds itself isolated between the state's two east-west limited access highways - the Pennsylvania Turnpike and Interstate 80. Route 219 only furnishes limited access from Somerset to Carrolltown.

Route 53

Local highways remain as Summerhill's link.

Portage Street is part of State Route 53. The highway, a two-lane ribbon, winds from Johnstown northward through Summerhill, Portage, Cresson, Lilly, Cresson and Gallitzin, essentially following the course of the Pennsylvania Railroad.

In 1964, the State began a relocation project between Summerhill and Wilmore to improve this route. Stock's Tavern and the residences of Harry Varner, Fred Urda, Edward Beyers and John Figula were purchased and demolished. The highway was widened. From Summerhill, bridges replaced four dangerous arches passing under the railroad at unsafe angles on the old road. At Summerhill, the former Portage Railroad bridge was razed to make way for the relocated portion.

Ribbon cutting was held in 1965. Eldred B. Jones, Summerhill resident who at the time was county treasurer, represented the Summerhill-Wilmore area.

Summerhill's Croyle and Main Steets lead off from Route 53. These two roads lead to the bridge over the railroad tracks. After crossing the bridge, motorists have a choice of two ways to Ebensburg -- up Jackson Street to Legislative Route 11021 or via Legislative Route 11025, the Ebensburg Road.

U.S. Route 219

It took eight years (1962 to 1970) to complete a new U. S. 219, a four-lane, divided concrete highway from Somerset to Ebensburg. Construction costs were approximately $58 million. The length of the project was 38 miles.

Route 219 North was extended, in 1991, toward Carrolltown. Also, in 1991, new exits were constructed to serve the Johnstown Airport Road, the Johnstown Industrial Park and the proposed site of the Galleria, a new shopping mall.

The original construction of Route 219 took eleven Summerhill homes for a 0.42-mile section over the northwest corner of the borough. The homes were those of Robert Sigg, Karl McGough, Marlin Mervine, Mrs. Charles Hettle, Herbert Bodenschatz, Mrs. Mary Mulvihill, Mrs. Fred Werfel, Louis Weinzierl, Ben Gallardy, John Gilbert and James Henry.

One of the longest highway bridges in Cambria County is part of Route 219. This bridge passes between South Fork and Summerhill. The 5-span, 458-foot bridge carries traffic over the mainline tracks and over Route 53. There are entrance and exits ramps at the Route 53 interchange. To handle interchange traffic, Route 53 was widened to four lanes around the bridge area.

Summerhill is located several hundred feet from the ramps. The town is clearly visual from the span. Motorist can see the straight railroad tracks and the overhead bridge which crosses them at Summerhill.

Immediately following this long span are two other bridges of much shorter lengths. One goes over the Little Conemaugh River at Ehrenfeld; the other is the portion previously mentioned over Summerhill's Jackson Street.

Downtown Johnstown is connected from Route 219 with a four lane, divided expressway that cost $10.5 million in 1972.

Route 22 & Connecting Highways

At the Ebensburg interchange is U. S. Route 22, which has been improved to a four-lane divided highway to Altoona.

In the opposite direction, there is Route 22 to Pittsburgh and Route 422 to Indiana, Kittanning, Butler and New Castle.

Route 219 North from Carrolltown to Interstate 80 is a curving two-lane highway not conductive to pleasurable driving.

Route 30 (Lincoln Highway)

Another possibility for Summerhill motorists to travel east or west is Route 30, the Lincoln Highway, about 20 miles on 219 South.

The American Automobile Association's tour book of 1939 described Route 30 as "the nation's major transcontinental route " with the claim that it "connects the country's greatest metropolitan areas without encountering their congestion" and affords "excellent connecting roads to most of the outstanding attractions of the west."

Another virtue of Route 30, according to the tour book, the highway is "now all paved from coast to coast and the best motor link between east and west."

Compared to current multi-lane highways, Route 30 is now an antiquated road. There are massive traffic jams in the Chambersburg-York section. Western Pennsylvania furnishes many sharp turns and mountainous climbs. However, it does provide some beautiful scenic views for leisure drivers.

Route 30's history is quite interesting. Lincoln Highway Association suggested, in 1913, that a continuously paved, toll-free road from New York to San Francisco be established as a memorial to Abraham Lincoln.

Financing, improvements and federal numbering started in 1925. Lincoln Highway was renamed Pennsylvania Route 1 until 1928 when it became U. S. Route 30.

Pennsylvania Turnpike

For points west on the Pennsylvania Turnpike, Summerhill residents can make suitable connections after about 30 miles travel on Route 219 South.

However, for points east on the turnpike, travelers must exit at the Richland exit of Route 219 and follow Route 56 through Windber, through Ogletown, down Pleasantville Mountain to the Bedford interchange. This road is quite often foggy. It is two lanes and with few areas where a motorist may pass slower-moving traffic.

The general consensus is that Summerhill is in an area which lacks a modern highway system for statewide and interstate travel. Unlike its

Summerhill Streets and Highways (Cambria County Planning Commission 1979)

strategic national position on the railroad network, it is, like most of the region around it, lost in a new wilderness of inadequate highways.

The only bright spot is that with the 219 and 22 projects, local travel has improved. Summerhill finds itself seven miles from Hills Plaza in Ebensburg, eight miles from Richland Mall, 15 miles from downtown Johnstown and 30 miles from Logan Valley Mall in Altoona.

Driving distances to its neighboring communities, via Route 53, are: Wilmore, 2.6 miles; Portage, 5.2 miles; Ehrenfeld, about a mile; and South Fork, 1.6 miles.

Roads Within The Borough

The Cambria County Planning Commission, in its 1979 comprehensive plan, records 4.57 miles of road within the borough of Summerhill. The identifications and lengths of each road follow:

Name of Road	Length
U. S. 219	0.42 mile
Portage Street (Rt 53)	0.74 mile
Ebensburg Road (LR 11025)	0.23 mile
Main Street (LR 11025)	0.49 mile
Jackson Street (LR 11021)	0.44 mile
Croyle Street	0.14 mile
Dibert Street	0.17 mile
First Avenue	0.12 mile
"K" Street	0.04 mile
Laurel Street	0.06 mile
Madison Street	0.06 mile
Main Street	0.14 mile
Manor Drive	0.09 mile
Market Steet	0.06 mile
McArdles Street	0.06 mile
Mill Street	0.24 mile
Orchard Street	0.06 mile
Portage Lane	0.13 mile
Pringle Street	0.11 mile
Second Avenue	0.15 mile
Spring Street	0.06 mile
Wendroth Avenue	0.11 mile
West Jackson Street	0.25 mile
T 607	0.20 mile
	4.57 miles

The study drew the following conclusions: (a) McArdles Street, "K" Street, Manor Drive and Portage Lane provide 20 or less feet of right-of-way widths and can support only one lane traffic; (b) the majority of borough streets, with a few exceptions, are within the recommended pavement width of 20 feet for local roads; and (c) the borough's street system was developed to serve the sloping land in the best way possible.

Naming of Streets

There is no apparent pattern for the naming of Summerhill streets. The southern section of Main Street was the business district. Obviously, Portage Street was taken from the Allegheny Portage Railroad. Ebensburg Road needs no explanation.

Croyle Street commemorates the Croyle family who left a legacy of the town's cemetery and the first church. Mill Street is in the area where the J. T. Long Planing Mill was located. Pringle Street leads to Pringle Hill.

It is logical to believe Wendroth (Wentroth) Avenue was named because John D. Wentroth owned most of the land in this section.

John D. Wentroth was one of the first six councilmen, the first postmaster and proprietor of the Summer Hill House. His father, George Wentroth (1809-1895), was a native of Hesse Cassel, Prussia. According to the 1896 Cyclopedia, George came to Summerhill in 1851 and farmed the rest of his life. Another son, George, was a farmer and merchant of Wilmore in 1896.

Old railroad bridge constructed about 1903. (Credit: Jack Bodenschatz)

Approach to the old railroad bridge. (Credit: Jack Bodenschatz)

Old Summerhill railroad bridge 1984. (Credit: Charles Huber)

Walk bridge during construction of new railroad bridge. (Credit Elsie Mervine)

Summerhill's Bridges

The northern and southern sections of Main Street were connected by a bridge about 1903 by the Pennsylvania Railroad to avoid the dangerous crossing of its four mainline tracks.

The bridge was about 120 feet long with a wood-plank deck, carrying an 18-foot wide roadway and a six-foot wide sidewalk on each side. The span over the railroad tracks was approximately 60 feet long and supported by steel girders.

During the 1970s, after a number of Public Utility Commission hearings, several improvements were ordered. Traffic lights were installed along bridge approaches. A 12-ton weight limit and one-way traffic was imposed. And, in 1977, Conrail replaced the wood decking.

Total replacement was subsequently mandated. Four plans were advanced. Public meetings and PennDOT conferences with Borough Council were held in 1982.

Construction of a reinforced concrete structure, at an estimated cost of $1.5 million, began in 1984. The old bridge was replaced under the Federal Critical Bridge Program with 80% federal and 20% state financing.

During the construction period, the two sections of Summerhill were separated. A detour between the north side to the south side of town was 4 miles in length, through Ehrenfeld, Fifficktown and South Fork.

Summerhill's other bridge, a 70-foot, reinforced concrete arch-type, on Route 53 was replaced in 1991. In its place is a single-span, pre-stressed concrete I-beam bridge which spans over the Little Conemaugh River. The contractor was A & L, Inc. of Belle Vernon, Pa. It was a $1.7 million project.

Public Transportation

Public bus transportation made its appearance with paved roads.

For a time, Johnstown Traction Company held the franchises for South Fork and Summerhill. Blue & White Bus Lines of Altoona took over the Summerhill rights in the 1960s and only picked up and discharged passengers along Route 53. It also was authorized to transport South Forkers when the Traction Company gave up that franchise.

Greyhound Bus Lines had a regularly scheduled route through Cambria County. Now, they operate from a terminal in Johnstown and via the Turnpike and other major highways.

There was a time local people were in the bus business, like Raymond Betz who transported Bethlehem Steel Company employees to Franklin during the World War II years. He provided three trips daily.

Cambria County Transit Authority's Rural Division was advertising service on the "Mainline Express" in 1987.

A van, on weekdays only, left the Johnstown Transit Center at 8:45 a. m. and made stops at Richland Mall, Lamb's Bridge, Burkey's Store and Sherer Service Station in South Fork, the Ehrenfeld Bridge before arriving at Redwood Restaurant (9:16 a. m.) and Ray's Lawn Mover (9:17 a. m.). From Summerhill, the van ended its run at Mainline Pharmacy in Portage.

A second van left the transit center at 5:10 p. m., made its two Summerhill stops at 5:41 p. m. and 5:42 p. m. and continued along the mainline to Gallitzin.

There also were two trips from Gallitzin to Johnstown. The scheduled stops at Summerhill were 8:09 a. m. and 8:10 a. m. and 4:16 p.m. and 4:17 p. m. Arrival times at Johnstown Transit Center were 8:31 a. m. and 4:38 p. m., respectively.

Senior citizens, 65 or older, rode free. Their fares were paid from the Pennsylvania Lottery Fund. For others, the cost was $1.10 from Summerhill to South Fork and $1 from Johnstown.

This service didn't last very long due to insufficient ridership.

Now, the only bussing in Summerhill is for school children attending Forest Hills Schools and two area parochial schools. Individual contractors transport these students under agreements with the schools.

Air Transportation

Air transportation is available at the Johnstown-Cambria County Airport located in Richland Township, southwest of Summerhill Borough via U. S. 219 or Route 53. Passenger and air freight services are afforded to many destinations throughout the State and the Nation. Commuter air service between Johnstown and Pittsburgh is provided on a regular schedule.

High Speed Railroad

In recent years, there has been talk about the possibility of high speed railroad between Philadelphia and Pittsburgh with intermediate stops in Paoli, Lancaster, Harrisburg, Lewistown, State College, Altoona, Johnstown and Greensburg.

One study projects that between 5.5 and 8.8 million passengers could be riding high-speed trains across Pennsylvania by the year 2000. The study indicates that a steel-wheel-on-steelrail system would be used at speeds of 180 miles an hour or a 250-miles-per-hour magnetic levitation system.

The total cost is projected at $3 billion.

If such a system would become a reality, Summerhill is expected to be along its route.

Chapter 8

Who's Doing Business Here?

Summerhill's Historic Mill

Thelma Jones at the mill dam. (Credit: Eldred Jones)

Summerhill was never considered an industrial town. Its economic base was dependent upon the neighboring coal mining industry and the extensive railroading activities at South Fork.

But, the gristmill, started by Thomas and Barbara Croyle, had a great impact and contributed to the town's history for over a century.

Gristmills were an important necessity for regional farmers. It was a place they could have their grain converted into flour. And, for Summerhill, the gristmill was the reason the county decided to finance its first road project with a route from Ebensburg to what was then known as Croyle's Mill.

According to Historian John McCormick, Thomas Croyle sold his mill to George Murray on July 14, 1839. It became known as Murray's Mill.

George Murray (1810-1887) was an aggressive and adventurous individual who emigrated from Scotland, alone, at the age of 18. Upon locating in Summerhill, he married Esther, a daughter of Thomas and Barbara Croyle. This was 1833.

Murray help build the Allegheny-Portage Railroad and, at the same time, established the Half-Way House to provide a combination hotel-store for the construction crews.

He invested in real estate; picked up 1,200 acres at a sheriff sale. When the post office was established (1840), he was named postmaster and held the position for 14 years. He engaged in railroad construction -- 65 miles for the Pennsylvania Railroad, several miles of canal along the Sandy and Beaver Rivers in Ohio, at Pottsville and, in 1852, the Iron Mountain Railroad in Missouri.

George convinced his brother, William, to leave Scotland in 1842 and join him in Summerhill. Here, in 1848, William married Catherine Jane Plummer and set up their own home.

Esther Murray died in 1853. George remarried a widow -- Mrs. Harriet (Wilson) Morgan -- and moved to a large farm in Davenport, Iowa.

William Murray took over his brother's business in Summerhill. In 1859, George sold the Half-Way property to William for $600. Then, William left Summerhill in 1866. He went to Altoona, opened a store, founded a bank, served as one of the first city councilmen and retired in 1894. A year later, he died.

There's a record that shows that William Murray sold 102 acres to John D. Wentroth in 1873 for $8,000.

The mill property passed through a number of deals in which John S. and Solomon Oster, Nicholas Altimus and James Murray (George's son) were involved. By 1868, a partnership of George Wike and the father of Attorney William H. Sechler were operating the mill.

September 10, 1870, George B. Wike and his wife deeded the mill property to Daniel A. Sipe.

A native of Allegheny Furnace in Blair County, Daniel learned the trade of miller at the age of 10 and worked in various mills until he was 31. This was the time, he purchased the Summerhill mill, repaired it and operated it successfully until an 1892 fire.

Sipe rebuilt with a 30' x 40' building, three stories high and a basement and equipped it with the latest and most modern milling facilities, including rollers, bolting chests, reels, purifiers and elevators. The operation was renamed Eclipse Roller Mill at Summerhill.

The new mill had the capacity to produce 35 barrels of flour a day. Feed also was manufactured. Sipe expanded and dealt in salt and grains of all kinds. His customers came from several adjoining counties. He marketed choice brands like White Rose and Minnesota Patent.

However, a second fire brought more grief. According to **The Cambria Freeman (April 21, 1893)**, the blaze completely destroyed the mill along with the stable, sheds and other outbuildings. The loss was estimated between $8,000 to $10,000; insurance coverage was only $5,000.

"People turned out with buckets and their efforts succeeded in saving adjoining property," said the story. Sipe, now 54 years old, "fell exhausted and now lies crtical at home."

When John McCormack wrote his history of Summerhill in 1906, he said Daniel Sipe was being assisted by his son, G. I. Sipe, and the capacity of the mill was 40 barrels of flour and four tons of chop daily.

"The water power is, however, becoming considerably diminished," wrote McCormack, "for which Mr. Sipe has already been awarded damages to the amount of $4,000, and the building of the new reservoir on the North Branch in Summerhill Township will further very materially diminish the supply of water."

Borough tax records show that Daniel Sipe owned 49 acres, assessed at $3,200, from 1895 to 1913. He died in 1912 at the age of 73. He had been the miller at Summerhill for over 40 years.

Ownership changed frequently during the next twenty years:
1914--David Dibert
1917--Henry Berschneider
1920--W. P. Cole
1924--Louis Sherer
1933--Franklin Penrod

When Penrod took over, mill operations were about finished. He used the building as a place for "The Handy Place For The Handy Man." Area residents quipped that "if you couldn't find it at Penrod's, you wouldn't find it anywhere."

The Stone Quarry

According to the 1890 Atlas, the Summer Hill Stone Quarry was located "a few hundred feet" west of Summer Hill, in Croyle Township, on the line of the Pennsylvania Railroad.

"John Brown leases a large quarry, in the Mahoning sandstone, from the Cambria Iron Company. The stone is used for building purposes."

The Women's Club history of 1966 notes that the quarry provided work for a number of men over a period of years. "Stones were cut and shipped to Philadelphia and Pittsburgh by railroad. Some stones quarried here, were used in the construction of the old Portage Railroad."

Coal Explorations

Coal was discovered in Cambria County long before the Allegheny Portage Railroad was built through the mainline section.

There was a coal mine along the Stonycreek River, near Moxham, prior to

1769. Another mine, west of Lilly, was operated by two brothers, Matthew and Michael Myers in 1825. This mine is believed to be the first commercial operation in the county. The Myers hauled their coal across the mountain by pack horse to the Juniata Valley where it was used by blacksmiths.

Construction work for the Allegheny Portage Railroad uncovered the coal reserves near Ehrenfeld and South Fork.

Several Summerhill men were involved in the early explorations of this natural resource.

Nicholas S. George began to prospect for coal on the south bank of the Little Conemaugh River (probably the so-called Sunshine area between South Fork and Summerhill) and on the east side of South Fork Creek. He located the E, or Lemon, seam which had limited use at the time.

George and William Murray opened banks at the Half-Way House to mine coal for blacksmithing purposes. However, they were involved in many other ventures and probably did not have the money or interest to further develop their find. Besides, George Murray left Summerhill in 1854 and William went to Altoona in 1866. Nicholas S. George directed his attention to the mercantile business in 1869, first in Summerhill and later in South Fork. (More about his mercentile experiences is related later in this chapter).

The Stinemans teamed up with Joseph Croyle and others to establish the South Fork Coal & Iron Company in 1867, followed by Dan Luke on the Fifficktown hill in 1875 and John C. Scott at Ehrenfeld in 1883.

Soon, the whole valley around Summerhill was a beehive of industrial activities involving coal mining and railroading. And, with land for housing and building at a premium and the hustle-and-bustle of the South Fork-Ehrenfeld development, Summerhill was the logical place for residental expansion. This probably led to the decision of making Summerhill a selfgoverning borough in 1892.

According to Caldwell's Atlas, there was a mine one mile west of Summerhill "on the line of the PRR and 100 yards east of Ehrenfeld station, on the south side and 8 feet higher than the railroad" operated by J. W. Haywood. He mined about 125 tons of D-seam coal daily.

There was an old opening about 50 feet above the Haywood drift, where it was reported, the penetration was only about 50 yards into an E-seam of coal.

Caldwell's report was in 1890. By 1900, the coal industry had expanded to other mainline communities, like Portage, Lilly, Cassandra and Gallitzin. Another development moved northward from Summerhill to Barnesboro, Vintondale, Revloc, Twin Rocks, Bakerton, Colver and Nanty Glo. And, to the south, there was Dunlo, Lloydell, Llanfair, Beaverdale and, later on, St. Michael.

From the serene atmosphere of its grist mill, Summerhill found itself surrounded by a maze of mining towns which sprang up from forested lands and farm sites.

John T. Long Planing Mill 1910 (Credit: Jack Bodenschatz)

Oaks Lumber Mill located at present day playground area. (Credit: Jack Bodenschatz)

And, even though Summerhill never had a coal mine within its boundaries, it shared in the prosperity of the industry.

Other Industries

The shook business was extensive in Ebensburg, Conemaugh, Summerhill and Chest Springs.

A Mr. Cooper had the shook factory in Summerhill. Oak logs were hauled to his store, cut, shaped into staves of various lengths and made into barrels, buckets and tubs. The finished products were sold in his store; some were exported by rail to Philadelphia and Pittsburgh.

There was an early furniture factory begun by John Brown who also operated a sawmill.

Anthony Werner had a tin shop. And, there were a number of blacksmith shops.

The Hare family had a tannery within the 500 block of Main Street.

On the Little Conemaugh River, about half a mile from Summerhill's eastern boundary, Fred Emigh had a forge with a trip hammer powered by water. John McCormack described him as a skillful whitesmith who fashioned axes, adzes, broad-axes, knives, chisels, hammers and all sorts of edging tools.

The history written by the Women's Club claims that early industries in Summerhill also included a rifle-gun factory and a brewery on Madison Street.

An industry which lasted for a long time was lumbering with operators like John T. Long, A. J. Oaks, Charles Oaks, John Hoover and Edward Bodenschatz.

This prompted John MCCormack, in 1906, to write that the"chief industry of Summerhill is the planing mill of Squire John T. Long, a veteran carpenter, contractor and builder. The mill now in operation was built several years ago at a cost of about $14,000. It is located on Market Street, employs a considerable force of competent workmen, and is run to its full capacity."

Concluding this portion on early industries, the following news story in the August 12, 1892 issue of the **Cambria Freeman** is noted:

"One night last week the sawmill of Mr. John Brown of Summerhill was visited by some evil disposed person, who deliberately cut to pieces about 300 feet of gum and leather belting. A few days previous the mill had been visited and a can of varnish worth about $40 was emptied on the floor."

Vandalism even in those days? Today, there is no trace of this profitable industry within the boundaries of Summerhill Borough. Timbering still strives, however, in New Germany several miles to the north.

In an unpublished history, John McCormack claimed that the first steam sawmill in Cambria County was erected between Wilmore and Ebensburg (the area known as Pensacola) by Lloyd & Hill, merchants from Hollidaysburg and Wilmore.

Squire Alexander Skelly of Wilmore laid claim that he was the first sawyer at the mill.

The first work was to saw planks and string timbers for the old plank road between Ebensburg and Wilmore "laid out in 1852 and completed soon afterwards and perhaps the Ebensburg Carrolltown plank road."

The planks were 8 feet long, 2 1/4 inches thick and of varying widths. The string timbers, about 2 1/4 by 6", were laid apart for a four-foot-six-inches gauge for wagon wheels to be directly over them. The road was used to "haul great loads to Wilmore."

Denise Dusza Weber, **Delano's Domain**, reveals that David and Agnes Pringle of Summerhill purchased a farm in 1871. The 127+ acres was shown on an early Vintondale mine map. The Pringles bought the land from Ephriam McKelvey of East Wheatfield Township for $350. The Pringles operated some type of grist or lumber mill there and, later, sold it to Thomas Griffith of Ebensburg for $300.

Wirfel and Wess, New Germany Memories, tell about the grandfather of Simon Wess coming from Germany and engaging in the trade of cooper here. He made hoops and barrels.

That Joe L. Wess was a blacksmith and also pulled teeth. After the extraction, he gave his patients a drink of whiskey or a big chew of tobacco. Wess also repaired guns.

That George Bimle recalls that his grandfather on his mother's side was a wagon maker who lived on Pringle Hill. He used a ox and sled all year. He made rough box coffins and used the shavings for padding, lined the coffin with muslin, and made them to order for the deceased measurements. He charged $3. His father butchered for lot of the people around New Germany. He also spent a week in Summerhill to butcher pigs. He went door-to-door because about one-third of the people in Summerhill had one or two pigs.

The Commercial Scene

In preceding chapters, Summerhill's business establishments of the 19th century were documented from tax records and an early atlas.

Business houses change periodically with the needs of a community. Early days required a complete line of retail establishments since travel was very limited. As people became more mobile, some stores gave way to competitors located in neighboring communities.

As Johnstown developed into a city, it was able to support department stores like Glosser Brothers and Penn Traffic and become the central trading area. A train ride from surrounding communities made an enjoyable shopping trip. Trains also delivered merchandise ordered from mail catalogs of Sears and Montgomery Ward.

Also, larger neighboring towns, like Portage and South Fork, attracted Summerhill shoppers with special sales and promotions.

Within the past decades, Main Street has succumbed to a larger conglomerate of stores under one roof -- the regional enclosed, air-conditioned mall. Here can be found from three to five anchors consisting of department stores with national recognition -- Sears, Penney, K-Mart, Hess, etc. They are complimented with up to 100 other specialty shops and outlets.

Summerhill shares this "New Main Street" with many strangers who flock to centers at Ebensburg, Richland, Somerset, Altoona and the Pittsburgh area.

The need for many locally-owned community stores has passed. What remains are convenience stores, service shops, restaurants, car businesses and others not threatened by mall competitors.

The business directories which follow demonstrate the changes that have taken place this century in Summerhill.

1906

John McCormack's list of business places include:
  -- John T. Long -- contractor and builder
  -- Daniel A. Sipe -- Eclipse Mill, roller flour, chop, etc.
  -- C. O. Askey -- general merchandise, Main Street

-- Miss Emma Sherbine -- dry goods and groceries, Center Street
-- Griffith House -- John Griffith, proprietor, Center Street
-- H. A. Brummert -- meat market, Center Street
-- Gardner Seaman -- blacksmith, Center Street
-- Kane Hotel -- James Kane, proprietor, Center Street
-- Carpenter House -- Frank Kurtz, proprietor, Main Street
-- Edmond Goss -- restaurant, Main Street
-- Elmer F. Dimond -- meat market, Main & Market Streets
-- W. R. Kirby -- general store, Madison & Market Streets
-- Thomas Seaman -- groceries, Jackson Street

An approved list of mercantile licenses in the May 25, 1906, **Johnstown Tribune** indicated that John Griffith, F. C. Kurtz and James Kane were granted licenses to sell cigars. Grocer licenses were approved for H. A. Brummert, Jacob Myers, Mrs. J. Mathieson and T. J. Seaman ; general merchandise to C. O. Askey, W. R. Kirby and Emma Sherbine. E. F. Dimond's license was for meats only.

The rest were for clothing, Judge Jloid; lumber, John Long; wholesale dealer, S. A. Sipe; and restaurant, Edmond Goss.

Emma (Sherbine) Griffith (1864-1935), who operated a grocery store for a number of years, was also a school teacher in Croyle Township and Summerhill's postmaster from 1907 to 1914.

In comparison, a look back to 1902 included these mercantile licenses according to the **Johnstown Weekly Tribune**:

general merchandise -- K. Getz, Emma Sherbine, Wallace Plummer, Nick Martin, M. C. Dimond and Anthony Werner;

cigars -- John Griffith, E. J. Jones, Frank Kurtz and J. A. Burk;

confectionery -- J. D. Plummer, Tony Test and George Dimond;

miller -- D. A. Sipe;

meats -- Michael Lordich and W. C. Dimond;

grocer -- Martin Kick;

pool rooms -- Joseph Brown and Thomas Kane.

According to a 1909 publication, Summerhill advertisements appeared for John T. Long -- established in 1872, dealer in lumber and builders supplies and manufacturer of fine interior finish; H. A. Brummert, dealer in all kinds of meats and groceries; Emma Sherbine, dealer in dry goods, notions, groceries, shoes, etc.; and W. R. Kirby, general merchandise.

1925

The tax assessment book for 1925 offers a much more complete listing:
-- John Bodenschatz -- repairman
-- Edward Bodenschatz -- teamster
-- Hugh Brummert -- meat cutter
-- C. P. Betz -- meat cutter
-- Raymond Betz -- garage manager

-- C. E. Claycomb -- merchant
-- Fred Dierling -- meat cutter
-- Robert M. Duffy -- merchant
-- Thomas J. Gilbert -- grocer
-- Thomas E. Kime -- hotel
-- W. R. Kirby -- merchant
-- Ira Lentz -- restaurant
-- Charles E. Myers -- boiler maker
-- Gussie Plummer -- postmaster
-- Samuel Rose -- policeman
-- Bernard Seifert -- paper hanger
-- Homer Seaman -- plumber
-- Anthony Werner -- tinner
-- Edward Wicks -- restaurant keeper
-- John Whiteley -- plasterer
-- William J. Yahner -- barber

1940

Fifteen years later, 1940, the assessor's classifications were longer and contained some new categories:

auto dealers -- Raymond Betz and Herman J. Werfel;
repairmen -- Francis Bodenschatz and Frank Burns;
confectioners -- Ethal Betz and Edwin Wicks Jr.;
seamstress -- Elva Betz and Bertha Hardy;
meat cutters -- James Bantley, Fred Dierling and Thomas Gilbert;
merchants -- C. E. Claycomb, Robert M. Duffy, Thomas E. Kime, W. R. Kirby, Ira A. Lenz, Charles F. Plummer, Stella Wilburn and John D. Wilson;
hairdressers -- Josepha Gallardy and Violet McCall;
music teacher -- Leroy Dierling;
blacksmith -- John G. Long;
boiler maker -- Charles E. Myers;
painter -- Charles Seifert;
salesman -- Ferdinand A. Werfel; and
barber -- William J. Yahner.

1953

Advertisers in St. John's Jubilee Book of 1953 provided the following: Bonny's General Service Station; Kirby's Super Market; Summerhill Beverage Co., John J. and Joseph W. Chimelewski, PLCB "D" 2416; Stock Coal Company; Kime Hotel, William J. Shay; John G. Long, blacksmith; Costello Brothers; Claycomb's Store; Hoover Lumber Company, Main Street; Franklin H. Penrod; Peter Brown; Summerhill Heating Company, Regis Shrift; Kick's Service Station; Henry Malonek, Kaiser-Frazer and Henry-J dealer on Route 53; Little Chef Drive-In, Pershing Harris, Take-Out Orders on Route 53; Stella Cullen, Justice of the Peace; Duffy's Where-U-Save; Oak's Dairy Farm pasteurized and homogenized dairy products; M. V. Beyer; Raymond C. Kirby, Capehart Sales & Service, Toastmaster Hot Water Heaters and Dexter Washers; McCall's Hudson Sales & Service, John W. and Frank J. McCall; Bob's Radio & Television; Ira A. Lenz; and Werfel Motor Company, DeSoto-Plymouth Automobiles.

1956

For South Fork's St. James Catholic Church Golden Jubilee program book, in 1956, those who chose to advertise from Summerhill were:

Kime Hotel -- fish and shrimp fires every Friday.
Werfel Motor Company -- DeSoto-Plymouth
General Service Station -- Francis Bodenschatz
Kirby's Super Market
Summerhill Heating Service -- Armstrong and Luxaire warm air furnaces, Regis Shrift, proprietor
Little Chef Drive-In -- sandwiches, french fries, milk shakes, sundaes, Eat Here Or Carry Out, open from 9 a. m. to ?
Hoover Lumber Company -- established in 1872
McCall's Hudson Sales & Service -- general service on all makes of cars, also Rambler automobiles
Duffy's Where You Save
Greater Beneficial Union of Summerhill, District 291, fraternal life insurance

1960

The list began to shorten in 1960, as evidenced by the following tax assessor's record:

Joseph Claycomb, Robert M. Duffy, Joseph F. Kirby, Mildred Reade, Regis Shrift and Walter Stock were classified as merchants; Francis Bodenschatz, repairman; Samuel Basile, Joseph Chimelewski, Henry Malonek, John W. McCall and Ferdinand A. Wefel, sales; Daniel Betz, bartender; Dominick Connonie, meat cutter; John M. Costello and Herman J. Werfel, dealers; Leroy Dierling, teacher; Josepha Gallardy, hairdresser; George Kick, gas proprietor; Franklin. Penrod, electrician; Thomas Tully, plumber and Edgar White Sr., painter.

1978

St. John's advertisers in 1978 came up with an almost completely new list of Summerhill merchants:

McCall's American Motors & International Scout (AMC and IH, Inc.) at 500 Main Street -- John W., Geoffrey A. and John W. II McCall.

Ralph Jones -- Dodge and Jeep Agency
Ace Drilling Company -- E. L. Jones
Brown Brothers -- Summerhill Construction Company
Costello Company -- Heavy Equipment
Kime Hotel (Herb's Place)
Vince's Bar
Stock's Tavern
Robert Penatzer Garage
Richard McCall Optical
Ray's Lawn Mower (Ray's Lawnmower Sales & Service) on Route 53
Scottie's Market

John D. Wentroth's Summerhill House. (From Caldwell's Atlas of 1890)

Carpenter Hotel on Market Street around 1910. (Credit: Gertrude Brummert)

Long's blacksmith shop on Croyle Street, now used as borough garage and storage.

Summerhill's Hotels

So far, this history has established that the Half-Way House had to be the first hotel in Summerhill.

The early hotels probably began as a rest stop to get a meal and refreshments. They consist of frame buildings with sleeping rooms, a bar and a dining area. Fancier ones had a display or sample room where traveling salesmen could show and sell their wares.

The Half-Way House was a one-story log building built by George Murray in 1839 as a place for lodging, dining and buying consumer items. In 1859, George sold Half-Way House to his brother, William, who operated it until leaving the area in 1866. And, since this hotel was not listed in the 1890 Atlas, it is reasonable to assume 1866 was the end.

The Railroad House appears in the 1890 atlas located along the mainline tracks and east of Laurel Run. Its origin is not documented. However, the Johnstown Weekly Tribune (July 29, 1898) verifies its existence in a story that Peter Brown, 65, was killed by a fast rain in crossing the tracks about 100 yards from his home. He was the owner of the Railroad House and a shoemaker.

The article says that Mr. Brown was a well-known resident of Summerhill who had owned the"Railway House" until six years ago -- 1892.

Lewis Brown, a great-grandson who currently operates a sawmill below the hotel's site, has found evidence that the hotel was located here. He claims that his grandfather, Joe Brown, also operated the Railroad House.

Summerhill House also was located alongside the railroad tracks, but on the western side of Laurel Run. It was the property of John D. Wentroth.

John D. Wentroth (1841-1913) was quite a mover, in more ways than one.

Born in Germany, he came to the United States at the age of 10. He lived on a Croyle Township farm until he left to seek work as a shoemaker for eight years. He did well in,both, boots and shoes.

He fought in the Civil War, enlisting at Wilmore in 1863 when the confederate forces under General Robert E. Lee invaded Pennsylvania.

Wentroth married a Summerhill native in 1864 -- Mary Ann, daughter of James and Elizabeth Patterson. She was a granddaughter of Thomas Croyle.

In 1872, the Wentroths built a house in Summerhill and engaged in the mercantile business six years later. Next came the Summerhill Hotel (1881) with a large dining room, a spacious porch and a sample room.

John Wentroth was postmaster twice -- from 1870 to 1877 and from 1889 to 1893. He took over the management of Vintondale Inn in 1895 under a lease arrangement with the owners. He terminated this lease in 1900 and retired.

Both, John and Mary Ann Wentroth (1844-1930) died in Kernville, a Johnstown suburb.

The Johnstown Tribune reported that in 1900 that the hotel had changed hands with "Landlord Jones taking charge."

Caldwell's 1890 Atlas characterized John Wentroth as "one of the most energetic business men of Croyle Township."

The Summer Hill House, the atlas says, had first-class accomodations and "for neatness in all its appointments it cannot be excelled. The fare is perfection, both in quality, variety and the manner serving. The dining room is large and airy. There is also a large sample room and commercial men make it a point to stop with him."

Wentroth, the biographer wrote, "learned the boot and shoe business, and during the war did a large business. In 1889 he was appointed postmaster of Summerhill."

A fire of suspicious nature struck the hotel September 25, 1903. The newspaper reported the hotel was saved by the "hand work of citizens" and the South Fork Fire Company.

A Portage man was arrested two years later. The lot on which the Summerhill Hotel stood is now vacant. Some of it is being utilized for parking.

The Carpenter Hotel was situated in front of the railroad station in the southern portion of Summerhill.

The following research is from the files of the Cambria County Historical Society, Ebensburg:

1794 -- warranted to Benjamin Williams

1797 -- conveyed to William Clark

1886 -- (January 31) Thomas Croyle sold to Elizabeth Patterson for $92

1886 -- (September 29) Mary Wentroth, sole heir of Patterson, sells to Albert Carpenter for $200

1920 -- John C. & Florence Carpenter and Eugene & Mary Myers of Altoona -- Carpenter's heirs -- sell to Robert M.Duffy for $7,000.

Robert M. Duffy established a store in this building and prospered here for many years as a prominent merchant. Patrick Dumm of New Germany has remodeled the structure into apartments.

Kannah Hotel was located in the northern section of Summerhill at the corner of Main and Railroad Streets. It was demolished in the 1960s to make room for the GBU parking lot.

Griffith Place was started in 1890 by John W. Griffith (1836-1910), a native of Bedford County where he worked as a blacksmith in his youth.

He was awarded the purple heart for his services as a private in Captain Webster B. Lowman's Company D, 5th Regiment of Pennsylvania heavy artillery volunteers. He enlisted September 3, 1864 and was discharged June 30, 1865 at Vienna, Virginia. Griffith spent the last days of his enlistment as a prisoner of war in Libby prison of Richmond, Virginia, where his daily rations were confined to bread and water.

Upon his death, the business was handed down to his son-in-law, Thomas E. Kime, and has continued as Kime Hotel. More about this hotel in the next

Kennah Hotel, Summerhill, PA about 1910

Plummer House used as a hotel and early post office.

Celestine Betz meat market and possibly the first building of Francis Duffy's radio service shop. (Credit: Jack Bodenschatz)

Hugh Anthony Brummert meat market and groceries of the early 1900s. (Credit: Gertrude Brummert)

Wilburn's grocery store on Main Street. (Credit: Stella Wilburn)

L. Weinzierl Shop advertising Honest Scrap. (Credit: Lillian M. Pisarski)

The original W. R. Kirby General Merchandise selling Goonow harness oil and Dr. A. Daniels home treatment medicines. (Credit: John "Woody" McCall)

W. R. Kirby's store on Main Street. (Credit: John "Woody" McCall)

W. R. Kirby at his desk. (Credit: John "Woody" McCall)

Today's Kirby building coverted into apartments.

Long's Theatre in the background of this 1900 photo. (Credit: Eldred B. Jones)

Long's Theatre Building as it appears today on Main Street.

chapter.

Other hostelries of the past carried names such as Frank Kurtz's Hotel, West End Hotel on Mill Street, Plummer's Hotel and Burk's Hotel.

About the turn of the century hotels were generally places with licenses to sell liquor. In those days, licenses were granted annually by county judges. While some retailers retained their licenses, others were refused or dropped from prior years. Politics appeared to play an important role.

Hotel ownership did not necessarily grant a license. It appears that there were times when licenses were granted to individuals who did not own the property. For example, in 1898, three licenses were approved for Summerhill: John Griffith, Main Street; Francis Kurtz, Carpenter House; and P. C. Yahner, Summerhill House.

Historical Perspective

There is no question that the first qeneral store in Summerhill was George Murray's Half-Way House. There are no records to indicate differently. Putting everything in proper perspective is practically impossible. What is possible is to relate some random bits culled from available individuals and written sources.

One of these early sources lists the commercial activities of the **George Family.**

Nicholas S. George was an early businessman who began his mercantile experience in Summerhill.

Born in 1834 near Mechanicsburg, Pa., he worked on the farm and in an iron furnace. From 1857, he followed the trade of cooper for three years in Summerhill and Benscreek along with five years as a school teacher.

He was rejected for military service in 1861 because of physical disability, but served as a sergeant in an emergency company at Antietam. At the time of Lee's invasion, he was accepted for enlistment, September 1, 1864, in a company of the Pennsylvania regiment.

At the end of the Civil War, he returned to Summerhill and got a job with the Pennsylvania Railroad as a laborer. Soon, he was promoted to foreman.

By 1869, he assumed the position of manager for the **P. M. and J. Brown's large general mercantile business** in Summerhill. After nine years with the Browns, he returned to farming.

In 1884, at the age of 50, Nicholas S. George went to South Fork to open a general store. This led to a partnership with P. M. Brown, Wilmore; Jacob C. Stineman and Dr. J. C. Luke, both of South Fork. The business, known as Brown, George and Company, was sold to the Stineman Brothers in 1890.

Nicholas and his son, Harry J. George, started a hardware furniture-undertaking business on Main Street, South Fork. Members of the George family continued in the hardware business until 1948 when it was sold to Michael Catchen and David Goldblatt, both of Westmont. Catchen now operates the store as a True value Hardware.

The undertaking part of the business remains in the George family and is now operated by Nicholas' great-grandson, Homer J. George.

Another early family who were Summerhill merchants were the **Dimonds.**

Casper Dimond was born and raised near Baltimore, Maryland. He migrated to Croyle Township and started with the purchase of 70 acres, neighboring Thomas and Barbara Croyle. It was on this Croyle Township farm that his son, Charles A. Dimond, was born in 1835.

Charles A. Dimond married Malinda C. Cullen. Her father was a superintendent of the Old Portage Railroad. For a number of years, Charles A. was associated with Jacob C. Stineman in the coal business but around 1880 he decided to go into the butchering business at Summerhill. His first store was located near the mainline railroad. Soon, he had meat markets and stores at North Branch, South Fork, Dunlo and Ehrenfeld.

A son, Arthur L. Dimond, was in business with his father until 1892 when he purchased the 14-room Hotel Ehrenfeld. He went on to own the Merchants Hotel, a large store building, the Star Bottling Company in South Fork, in addition to being a wholesaler.

Another son, **Charles O. Dimond**, was born in Summerhill on April 28, 1881. Educated in the Summerhill School, he completed studies at the Pennsylvania College of Embalming, Pittsburgh. He began an undertaking practice in Summerhill at the age of 19 in 1899. In 1903, he moved his funeral home to South Fork and noted as the youngest funeral director in Cambria County.

Charles O. Dimond operated the business until his death in 1944. He was succeeded by his son, Charles O. Dimond, Jr. who continued until his death in 1981.

Today, Charles O. Dimond Funeral Home, Inc., South Fork, is operated by Charles O. Dimond III who also manages the South Fork Insurance Exchange.

Like his great-grandfather and grandfather, he and his wife, Susan, make their home in Summerhill -- at 709 Madison Street.

Claycomb's Store took over the Dimond location in Summerhill. Charles Edwin Claycomb came from Bedford County, in 1905, to take over the business. After two years, Claycomb sold to Frank Sloan of Indiana. Claycomb went to Portage with Moudy's. Meanwhile, Sewell Claycomb was at Eureka Stores in Windber from 1909 to 1910.

In 1911, the two brothers -- Sewell and Charles Edwin -- decided to form a partnership (Claycomb Brothers) at the former Dimond location. This partnership lasted until 1943. Sewell became the sole owner and renamed the business Claycomb's Store.

In 1950, Sewell sold the store to his son, Joseph D., and Joseph's wife, Twila H. They conducted the business until 1964. Joseph also was a licensed Nationwide insurance agent and drove school bus for George Hillegas of

South Fork. He recently retired from Pennsylvania Electric Company. Twila is a retired Forest Hills school teacher. They make their home in Summerhill.

Joe recalls that in his father's days, deliveries were made door-to-door by horse and buggy and on the way back from Ehrenfeld they would haul coal for Summerhill customers. He also remembers the store almost went bankrupt during the Depression because customers defaulted on their credit accounts. Credit accounts for groceries and home deliveries no longer are available. Chain supermarkets have replaced the former community groceries and meat markets. They operate on a cash or credit card basis. Customers haul their own purchases.

William R. Kirby was a native of Summerhill and a son of Patrick and Ellen (Neff) Kirby. His grandfather, John, emigrated from Ireland to Johnstown about 1850 where he engaged in the retailing and wholesaling of flour and feed and, also, served three terms as county commissioner.

His father, Patrick E. Kirby, was born in Ireland in 1846, operated a general store in Wilmore for 25 years and moved to Conemaugh to take a job as shipping clerk for Cambria Iron Company.

William R. Kirby clerked in Anthony Werner's general store, Summerhill, from 1896 to 1902. William bought Werner's business in 1902 and began the William R. Kirby Store.

By the late 1920s, the business had expanded into the sale of appliances, shoes, dry goods, feed, hardware and other lines. The name was changed to W. R. Kirby Department Store. A 1930 letterhead listed a Johnstown telephone number of 37-L.

During the years of the miners strike and the 1936 Depression, Kirby extended credit to carry over many of his customers, most of whom were appreciative and loyal while some failed to repay.

Arzella Seifert worked for Mr. Kirby from 1938 to 1947 and remembers wartime rationing when they spent many evenings to fairly distribute available supplies. In 1945, she married Joe Kirby, one of W. R. Kirby's sons who was the store's butcher.

At the end of World War II, Joe and his brother William bought the business from their father and, by the 1950s, had converted it into a self-service supermarket. (The father, William R. Kirby passed away about 1960).

As the shopping patterns changed, the Kirby brothers found it more difficult to earn a living with the store and they began to supplement their income by other means. Joe became well-known throughout the area promoting the Dale Carnegie program.

About 1972, Kirby's Store was no more -- ending 70 years as the last of Summerhill's big grocery stores. Claycomb's and Duffy's had closed earlier.

The W. R. Kirby name, however, is still visible on the brick building. John W. (Woody) McCall bought the building in the late 1970s and made it into the Mid-Town Apartments. The adjoining lot is used to display McCall's new and used cars.

William Kirby died in 1978; Joe, in 1979.

Arzella Kirby, Joe's widow, recalls that at its peak, the store furnished jobs for up to five people. There were home deliveries; first by horse and wagon and later by motor truck. Two principal drivers and deliverymen were Robert Mathieson and Ralph Shrift.

William R. Kirby brought his nephew, **Robert M. Duffy** (1899-1964) to Summerhill to work in his store. Duffy, a native of Portage, spent his early childhood in Johnstown where at the age of 16 he had his own store on Franklin Street. He sold his inventory to his Uncle Kirby when he was drafted for World War I.

In the early 1920s, Robert Duffy rented space and sold meats only in Summerhill. By the mid-1920s, he purchased the Carpenter House and placed a general store in the half formerly occupied by Frank Kurtz' Bar.

He married Mabel Boyer of Meyersdale, a nurse at Johnstown Memorial Hospital, in 1930. They made their home in the other half of the former Carpenter House building.

Upon Duffy's death, Peter, his son, and other members of the family continued the operation of the store into the late 1960s. Mrs. Mabel Duffy was the sole operator for the last three years. She closed the doors in 1971.

Mabel made an agreement with Patrick Dumm of New Germany that he could take ownership of the building if he built her a home on Ebensburg Road. Dumm converted the building into six apartments. Mrs. Duffy currently resides in her new home on Ebensburg Road.

Peter Duffy, her son, has been the meat manager of Ebensburg's Shop-N-Save for nearly 30 years. Robert M. Duffy, Jr. specializes in energy systems with the W. A. Kraft Corporation, Boston, Massachusetts.

The early 1900s saw the establishment of other local commercial establishments.

There was a **Summerhill Industrial Company** along the Ebensburg Road in Croyle Township, titled to Charles P. Kime, Thomas E. Kime, John M. Scott and Zachariah Dunmire. The company, in 1903, owned a large building that was used as a planing mill and furniture factory.

Summerhill Construction Company Limited, was chartered in 1905. William Leap, chairman; Thomas James Morgan, secretary; and Castleton Ake Pringle, treasurer, each subscribed to $400 in stock. The incorporation was for "general contracting for the construction of roads, street railways, sewers and pipe lines." The predicted duration was recorded at 20 years.

Another charter recorded at the Cambria County Courthouse showed seven stockholders who banded together to form **Summerhill Coal & Coke Company** in 1882 on lands of P. M. and J. Brown. Five stockholders were listed with 10 shares each: P. M. Brown, John Brown, John Reilly, Thomas H. Carland and William A. Fulton. Subscribed to one share each were N. S. George and W. J. Buck.

From the 1910s to 1930s, **Minnie Betz** baked and sold homemade bread and baked goods from her home at 402 Jackson Street.

Harry F. Snyder was Summerhill's photographer who worked out of his home on Ebensburg Road in the 1930s and 1940s.

Francis Duffy, a brother of Robert M. Duffy, had a radio repair shop in Summerhill from 1933 to 1936. He moved this business to South Fork and is now associated with Duffy TV Sales, Inc., 2212 Bedford Street, Johnstown.

A pioneer radio enthusiast, Francis taught in New York City during World War II, offered NYA programs at Berkley Hills and the Johnstown Post Office after the war. He operated a short-wave radio transmitter in South Fork.

He assembled his first crystal radio set when he was seven years old. Francis was the first to televise a signal -- a boxing match -- from an airplane in this area (Stratovision) and aired the first test patterns of WDTV, Pittsburgh's channel 3, about 1948.

Stella Wilburn opened a store on Main Street in the old Sherbine Store building which had been purchased by Joseph V. and Pearl Gallardy from the heirs of Emma Shervine Griffith, according to a note in the Cambria Dispatch of August 28, 1936.

The Hoover Sisters -- Violette McCall, Jo Gallardy and Blanche Kinley -- teamed together on Main Street as the Flower-In-Bottle Beauty Shop.

Violette's sisters had started a shop under the same name in Portage about 1931. When they moved the business to Summerhill, in 1939, Violette joined them. The shop operated in this manner until 1962. Violette, who is now the widow of John W. McCall, went on her own with a shop in the basement of her home until 1970.

John Hoover, the oldest living male in Summerhill in 1991, tells that **Louis White** sold beer before the 1912 prohibition; and had a wholesale house. At one time, Hoover says, there were seven beer gardens and one wholesale house. The town supported them because people "had no where to go except by horse and buggy."

From February 1947 to February 1972, two Fifficktown natives -- Joseph and John Chimelewski -- operated **Summerhill Beverage Company** in Summerhill along Route 53 as a beer distributor's business licensed by the Pennsylvania Liquor Control Board. Under the laws of those days, distributors could sell beer only; other liquors are sold in state-owned stores.

The Chimelewskis had a D license which permitted beer sales in keg and case lots to licensed bars and clubs as well as indiviudals. In 1955, they bought the ID license of Anthony J. Basile of South Fork. Now, they could expand their sales to other licensed distributors and secure protected territories as brewing company franchisees.

John Chimelewski left the business in 1965 and relocated in California. Joe continued as sole proprietor until 1972. The license was sold to West End Beverage, Morrellville, who chose not to continue a distributor location in Summerhill.

The building, now vacant, had been rented for a short time as a manufacturing site -- a venture which did not meet with much success.

Stock's Tavern came about after Walter Stock was one of 15 property owners who was burned out in the disastrous Fifficktown fire of 1941. He located his business along the southern side of Route 53, near Laurel Run.

When the highway was widened, Stock's ground was needed and he moved to Mill Street. The tavern closed in 1989.

Long's Hall is the largest commercial building in the borough today. It has a history of many uses.

The two-story rectangular structure with a finished basement, at the lower end of Main Steet, was built for John T. Long by Fred Crosser in 1912.

Prior to the construction, there was another long building, reportedly resting on stilts that was used by some visiting merchants who stored wares they peddled door-to-door throughout the area. This site, between Main Street and Laurel Run, also was the location of John T. Long's first sawmill.

The basement once was used by Raymond Crosser and John Manahan for a soda pop/carbonated beverage factory. It also was used as an extra school classroom about 1912. Later, it was a place to work on cars.

John T. Long brought burlesque shows from Chicago to the building's theater. Community complaints, however, forced a change in billings and it was used for traveling medicine shows, silent movies, minstrels and vaudeville.

One early show card, displayed in Wicks Store, advertised a three-act comedy, "All A Mistake" at Long's Theatre on August 21, 1910.

Local talent was staged into the 1920s. A revival came about 1931-32 when Father Claude Geary, OSB, organized a dramatics club that produced home talent shows here and in neighboring communities. School programs and graduation exercises shared the stage, too.

John Hoover says he managed a movie theatre in the 1920s. Movies were shown Saturday nights with admission prices of 5¢, 10¢ and 15¢. Later on, there also were showings on Wednesday nights. Along with John McCall, Hoover was associated with Summerhill's only movie until the advent of television.

The second floor was used as a dance hall, for card parties and other community social events.

The dances were held every Saturday nights with a live orchestra, according to John Hoover. "There were about a couple of hundred who attended." He remembers there was a 7 p. m. train from Pittsburgh which would bring dancers who returned to the city on the midnight train.

The dance floor was above the theater and sometimes, Hoover said, "the dancers made so much noise it bothered the movie patrons below."

During the 1950s, Summerhill-New Germany Industrial Development Committee offered the building for industrial purposes. Promotional literature listed 2,700 square feet with a high ceiling, a dance floor of 2,700 square feet and a roller rink with 2,400 feet with additional ample office space, display room and a small apartment. The brochure said the building was ideal for a needlecraft or an assembling plant.

About 1962, Regis Shrift purchased the building and converted it into four apartments. Upon his death, Thomas Madison, a nephew, inherited the property. He maintained it for several years and sold it to Farel Corporation of Charlotte, North Carolina. The corporation's plans were to expand its South Fork garment plant to Summerhill with additional sewing and cutting operations. A Summerhill Printing Company had been organized in the basement to print labels. However, at this writing, none of the building was being used for these purposes.

John Hoover, born September 8, 1899, has had a long career in trucking, lumbering and bus driving.

Upon his grandfather's death, John T. Long, the planing mill at Mill Street became the business of his father, Jacob F. Hoover (1872-1944). Jacob Hoover operated the mill for 15 years under the name of Hoover Lumber Company. Upon his death, the business went to John Hoover. He and his mother continued for 20 more years. The business was sold to John Costello in 1964; Costello discontinued the lumbering and later sold the lot to Portage National Bank for its Summerhill Office.

In reviewing his working years, John Hoover said he was hauling lumber with horses and wagons into South Fork, Fifficktown, Wilmore, Portage and St. Michael at the age of 18. He also hauled coal from Mineral Point from Page's coal mine.

By 1927, he was hauling coal and lumber by truck. He stayed in the trucking business until 1974. He also drove bus to Bethlehem Steel for Raymond Betz. And, until 1974, he was a school bus driver. He claims he had to quit at age 75.

From available council minutes, notations appeared about other business ventures: Burk's Hotel (1902), Opera House (1922), Hampson Tea Room (1926), Wilson Service Station (1938), Penatzer Service Station (1972) and Fran's Beauty Shop (1976).

Chapter 9

The New Commercial Look

Summerhill's commercial look has changed over the past 100 years.

In the 1890s, there were 3 hotels, 3 general merchandise stores, a grist mill, a planing and sawmill, a blacksmith, 2 building contractors, a lumber company, a town doctor and a surveyor-engineer.

All these are gone now. In their places, there is a new mix. There is no Main Street business district. Current establishments are primarily located along Route 53.

The one exception is the business of selling alcoholic beverages. In the 1890s, drinks were dispensed in the hotels. Today, they are available in the two state-licensed barrooms and the GBU clubhouse.

The 1990s present 2 new/used automobile dealers, 2 used car dealers, 2 barrooms, a club, a convenience store, a beauty salon, a restaurant, an area ambulance service, an automobile service garage, a lawnmower/outdoor equipment sales and service, a coal yard, a wood fabricating shop, a contracting firm, a bank office and offices for E. L. Jones.

The major employer is Redwood Restaurant.

The community's common meeting place is the post office where residents have individual mail boxes and where retirees get their monthly social security and pension checks.

There is no town doctor, dentist, lawyer, accountant, barber, theater, hardware, supermarket or industry.

Summerhill Post Office. (Credit: Lois Rosenberger)

Summerhill Postal Service

The first post office was established July 29, 1840 with the name SUMMER HILL because the Allegheny-Portage Railroad needed an address to drop off mail between Cresson and Johnstown.

The name was changed to SUMMERHILL on May 2, 1894.

Since George Murray was the first postmaster in 1840, the post office must have been located in his Half-Way House.

Summerhill has had its own post office building since 1975 -- a newly-constructed brick structure complete with a paved parking lot along Route 53, next to Redwood Restaurant. Other known locations were at Sherbine's, on Main Street; Charles Plummer's, across from Shirley & Vince's Tavern; Kannah Hotel, now the GBU parking lot; and Joe Hettle's, on Wentroth Avenue.

There has never been free delivery because of the third class status. Local residents rent boxes and pick up their own mail. Currently, there are 310 rented boxes.

Rural delivery encompasses an area of about 50 miles in parts of Croyle, Cambria, Jackson, Portage and Summerhill Townships. During the summer of 1991, Jean Beyer of Ebensburg R. D. #3 was the rural carrier; Robert Vorgelbacher of Summerhill R. D. #1, rural carrier assistant. Laverne Casey, Summerhill has been postmaster relief since about 1985. A recent longtime employee, now retired, is Catherine Hettle.

Martha M. Smith has been postmaster since June 23, 1984. A native Johnstowner, high school class of 1956, she served three years with the U. S. Women's Army Corps after high school graduation.

In 1968, she began work with the postal service as a clerk in New York City and returned to Johnstown in the same capacity in 1972. Through the career enrichment program, Martha qualified as postmaster; her bid for the Summerhill opening was accepted in 1984.

In earlier years, the postmaster was a political appointee. Now it is regulated by civil service. Also, it formerly was a requirement that the postmaster be a registered voter and resident of the community. In recent years, these requirements have been dropped. Martha M. Smith, by choice, has opted to reside in Summerhill.

Between 6,000 to 8,000 pieces of mail are handled daily by the Summerhill post office. Pickup and delivery is made twice daily, morning and evening, by truck from Johnstown. The trucking contractor, for over 35 years, has been Woodrow Fry & Sons of Salix.

Mailbox rentals in 1932 were $1.40 a year. In 1991, the rental is $7.25 a year for a 4 by 6-inch box. Postal rates in 1917 were 1¢ for an unsealed, printed circular letter; 2¢ for a typewritten one, whether sealed or not. The summer of 1991, first class postage was 29¢.

Whereas postal money orders once cost from 3¢ to 30¢, according to a sliding scale for amounts up to $100, today's rate is 75¢, regardless of the amount.

Summerhill's post office is open from 8 a. m. to noon; 1:30 to 5:00 p. m. weekdays and 8:30 to 11:45 a. m. Saturdays.

September 26, 1990, the local office celebrated its 150th anniversary with an open house.

The custodians of the mail since 1840 are:

	Title	Date Appointed
George Murray	Postmaster	July 29, 1840
William Murray	Postmaster	May 20, 1854
Benjamin F. Slick	Postmaster	June 28, 1860
James D. Plummer	Postmaster	October 29, 1866
John Brown	Postmaster	May 4, 1869
John D. Wentroth	Postmaster	July 12, 1870
Elias Paul	Postmaster	November 2, 1877
John Brown	Postmaster	April 19, 1878
Charles A. Dimond	Postmaster	October 22, 1885
John D. Wentroth	Postmaster	April 19, 1889
Patrick F. Lewis	Postmaster	July 10, 1893
Minnie M. Dimond	Postmaster	May 2, 1894
James D. Wentroth	Postmaster	October 23, 1897
Emma E. Sherbine	Postmaster	June 24, 1907
Gussie L. Plummer	Postmaster	August 10, 1914
Thelma Wicks	Postmaster	November 17, 1928
Gussie L. Plummer	Assumed Charge	February 3, 1934
Gussie L. Plummer	Acting Postmaster	February 7, 1934
Stella K. Simendinger	Postmaster	August 3, 1934
Victor C. Rosenberger	Postmaster	March 19, 1935
William R. Kirby Jr.	Assumed Charge	February 1, 1940
William R. Kirby Jr.	Acting Postmaster	March 1, 1940
William R. Kirby Jr.	Postmaster	July 1, 1940
Mary E. Callahan	Assumed Charge	January 1, 1942
Mary E. Callahan	Acting Postmaster	January 3, 1942
*Mary E. Callahan	Postmaster	July 17, 1942
Beatrice M. Cameron	Acting Postmaster	April 39, 1968
Beatrice M. Cameron	Postmaster	June 30, 1971
Martha M. Smith	Officer-in-Charge	December 1, 1983
Karen H. Ondo	Officer-in-Charge	March 21, 1984
Martha M. Smith	Postmaster	June 23, 1984

*Name changed by marriage to Mary E. Sherlock July 23, 1966

Redwood Restaurant

Redwood Restaurant

Redwood Restaurant was established in September 1982 as a trust for Evan L. Jones' three daughters -- Bonnie Jean, Ruth Marie and Louise.

Bruce and Diane Walkovich and Larry and Karen McCabe, all from Portage, purchased the business September 1, 1986. The Walkovichs assumed sole ownership in 1988.

The restaurant was expanded, in 1990, with the addition of a banquet room to seat 50. In the main dining room, groups up to 100 can be accomodated. Catering services for upwards to 450 people are available. Church groups have provided much of the catering business. Walk-in diners come from a five county area.

Bruce Walkovich, who is a 1973 graduate of Portage High School and a 1977 graduate of Dickinson College with a B. S. degree in economics, had been employed in management by K-Mart for ten years. He chose the Summerhill business during his search for self-employment.

Redwood Restaurant features a lot of ethnic specials during the week along with the traditional dishes of steaks, pork chops, chicken, turkey, roast beef and seafoods. It is geared to casual dining with a full breakfast, lunch and dinner menu.

Bruce says they "strive to do things differently" and provide as much quality as possible at the lowest prices. "We use all first quality produce and we don't concentrate on prepared portions." Specials, he said, are prepared from scratch. Desserts are made in-house. "We don't serve alcohol, therefore, we don't compete with those that do." He claims that 60 to 70 percent of the business is from senior citizens.

During the Johnstown Flood Centennial of 1989, newspaper ads exhorted visitors to drive just two miles north of the Johnstown National Memorial to the Portage/South Fork exit of 219 with the following historic note:

> "chances are that if you sat down to dinner at a restaurant in 1889, you would have been treated to fresh baked bread, made on premises, homemade soup made from scratch and your entree would have been a large portion chosen from a wide selection of traditional dishes. Your mashed potatoes would have been made from fresh potatoes, your coffee cup kept full, and for dessert you could have chosen from a vast assortment of fresh baked pies and cakes...we humbly invite you to sample a taste of the past in the Redwood tradition of quality and value."

Redwood Restaurant employs from 30 to 35 people. It is open Sundays from 8 a. m. to 7 p. m. -- Mondays through Thursdays from 6:30 a. m. to 8 p. m. and -- Fridays and Saturdays from 6:30 a. m. to 9 p. m.

The Automobile Businesses

Raymond A. Betz (1897-1945) pioneered the sale of new cars in Summerhill. His father, George, came from Germany and settled in Summerhill at the age of 6. His mother, the former Philomena Long, was a native of Summerhill.

Raymond was born and raised here, attended the Summerhill Schools, clerked in Kirby's General Store for five years and worked two years at South Fork Lumber Company.

In 1922, he went into the garage business on Jackson Street and obtained a Chevrolet dealership.

During gas rationing of World War II, he furnished bus service for Summerhill mill workers to Bethlehem's Franklin shops.

Werfel Motor Company was a partnership organized in 1932 by two brothers -- Herman and Ferdinand Werfel. They first sold plymouth automobiles.

When Herman moved to New Jersey, Ferdinand remained as the sole owner. Mary, his wife and a Summerhill school teacher, helped out with the book work.

Ferdinand Werfel (1903-1964) was a native of Pringle Hill. He spent his youth on the farm. He and Mary set up housekeeping in Summerhill upon their marriage in 1934.

Ferdinand had gotten his initial training in the automobile business as an employee of Raymond Betz.

Mrs. Werfel, who still resides in Summerhill, recalls that the motor company's first customer was "Bony" Bodenschatz.

She also saved a Portage Dispatch advertisement of August 15, 1957, which pictures the staff of the company -- William E. Werfel, Joseph F. Werfel, Stephen Werfel, Joseph F. Stoke, Robert J. New and Dorothy E. Grattan.

An interesting invoice in the hands of Stella DeLozier shows the purchase of a Plymouth Sedan by her father, C. W. Simendinger, on October 25, 1932. The purchase price was $475 less $135 for a trade-in. The $340 balance was financed by a note for $55 and a lease for the remaining $285. Payments were spead over a year at $27.75 a month.

Wefel Motors terminated as a Plymouth-Dodge-DeSoto new car dealer in 1964. Its franchises were purchased by E. L. Jones.

Werfel Motor Company (Credit: Lillian M. Pisarski)

Werfel Motor Co.

McCall's Jeep-Eagle

McCall's Jeep/Eagle, Inc. is a new car dealership which dates back to 1945 when two brothers -- John W. and Frank McCall -- formed a partnership.

John, a 1915 native of Summerhill, graduated from Johnstown Catholic High School and Cambria-Rowe Business College. He was employed by Bethlehem Steel Corporation in Johnstown as a timekeeper and also worked as Raymond Betz's bookkeeper.

Frank, a 1905 native of South Fork, worked in Altoona until 1937 when he purchased a home in Stonycreek Township and worked as a supervisor at Johnstown's Bethlehem steel mills. He also worked at Betz's garage and got him his state inspection station.

Raymond Betz's death in the Spring of 1945 saw the two McCall brothers operating the garage for Mrs. Ethel Betz. John managed the business; Frank handled the service work.

In 1946, they rented the garage from Mrs. Betz and started with a Hudson franchise.

Frank recalls that during the first year they got only two new Hudsons to sell because the priority of automobile manufacturing plants was for the war effort. In 1947, he said, they had six Hudsons to sell. Some came without bumpers; others without backs. The dealer had to complete the assembly.

Then, there was the Hudson-Nash merger which, in 1954, merged with American Motors. And, the, Chrysler bought out American Motors in 1987. From 1962 to 1980, McCall's also sold a light duty line of International-Harvester trucks and, in 1981 were awarded the Jeep franchise.

After renting one year, the McCalls purchased the garage building from Mrs. Betz. During the sleet storm, either in 1948 or 1949, Frank remembers that two-thirds of the roof collapsed and pushed out the brick walls. They rebuilt with wood truces -- one to two feet long -- purchased from the demolition of the former Auditorium Building in Johnstown.

Frank also recalls that Raymond Betz had purchased a school bus in 1929 to transport Summerhill youngsters to South Fork High School and during World War II used a 32-36 passenger bus to transport employees to Bethlehem's Franklin plant. The mill bus was discontinued in 1945. The McCalls got into school bus transportation in 1946.

McCalls

The school bus garage was constructed under the show room in the latter part of the 1970s. Now, about 10 regular and part-time school bus drivers are employed to transport pupils for Forest Hills School District and two area parochial schools.

Frank McCall retired in 1969; the business was retained by John. About 1980, the business was incorporated as McCall's Jeep/Eagle, Inc. with John W. McCall, president; and sons John W. McCall II, vice president; and Geoffrey A. McCall, secretary-treasurer.

Upon John W. McCall's sudden death September 1, 1990, the new corporate officers have been Geoffrey McCall, president; John W. McCall II, vice president; and Geoffrey's son, Brent, secretary-treasurer.

McCall's continues to offer full service facilities, sell new and used cars, stock Chrysler motor parts, conduct an auto leasing program, provide daily auto rentals and operate flat bed towing services.

The garage has been pumping Mobil gasoline since 1945. There are 8 full-time and 2 part-time employees. For three consecutive years, the dealership has been cited with the Chrysler award for excellence and is one of 15

Jeep/Eagle dealers in the United States nominated for People's Magazine award.

The late John W. McCall was a well-known and respected community leader. He served 22 years as borough councilman and 12 years as mayor.

During the 1950s, he was second vice president of the Mainline Industrial Development Association, a group which united seven mainline communities into one unit to attract new industries. John headed the Summerhill-New Germany affiliate.

His membership credits included the Knights of Columbus, South Fork Lions, South Fork Eagles, St. Michael American Legion, St. John's Catholic Church, Chrysler Motors dealer advisory board, Adams-Summerhill School Building Authority, South Eastern Cambria County Authority and Cambria County Industrial Development Committee.

E. L. Jones Dodge, Inc. is located in the former Werfel Motor Company building along Route 53. It is now owned and operated by Ralph Jones Sr. His father, Evan L. Jones, purchased the property and opened his own new and used car business. Across the street, he constructed a new, large show room about 1967 and sold new Dodges and Plymouths. Two years later, he added Jeeps.

The Werfel property was used for repairs and display of used cars.

E. L. Jones Dodge

The Jones agency was refranchised in 1980 for Dodge cars and trucks. In 1982, the new show room was converted into the Redwood Restaurant. All car sales and services solidated into the former Werfel building.

E. L. Jones Dodge is a family owned business of Ralph Jones Sr. His wife, the former Patricia Noel of Portage, is the bookkeeper and title clerk. Their daughter, Stacey, is the warranty manager and son, Ralph Jr., parts manager and body man.

In addition to selling and servicing cars, they are licensed as an inspection station. They offer wrecker service within a 25-mile radius and hold a service contract for state-owned vehicles. Unitl 1990, it was a Texaco gasoline station. The operation provides employment for 8 people.

Malonek Auto Sales, located along Route 53 across from the post office, is the used car business of Henry Malonek, a South Fork native who has been selling automobiles for over 45 years.

When he was 4 years old, the family moved to Summerhill in a house across the street from his current used car lot. His early years were spent working in the coal mines. He walked to Stineman's #4 mine in South Fork from his Summerhill home. Later, his walking distance was shortened when he got a job in the Ehrenfeld mines.

Henry became a local boxer at the age of 15, beginning as a lightweight and ending as a welterweight. He won 43 of 48 amateur fights and, in 1940, won the Western Pennsylvania Golden Glove championship. He turned pro in 1941, fought out of New York and New Jersey and ended with 29 victories and 4 defeats. He quit boxing in 1944, at the age of 25, and returned to the coal mines -- this time at Bethlehem's mines in Franklin.

Around 1945, Henry was selling used cars, part-time, from the lot in front of his Summerhill home.

1946, he secured the Kaiser/Frazer new car franchise and established a garage in Hutzel's Garage, Grant Street, South Fork. He moved the business to Summerhill in 1950 and added the Jeep dealership in 1951. He remained in business until 1956; the last Kaiser car was made in 1954.

For the next 18 years, Henry was a car salesman for Bingler Ford, Johnstown; Johnstown Auto Sales; E. L. Jones, Summerhill; and Raymond Brothers, Davidsville.

From 1974 to 1984, he served as deputy warden at the Ebensburg prison.

Malonek returned to Summerhill in 1985 and has been selling used cars, again.

Malonek (Boxer)

Malonek Used Cars

Rick's Auto Service

Rick's Auto Service and Petak's Auto Sales are two new automobile businesses owned by Rick Petak of New Germany. Across from each other, Rick handles both with the help of his father-in-law, Jim Kulback.

Petak, a 1978 graduate of Central Cambria High School of Ebensburg, had about 15 years experience in the automotive business before purchasing Penatzer's Service Station on old Route 53 in June of 1988.

At the garage, Rick does most service work including motor tuneups, state inspections, oil changes, brakes, shocks, etc.

As a service for his customers, he recently complied with DER regulations to sell BEST gasoline.

He started selling a line of dependable used cars in August, 1990, from a lot facing his service station.

Petak's Auto Sales

Portage National Bank's Summerhill office

Summerhill's Bank

Approval for the Summerhill Office of Portage National Bank was granted November 11, 1965. The office opened June 27, 1966 at the corner of Croyle and Wentroth Streets.

Herbert B. Wadsworth, a South Fork banker who joined the Portage National in 1960, was assigned to manage the Summerhill Office.

Upon Wadsworth's retirement in 1968, Paul J. Nigborowicz, of Portage, became the manager -- a position he still holds as an assistant vice president.

The Summerhill office offers employment to three fulltime and one part-time employees. Josephine Stein, of Wilmore, retired July 19, 1991 as community banking officer after 13 years of service. Ellen Pisarski, Portage, and Wendy Myers, Salix, have been the other employees.

The bank draws its customers from an area encompassing Summerhill, New Germany, South Fork, Ehrenfeld, Ebensburg, Summerhill Township and Portage R. D.

Among banking products available are checking and savings accounts, loans for all purposes, certificates of deposit, mortgages, night and mail deposits as well as two newer programs -- the Good Neighbor's Club for 55 or over and Money Mulitiplier for those under 55.

There is a drive-up window and a paved parking lot. A community room is available for local organizations like the borough council, fire company and women's club.

Regular banking hours are 9 a. m. to 4:30 p.m., Mondays through Thursdays; 9 a. m. to 6 p. m., Fridays; and drive-up services from 9 a. m. to Noon on Saturdays.

24-hour banking is available at the MAC/CIRRUS automatic teller machine at the bank's Route 53 Drive-Up in Portage Township.

The main office is located at 737 Main Street, Portage. Other offices are in Southmont and Ebensburg Mini Mall.

Portage National Bank is a locally-controlled institution with assests of $95 million in 1991.

Directors are Neal P. Stager (president), Attorney Ferdinand F. Bionaz (vice president), John M. Costello (Summerhill), Dr. Esker W. Cullen, Lawrence T. Giannone (executive vice president and CEO), Rohlen Kondisko, William J. Kristofco (retired executive vice president), Clifford F. Randall and Attorney Dennis McGlynn.

Ray's Lawnmower

Ray's Lawnmower Sales & Service

Ray's Lawnmower Sales & Service, Route 53, is owned by Raymond F. and Sandra Penatzer. Three sons -- Mark, Keith and Jeff -- are active in the business. Nelson Ringler is the other employee.

Raymond, a native of Summerhill and a South Fork-Croyle High School graduate of 1952, was drafted into the Army and saw duty in Kentucky, Korea and Japan during 1953-55.

He worked out of the area for three years, two years for Sears and 16 years as a sewing machine mechanic for Bestform Foundations, an area garment industry.

Beginning by repairing lawn mowers at his 412 Jackson Street home in 1970, he moved near the post office in 1974. In 1979, he built his own building at the current location on the south side of Route 53, near Laurel Run. The building is a two-story structure with 6,000 square feet to handle sales, service and parts.

Penatzer has developed this into a half-a-million dollar business with an extensive line of outdoor equipment. His customers come from several counties.

He is the authorized dealer for a wide variety of nationally advertised lines: Toro; Ariens mowers, tractors, tillers, sno-thros; Husqvarna chain saws; Echo hedge clippers, power blowers, chain saws, grass trimmers; Lawn-Boy; Homelite, Troy-Bilt and Noma power equipment; Mantis tillers and equipment; and Mighty Mac chippers and sprayers.

The business is open 54 hours a week: Monday through Thursday, 9 a. m. to 7 p. m.; Friday, 9 a. m. to 5 p. m.; and Saturday, 9 a.m. 3 p. m.

Wilson Refrigeration

Wilson Refrigeration & Appliance Service

Located at 160 Orchard Street, this is a one-man operation of Glenn Wilson. He started the service about 1979.

For 13 years, Glenn repaired appliances for Gearhardt Furniture, Conemaugh. He did refrigeration work for Sanitary Dairy, Johnstown. He participated in the General Electric on-the-job training in Pittsburgh and, later, completed another training program in 1948.

In 1964, Wilson was equipment inspector in airconditioning at Behlehem Steel Mills, Johnstown. He took an early retirement in 1983 and has since devoted full-time to his own service business.

With his own truck, Glenn services mostly household equipment -- electrical appliances like washers, dryers, garbage disposals, refrigerators, dehumifiers. He does some automotive air-conditioning work and some commercial repairs for neighboring clubs, bars and restaurants. His accounts are primarily in Cambria County and concentrated in the Ebensburg-Portage-South Fork area.

Born on a farm bordering New Germany, Glenn Wilson moved to Summerhill in 1954. He is a 1943 graduate of South Fork High School.

Kime Hotel

Kime Hotel is the oldest, continuing business in Summerhill. Herbert J. Kime has been the proprietor and operator since January 1, 1942.

His grandfather, John W. Griffith, located the business at this spot in 1890 and named it Griffith's Place.

Thomas E. Kime, Herb's father, married Griffith's daughter Lillian. When Griffith passed away, Thomas Kime took over the operations and continued the business until the end of 1941. The name was changed to Kime's Hotel.

Herbert Kime has continued the long tradition. He has offered many services to the community's citizens and children.

Kime Hotel

Kime Hotel

Brian Basile & Herb Kime

    The premises are well-kept, clean and neat. The brick building has 11 bedrooms which are even available now. The rooms are outfitted with furniture that is over 80 years old. It has been well preserved and serviceable.

For many years, Kime Hotel was famous for its Friday fish fries. Customers were attracted from a wide area. The last meals were served in 1988.

There are senior citizens who remember when Kime Hotel treated children of the community to the early Saturday kiddies programs on television. This was before televisions were common in private homes.

In addition, Kime sponsored many athletic teams in local basketball, baseball and softball leagues. To name a few, there were the Forest Hills Community Basketball, American Legion Baseball, and a night league at South Fork's Falcon Field. These sponsorships occurred over a period of 35 years -- from 1945 to 1980.

In recognition of the long tenure of bartending and community services, Herbert J. Kime was inducted into the 1990 "Bartender Hall of Fame" as one of 25 throughout the United States and the only inductee from Pennsylvania. His name was submitted by Brian Basile of Westmont to Bartender Magazine. The magazine presented Herb with a plaque and a gold ring. The inductees were noted in the publication's Fall Issue of 1990.

Herbert also worked as a draftsman from 1931 to 1969 at District 9 Pennsylvania Highway Office in Hollidaysburg. He is the only surviving member of the Kime family of four brothers and two sisters. Thomas R. was a draftsman; John worked at Laurel Crest; Paul was a Penn Central employee; Grace worked at the Ebensburg State School and in Virginia; Kathleen was employed in Chesapeake, Virginia.

Along with his wife, the former Sophia Figola, Herbert Kime has recorded nearly a half century in Summerhill as business and community leader.

Shirley & Vince's

Shirley & Vince's is the other tavern on Main Street. It is owned and operated by Vince and Shirley Kitchick. Vince also is the borough's street commissioner.

Their parking area is part of the lot which formerly contained the Summerhill House. Thereafter, it was the site of Jacob Meier's Store, Duffy's and Kirby's first grocery. Ira A. and Genevieve Lenz operated a general store here, too. It is remembered for its ice cream and a pool table in the back.

In 1933, the Lenzs got a liquor license and opened Lenz's Tavern. They were noted for hamburgers and sandwiches.

The Kitchicks acquired the property after the Lenzs and constructed a new building.

The business is open daily. Customers are local people who spend their leisure time here. Shirley notes that a lot of the "old timers" are gone; coal miners are gone, too. She claims that Katz Sliko has his name on the corner bar stool from which he "educates the other patrons."

Most of the bar's business is in the nights. There is seating at 8 tables in a pleasant atmosphere. It is the primary place for pizza and stromboli. Ham, hamburgers and nachos with cheese also are served.

A popular entertainment during winter months is the dart league which attracts 40 to 60 patrons from South Fork to Ebensburg.

Shirley & Vince's

Summerhill Construction Supply

Lewis Brown does custom work for contractors and other builders with an emphasis on millwork, mouldings and cabinets.

There is a lot of Summerhill history here.

Peter Brown, the builder of Railroad House, was the great grandfather of Lewis.

Joe Brown, Peter's son and grandfather of Lewis, was born in Summerhill and also was a hotelkeeper at the Railroad House. Later, he farmed where the Summerhill Coal Company is now situated. He also tended bar at Griffith's Place (now Kime Hotel).

Peter Brown (1905-1967) was Lewis' father. He worked most of his life as a carpenter and stone mason building and renovating many area properties. He worked as an independent contractor and, at times, with others.

Lewis began working with his father at the age of 12. He accompanied him to jobs and helped with building chores.

Upon his father's death in 1967, Lewis went on his own for three years. Then, along with his brothers Charles and Denne, they formed Summerhill Construction, Inc. and built homes as far as Cresson and Johnstown.

Charles and Denne went independent in 1984 with Denne based in Summerhill and Charles based in South Fork.

Lewis operates out of a small mill shed just off the location of the former Railroad House.

Summerhill Construction

Rosie's Watkins Cupboard

Rose (Beiter) Brown is Lewis Brown's wife. She operates Rosie's Watkins Cupboard at their home, 823 Spring Street, Summerhill.

The store occupies a room in the house and is open Mondays and Tuesdays from 8:30 a. m. to 3 p. m. Customers, however, can telephone anytime or visit whenever Rosie's home.

A sewing machine operator for 24 years at Bestform Foundations of Johnstown, Rose married Lewis Brown in 1976 and became a Summerhill resident.

She allowed Margaret McCormick to use her home for a Watkins party. This kindled her interest; she became a dealer in direct sales in 1984. Three years later, Rose was a distributor and, in 1990, she advanced to executive distributor. Now, she sponsors about 20 dealers in Johnstown and the surrounding areas.

Her line of products include extracts, spices, dessert mixes, soup bases, punch, cookbooks, water filters, health aids, household and cleaning products, room fresheners and deodorizers, pest control and pet supplies.

She does no door-to-door solicitation but does fund raisers for area organizations and about three parties each month.

Rosie's Cupboard

Mary Ellen Wess Beauty Shop

The only beauty salon now in Summerhill is operated by Mary Ellen (Werfel) Wess at her home at 437 Jackson Street. The wife of councilman Eugene "Mike" Werfel, she has been doing business here since November 1967.

A 1953 graduate of Adams-Summerhill High School, she was licensed in 1958 after training at the Hammond Beauty School of Johnstown. Three of her daughters also are hairdressers; one in Ebensburg and two in Virginia.

Mary Ellen cuts hair, gives permanents and applies color to make her customers "ready for their events in life." Her customers include men, women and children.

She has reduced her working hours to appointments only, usually Thursdays and Fridays. She serves a selected number of regular customers from the local area, including Portage, South Fork and Summerhill.

Mary Ellen is licensed as a cosemetologist by the Commonwealth of Pennsylvania, Department of State, Bureau of Professional and Occupational Affairs, Harrisburg.

Country Mart

Country Mart goes back to Edgar E. and Jessie (Sherbine) Wicks.

Edgar's name appeared for the first time on Summerhill's tax list as a confectioner in 1914.

Mary A. Wentroth transferred the property, valued at $2,500, to E. E. Wicks in March 1915.

Known as "Bus", Wicks, he catered to the general needs of the growing community. He sold Nelson's ice cream from Portage, candies, fruits, tobacco, cigars, lunches, roasted peanuts, Saturday Evening Post and the Gazette Times. He was the first to sell gasoline in Summerhill. Many remember the marble soda fountain and the two pool tables.

A daughter, Thelma (1906-1975), was a graduate of South Fork High School and Indiana State Teachers College. She started her teaching career in Portage where she met her husband, Eldred B. Jones.

Thelma also served as postmaster of Summerhill from 1928 to 1934. She retired from teaching in 1970 as a South Fork elementary instructor.

Eldred, a 1907 native of Portage, was a well-known representative of the American Tobacco Company and until 1963, a partner in Jones Candy Company of Portage. He is the only Summerhill resident to hold elective county office -- treasurer from 1964-1968.

Wick's Store

After three years in charge of the finance office at Ebensburg State School, he went into semi-retirement. He has been affiliated with the Cambria County Fair for 10 years and served on its board of directors until 1991. He also is a past commander of Portage's American Legion.

Country Mart

Eldred spent a year as a member of the Cole Brothers circus band in 1928. He played clarinet and flute. He performed with the Portage Concert Band in 1922 and Portage Amvets in 1945-46.

Three daughters -- Marcia, Karen and Sylvia -- were billed as the Jones Girls and performed at many church and community functions in the late 1930s and early 1940s. Their mother, Thelma, was the piano accompanist.

When E. E. Wicks died in the 1940s, the store changed hands a number of times. Among the operators were Guy Galosi, Scottie Truscott, Dick and Naomi Costello and John Brown.

Bill and Joyce (Brisini) Itle of Bellwood Farms, Munster, assumed ownership in September 1981 and have successfully provided employment for five people. They sell a little bit of everything including groceries, newspapers, dairy and deli products, snacks, sodas, over-the-counter drugs, etc.

"We even sell the screw-in types of electrical fuses," muses Joyce.

The store is an official Pennsylvania lottery sales station. It is open everyday except Christmas. Hours are 9 a. m. to 9 p. m. with an extra hour on weekends.

Joyce points out that it is the only store with a cast iron bath tub, part of amenities from former living quarters.

Summerhill Coal Company

On Route 53, Summerhill Coal Company has been owned and operated by Russell David Jones since 1986.

The building, erected by John M. Costello, was sold to E. L. Jones who used it in his coal operations. Russell is E. L. Jones' son.

The company deals in hard and soft house coal, topsoil, driveway shale, railroad ties and bagged hard and soft coal. Excavating and landscaping services also are available.

A recent ad lists "run of mine, stoker and nut" and "Anthracite: rice, pea, and bucksheat, nut". Energy assistance and emergency customers are welcome. "We will deliver to your residence -- call for prices!"

The yard includes scales, weigh sheds and six 60-foot coal bins.

Russell was born in Mineral Point and now resides in Summerhill.

John M. Costello and Costello Company

John M. Costello and his wife, the former Lois Jones of Portage, make their home at Two Manor Drive, the only Summerhill residence featured on the post card series of the early 1900s. Then identified as the Sherbine Residence, the house has a unique history of its own.

It was quite a show place. Built for Dr. J. B. Green, it was an elegant structure with a fabulous, working fountain that stood upon the hill on the northern banks of the railroad. Not only did it provide a spectacular view of the town but the town folk looked up to it in awe. It was the first house between Johnstown and Altoona to have a central heating system with big cast iron radiators. The bathroom was finished in solid copper. The doctor's office was located in the basement and reached by ascending a series of wooden steps from the railroad.

Courthouse deeds show that Dr. Green purchased lots #1 and #2 from Griffith, Brown and Stineman for $250, September 12, 1889.

By February 1900, the property was up for sheriff sale because of an unpaid debt of $1,313.33 with Pennsylvania Building & Loan Association. The specs listed a two-story frame building, 30 by 36 feet, with a 12 by 12 feet addition, stone foundation and water from a spring at Funk's cabin. It was sold, at the $750 highest bid, to John W. Dale, receiver for the building and loan association.

After several other transactions, Squire Milton A. Sherbine acquired ownership and, by 1909, sold it to his son-in-law and daughter, Richard Henry and Ada Costello.

Richard Costello (1877-1930) was a native of Croyle Township. He worked as a bookkeeper for Pennsylvania Coal & Coke Corporation in Cresson and was division operator at the PRR W Tower in Summerhill. He married Ada in 1901 and lived in Sherbine's "town house", the historic stone house on Main Street.

John was one of four children and after his father's death, he bought the property from his mother and two surviving brothers.

The century-old house has been periodically renovated and adapted to the needs of the Costello household. There now are 6 bathrooms, 3 kitchens and 7 bedrooms. It has provided separate living quarters for the mothers of John and Lois.

There is a large, in-ground swimming pool and a poolside area with an extra large umbrella. The grounds have been enhanced with walking trails and permanent benches. Trees shelter the property from the adjacent railroad. No longer can the residence be seen from the town.

Another unique feature is a 22-ton, 4-wheeled caboose built in the Altoona railroad shops in 1905. It was placed in the backyard area in 1963 for the couple's son John when he was 4. Uncle Miles Costello secured the caboose for his nephew at West Brownstown, near Uniontown, and hauled it to Summerhill on a 50-ton lowboy.

Used by PRR in 1918, the caboose is set up on 135-1b. rail, 39 feet long with 16 railroad ties.

A second, or back-up, caboose is located on the old Sherbine farm property, below St. James Cemetery and visible from Route 53.

A veteran of the U. S. Air Force and a life-long resident of Summerhill, John M. Costello is president of Costello Company of Summerhill. The firm's business was concentrated in contracting and leasing earth-moving equipment and trucks from 1944 to 1988. It was started by John's two older brothers, Richard and Miles. Richard was a well-known and respected area school teacher and school principal. Miles was a member of the PRR police department. John became sole owner about 1960.

The company did a lot of paving in Summerhill and South Fork, built earthen dams and constructed some homes. For many years, they cleared the PRR right-of-ways after accidents along the mainline from Pittsburgh to Altoona and the Punsutawney Branch. A related business -- Costello Garage -- was a public inspection garage along Route 53 from 1946 to 1989.

In 1969, John bought Schrader Brothers truck body shop in Fifficktown and as Costello Body and Manufacturing Company built truck bodies and trailers until 1980.

At its peak, Costello Company provided jobs for up to 40 people.

John Costello leases the Summerhill post office to the U. S. Postal Service and also owns the ancestral farm in Croyle Township and a number of homes in the area. One of them, the historic Stone House in Summerhill, he purchased in the 1950s from First National Bank of South Fork. After completely remodeling the interior, he has retained it as a rental property.

A 1939 graduate of South Fork High School and 1951 graduate of the University of Pittsburgh, John serves a long list of civic, fraternal, religious and corporate organizations.

He is past treasurer of the Cambria County Historical Society and past president of the Johnstown Flood Museum.

Currently, he is president of the First Lutheran Church council of Johnstown. He is past president of Allegheny Lutheran Homes and Lutheran Social Services in Johnstown and Hollidaysburg and former delegate, for 11 years, to the Central Pennsylvania Synod of Lutheran Church of America.

Masonic order affiliations include lodges in Ebensburg, Johnstown and Altoona. He also is a member of the Jesters, a fun organization of the Masons.

A past president of South Fork Lions Club, he also is a member of Elks, Bachelors Club and Sunnehanna Country Club, all of Johnstown.

John is chairman of the Girls Scouts development committee and a director of Portage National Bank and Johnstown Lee Hospital. Currently, he serves as board chairman of Lee Health Service Foundation.

John and Lois are parents of four children, all of whom have attained professional status: John Milton Costello, Jr., board certified internist on a fellowship in cardiology; Susan Lorditch, Mechanicsburg, a registered nurse at Harrisburg Hospital; Margaret Plank Etters, a registered nurse at Harrisburg Hospital; and Amy Suhr, an attorney with Commonwealth Court.

Evan L. Jones - Coal Mining Enterprises

Evan L. Jones, a man from humble beginnings who has achieved financial success from the coal-stripping business, is another prominent residence of today's Summerhill.

In 1969, after purchasing the former Dora Kick and Charles Dimond properties along Route 53, he drew the blue prints, excavated the foundation and had Summerhill Construction Company build a $136,000 home.

The 8-room stone house is 40 by 110 feet with a full basement and recreation room, 3 baths, two five-foot major fireplaces, 5 bedrooms, a laundry, a dining room and a 20 by 30 feet living room. There are complete vacuuming and intercommunication systems throughout the house.

Additional buildings include a 24 by 28 feet, two-car garage, a large 30 by 30 feet patio and a 30 by 40 feet camper garage.

An historic note related by Mr. Jones is that in his front yard, almost directly in line with his front door, he uncovered a 22-foot well, 5 feet in diameter, which was used by the stage coach when it made it runs through Summerhill. He restored the well, placed protective plates over it and piped a water line into his home. An electric pump furnishes this well water into the house, when needed. During the 1977 flood, Jones said, this water source was used.

Jones Warehouse

Jones Office Building

Jones Residence

He and his wife, the former Hazel Alberta Alexander of Mineral Point, have a second home in Florida. They spend the winters there.

Evan L. Jones is a 1924 native of Akron, Ohio. His father, David C. Jones, came from Cardiff (Wales) and at the age of 18 went into mining in New Mexico. His mother, Melanie, drove Red Cross ambulances in Ohio during World War I (1916-1918).

E. L. Jones left Akron in 1929 and settled in Nanty Glo, attended Catholic schools up to seventh grade and moved to Mineral Point R. D. in 1937.

He saw military duty from 1943 to 1946. Here, he got his technical training serving with the U. S. Air Force with General Stillwell in the Asiatic-Pacific Theatre. As a sergeant, Jones laid out construction to cross waterways and build jungle roads.

Returning to Mineral Point, E. L. Jones got involved with Page's and Walter Stock's house coal mines.

In 1946, he did some coal stripping in Coalport with a $4,000 loan from First National Bank of South Fork. By 1948, he formed E. L. Jones Coal Company and had expanded his stripping operations into Bakerton, Indiana and Blairsville.

He also furnished tipple management for Pennsylvania Coal and Coke Company at its Priscilla Coal mine in South Fork and did contract work at #20 steam station for Behlehem Steel Company.

In 1961, Jones leased Stineman's holdings in South Fork. He did extensive stripping which necessitated the construction of a tipple near the viaduct.

June 21, 1963, he bought all of Bethlehem Coal Company's rights at the former Argyle mines in South Fork, Cresson, Lilly and other locations -- over 9,000 acres.

In 1961, he organized the South Fork Equipment Co.,Inc. to handle all mining equipment and the Ace Drilling Coal Company as the main operating company for strip mining in Maryland and Pennsylvania.

Also, in the 1960s, he had four mining operations in Grantsville, Maryland. And, in the 1970s, his operations took him into Stoystown.

The present E. L. Jones Coal Company office building in Summerhill was erected in 1975. Evan had bought the old mill property of some 40 acres from the Franklin Penrod Estate. He also used part of area to construct a large truck garage in 1978 as a facility to serve as the central location of all mining supplies. This building is unusual in that it is constructed on a floating foundation which rises and falls with the river.

The remaining acreage was the site of his first office in the car dealership business which now houses Redwood Restaurant.

Lot of his coal was sold in Lancaster County. His two principal accounts included Pennsylvania Power and Light and Baltimore Gas and Electric.

Top quality coal was shipped to California horse ranches where it was used for blacksmithing until 1979.

E. L. Jones quit stripping coal in 1983 after having provided employment for 165 people. He estimates that, by this time, he had stripped 7 to 12 million tons of coal with as much as $5 million credit from Pittsburgh National Bank.

Two of his sons are Summerhill businessmen: Ralph at the E. L. Jones Dodge and Russell at the Summerhill Coal Company. A son, Roy, is in the auto body business in Stuart, Florida. Ray, the youngest, is living at home in Summerhill.

Three daughters are: Bonnie Jean and Ruth Marie, both residents of Florida; and Louise, Pleasantsville, Pa.

E. L. Jones owns some other businesses besides the coal companies. In 1965, E. L. Jones Building Supply Corporation was organized in Ocala, Florida. Other Florida enterprises include American Rock & Stone Corporation, Jones Septic Tank, Inc., and George's Body Shop, Inc.

At Summerhill, he currently employs four people. His business activities are now restricted to excavating, retailing and new and used equipment. His office is staffed by his niece, Helen Alexander Hebden, who has been administrator for 22 years.

E. L. Jones is proud that he ran a clean operation and provided a good pension system. He is especially proud that he put money back into the area.

E. L. Jones remains as one of the largest land owners in Cambria County.

He has generously donated land to the National Park Service at the Lemon House historic site in Cresson and continues to cooperate with area development plans.

When one looks at today's Summerhill, the stretch of Route 53 attest to his investment in the community. This portion is easily the current main business area.

McCall's Optical

Richard McCall is employed in the optical laboratory of Ophthalmic Associates of Johnstown and operates an optical wholesale from Summerhill. His office is located in his home at Croyle and Mill Streets and his wholesale operations on Main Street, the former Evangelical United Brethren church building he purchased in 1976 and converted into two apartments.

Richard has been in optical work for 35 years. His early experience was with Bausch & Lomb in Rochester, New York. In the 1950s, he completed four years of training as an optician at the New York State Institute of Applied Arts and Sciences, Buffalo, New York. He was associated with Keller, Irwin Optical Company, Johnstown, for 17 years prior to his present position with Ophthalmic Associates.

A Summerhill native, Richard McCall is a son of Thomas and Esther (Noon) McCall. His brother, Joseph L. McCall, was the owner of McCall's Optical Shop, New Germany, prior to his death August 28, 1989.

McCall's Optical

Gruss Electronics Repair

Joseph Gruss Jr., son of Joseph and Betty Gruss of Fifficktown, moved to 210 Mill Street, Summerhill in 1974 when he married Kathleen Tully. She is a life-long resident of Summerhill and a daughter of Bernard and Frances (Haberl) Tully.

A 1967 graduate of Forest Hills High School, Gruss' interests were directed towards electronics. He attended Electronics Institute of Pittsburgh for two years and passed the test for certified electronics technician. Since 1971, he has been a full-time technician at Bethlehem Steel Company in Johnstown.

About 1972, Joe answered an ad that Radio Shack was looking for individuals to do service work on their equipment. He did Radio Shack's repairs at his home on a contract basis until 1978.

In the meanwhile, his expertise spread by word-of-mouth and the demand for his services increased. Not able to handle all the repairs from the basement shop of his home, Joe opened Gruss Electronics Repairs, a factory authorized warranty service, in 1978 at Hills Plaza in Richland Township's shopping area.

October 1988, he moved his facilities to its newer location in the plaza. He furnishes authorized warranty services for 45 to 50 consumer electronics manufacturers. His is a large, independent service which is listed as an 800 number in the warranty information of the manufacturers who use his service. In many instances, Gruss covers the area midway between Johnstown and Pittsburgh and between Johnstown and Harrisburg. A lot of service work arrives through U. S. mail and United Parcel Service.

This business, started in Summerhill, has grown into an area enterprise which requires the services of five full-time employees in addition to the owner.

The repair shop is open 5 1/2 days a week.

Basile's Lunch

Samuel Basile, a South Fork native and now a resident of Summerhill, conducts a bar business in his hometown where his father, the late Joseph Basile, settled in 1902 and was a grocer for over 60 years.

Sam's brother, Carmel Thomas, bought the Jim Davis Bar on Lake Street, South Fork, in 1941. Sam purchased the business from his brother in 1953 and has operated it ever since as Basile's Lunch.

Sam and his wife, Doreen, make their home at 255 Croyle Street, Summerhill.

Ted's TV

Ted's TV at 536 Main Street, South Fork, is the business Edwin T. Walls started April 1, 1950 in his hometown. During the years, he held a regular job at Bethlehem's Johnstown steel mills and worked at his television sales and service part-time. Now retired from the mill job, he continues selling and servicing Sylvania sets.

About five years ago, Ted and Kathleen Walls purchased their current Summerhill home at 402 Jackson Street from the Clare Betz Estate. Kathleen returned to her hometown where her father, the late John Sloan, was mayor for over 30 years.

The Walls believe their new home is the third oldest house in Summerhill -- the original property of George Betz. It was the location from which a widowed Minnie Betz supported her family by baking, selling and delivering bread around the 1910s to the 1930s. The large baking ovens once stood where the remodeled kitchen is now located.

Summerhill Plumbing & Heating

Summerhill Plumbing & Heating is an extension of the original Summerhill Heating Company operated for many years by Regis Schrift.

Mike Wess, a Summerhill native, now heads a firm of three employees. He is a son of Eugene Wess, councilman, and Mary Ellen, operator of Mary Ellen's Beauty Shop.

Mike studied heating, ventilation and air conditioning at the Greater Johnstown Vo-Tech and worked with Ebensburg Plumbing and Heating for about seven years before establishing his own business with an office at his home, 435 Jackson Street. Since August 1991, he works out of his New Germany residence at R. D. 1, Box 402.

Two vans and one truck handle light commercial and mostly residential plumbing, heating and air conditioning work throughout Cambria County.

Lenz's Tavern at the present site of Shirley's & Vince's.

Bar in Lenz's Tavern.

Early General Service Station, now Rick's Auto Service.

Louis Rosenberger, the Jewel Tea Company representative, 1960.

Chapter 10

The Town's Religious Needs

The first church in Summerhill was a non-denominational church on Madison Street, according to the Women's Club history of 1966.

Free Will Baptist Church also is mentioned as another early house of worship. Rev. Samuel B. Seaman was the pastor. The Women's Club publication says that the pastor's tombstone was found in the Edward Bodenschatz yard at 429 Jackson Street with the following inscription:

"In memory of Samuel B. Seaman, Pastor of the Free Will Baptist Church. Died March 3, 1854, Age 43 years, 6 months, 29 days."

The 1910 tax assessor's book valued the Lutheran Church on Church Street at $2,000; United Brethren, Main Street, $1,200; and St. John's Catholic, Main Street, $3,500. Two ministers were on the tax records -- J. T. Fox, Jackson Street, and Clemence M. Stratman, Main Street.

The Evangelical Church on Jackson Street first appeared on the tax records of 1915 with a value of $1,000. The three other churches for that year included St. John's, Lutheran and United Brethren.

By 1917, only three remained on the tax assement rolls: the Catholic, Lutheran and Brethren.

Lutheran Church, Summerhill, about 1910. (Credit: Gertrude Brummert)

St. John's Lutheran Cemetery, 1991

St. John's Lutheran Church, 1991

The **Southern Cambria News of Portage** reported the following churches and services in 1927:

St. John's Catholic Church, Rev. Richard Krause -- Low Mass at 8 a.m. and sermon -- High Mass and sermon at 10 a.m. -- Vesper services at 7 p.m.

St. John's Lutheran Church, Rev. F. S. Schultz -- Sunday School at 10 a.m. -- Preaching at 7:30 p. m.

United Brethren Church, Rev. Buffington -- Sunday School at 9:30 a.m., Harold Roush, superintendent-- Preaching at 11 a.m.

St. John Evangelical Lutheran Church

Wallace Croyle, Margaret Croyle, Alice McGough and Fern Myers wrote and Helen Claycomb and Bonnie Novotny typed a history of St. John in 1987. They prefaced the publication with the following descriptive background of their Lutheran faith:

"The Reformation had its cradle in Germany and the Evangelical Lutheran Church is regarded as the church of the Germans and their descendants, according to a History of the Lutheran Church written in 1888 by Edmond Jackob Wolf, D. D. The Palatines were the first Lutherans whom religious persecution drove to our shores. Their history is one of tragic interest. Germany was in the Thirty Year War with France. Within a single generation their beautiful country, one of the fairest and most fertile regions of Europe, was thrice devastated by the armies of Louis XIV. When it was found impossible to hold what had been conquered, Louis gave the command to have the country turned into a desert. They granted the people three days of grace to leave the country. Then the destruction began, the flames went up from every market place, every hamlet, every parish, and every country seat within the devoted province. The fields where corn had been planted were ploughed up, the orchards were hewn down, no promise of a harvest was left on the fertile plains, where once had been Fankenthal. Not a vine or tree could be seen on the slopes of the sunny hills around what had been Heidelburg, Mannheim, Worms and Spires met the same fate, they were reduced to ashes. Protestant worship was broken up. Louis XIV was devout Catholic and he turned the country over to Roman Catholic Priests, while the Palatines fled to Protestant England. Under the stress of their misery, many thousand inhabitants of the surrounding countries, Baden, Wurtemberg and Hesse joined the Palatines and fled to England. The arrival of such a host of impoverished refugees created some alarm and the government quartered them in a camp like an army. The Queen took them under her personal protection and in time they accepted her proposal for their transportation and settlement in America, where she expected their thrifty and peaceable habits would render them a valuable accesion to her colonies. Such was the background of our Lutheran faith."

St. John Evangelical Lutheran Church of Summerhill had its beginnings in 1832 when Thomas and Barbara Croyle deeded 2 acres and 68 perches for a union church and burial ground.

A small frame building was erected and used by Presbyterians (Reformed) and Lutherans.

The first written record is a book of the Reformed Presbyterian Congregation November 6, 1833.

The first recorded baptism was Maryanne Knepper Crum, daughter of Nicolas and Mary (Knepper) Crum on April 5, 1823.

The first death recorded was Fleetwood Crum on January 28, 1834. The second was Charles Croyle, Thomas Croyle's brother, February 4, 1836 at age 75.

First marriages included James Williams-Mary Pringle, John Stineman-Catherine Strayer, Peter Glunt-Sarah Stineman, and George Murray-Esther Croyle.

The book noted that the first Holy Communion for 37 members took place October 20, 1833.

Another book in the church archives is entitled "Record of the Evangelical Lutheran Church at Jefferson and the HalfWay House." Jefferson was the original name of Wilmore. HalfWay House was the early name of Summerhill.

The Allegheny Lutheran Synod minutes read that in 1845 "The Half-Way House Congregation in Cambria County was received in the Synod." It was the first county church to unite with the Allegheny Synod.

At a congregational meeting of the Jefferson and Halfway Churches in "Mrs. Croyle's Church", Mr. Croyle and Mr. Palmer were elected Elders; Mr. Paul and Mr. Settlemyer, Deacons. Rev. A. Bosserman of Johnstown was supply pastor.

The list of communicants for the Summer Hill congregation June 6, 1849 were: Peter Barrick; William Burnhimer; Daniel and Maria Burtnett; Joseph, Margaret and Samuel Croyle; Enders and Margaret Englehart; John Flenner; John and Mary Karr; Elizabeth Ketner; Michael Knipps; Matthew Michael; Valentine Moyer; Barbara Myers; William Palmer; Elizabeth Patterson; Issac, John and Susanna Paul; Elizabeth Pringle; "Febby" Rhinehart; Adam and Maria Rorabaugh; Catherine Sell; Catherine and George Settlemyer; Elizabeth and George Slonaker; Jacob and Susan Stiffler; Elizabeth, Jacob, Leah, Mary and Susan Stineman; Eliza and Jacob Weaver; Anna, Joseph and Susan Wissel; and Eve Wright.

At a congregational meeting, February 9, 1856, Samuel Riddle and Charles R. Weaver were elected Elders; Peter Berg and Joseph Croyle, Deacons.

Some of the early church services were in German during the afternoons. English services were held in the mornings. A German Communion, September 24, 1854, had 21 communicants.

By 1864, there was a membership of 74. A larger church -- the third -- was constructed with donations from members and the community at a cost of $1,800.

The church council in 1886 consisted of John B. Brown, W. Sherman Croyle, William Gable, David Gardner Seaman, Daniel Sipe, Henry Croyle and W. W. Paul. (William Henry Croyle served on the church council for 50 years.)

Improvements were noted in 1896 in the church's property.

Alma Hull (1887-1982), well-known piano teacher at South Fork, was church pianist from 1914 to 1949 and also served as choir director. She gave piano lessons in South Fork from 1899 to 1982.

Other choir directors included Mrs. McGiffin and Thelma Wicks Jones.

In 1924, a rededication service was held to commemorate improvements costing $3,000. The ceiling was covered with metal and painted white, woodwork painted and varnished, platform remodeled, circular pews installed and the entire exterior refurbished.

More improvements were completed in 1932. A bell was donated by the Wilmore Church and placed in the belfry by the Everyman's Bible Class. An altar was donated by Mr. and Mrs. Kenneth McGough. The Ladies Aid, Luther League and Fidelity Class provided an altar missal, stand and paraments. Charles Viola and Violet Myers donated the altar cross.

The Sunday School or social room was constructed in 1940 at the cost of $1,954.

The Church was incorporated and secured a church seal in 1950. A new constitution was approved. Extensive repairs were made to the basement.

A new cornerstone was laid in 1956 and a box enclosed with coins of the day, an old Bible and signatures of church council and building fund committee members.

The South Fork Trinity Lutheran Church merged with Summerhill in 1959. Rev. Gordon N. Edwards served as pastor until 1968. He was Summerhill's last full-time pastor. Since then St. John's has been supplied by ministers from the Seminary or from the area.

During the 1970s and 1980s, renovations have included new carpeting in the nave, an oil furnace, a nursery, new choir robes, lowering and insulating ceilings, installation of storm windows and outside painting.

Much has been added through personal donations: parish hall carpeting (Richard and Naomi Seaman Costello), baptismal font built and presented by Mr. and Mrs. Fred Sablotski, new pulpit bible, Gordon and Ivella Croyle Smith; new altar paraments in memory of Vernon Lehman by his wife Ethel; banner stand in memory of George and Lucy Berghane by Sewell and Helen Berghane Claycomb chalice in memory of Florence Seaman by her family; paten in memory of Florence Seaman by James and Leona Goughnour and family; host box in memory of Jessie McGough; and Joseph McGough by Elwood and Genevieve McGough, landscaping by Wendell and Fern Myers.

Periodically, the Synod has suggested closing or joining with other churches but the Summerhill congregation has chosen to remain independent. The Gallitzin church affiliated with Summerhill until 1986. Rev. Paul F. Luebbe, who was supplying both churches, has continued to be Summerhill's pastor since 1979. He drives from Chambersburg each Sunday morning.

The current church council is made up of George Novotny (president), Kathy Hostetler (financial officer), Beverly Lehman (treasurer), Florene Hettle (secretary), Ernest Malloy, Bonnie Novotny, Jeff Arnold, Wendell Myers, David Arnold and Pastor Leubbe.

Recent projects have been a new porch, exterior painting, installation of exhaust fans, shrubbery upkeep and cemetery maintenance.

The congregation consists of 72 confirmed members. Services are held every Sunday at 10:30 a.m.

Margaret Croyle in her reflections of the 150th anniversary celebration of October 10, 1982 attributed these appropriate thoughts to Pastor Paul F. Luebbe:

"A valiant band of pioneers crossed to the west side of the Alleghenies and came together to worship. Frightened, they probably were -- uncertain about today and anxious about what might befall them tomorrow. But they knew that in spite of the distance they had moved from their roots in other lands and other provinces, the same Lord that had guided and strengthened their forebearers was with them and would be their constant companion on the frontier."

"And what of the future? Who but God himself knows! But this we do know; if we ascend to the heights, He is there! If we plunge to the depths, He is there! He is ours, we are His forever and ever! Praise be to God!"

Pastors Who Have Served St. John

Rev. Christian Berentz	1832 - 1839
Rev. Peter Mose Rightmyer	1834 - 1845
Rev. A. Bosserman	1845 - 1849
Rev. Peter Sahm	1850 - 1852
Rev. L. J. Bell	1854 - 1858
*Rev. J. F. Kuhlman	1860 - 1864
Rev. P. Sheeder	1864 - 1867
Rev. A. R. Height	1867 - 1870
Rev. A. J. Hartsock	1870 - 1872
Rev. S. Croft	1872 - 1874
^ Rev. W. H. Settlemyer	1874 - 1878
Rev. J. J. Kerr	1879 - 1881
Rev. George D. Gross	1882 - 1883
Rev. John Unruh	1886 - 1888
Rev. M. O. T. Sahm	1890 - 1893
Rev. A. B. Erhart	1893 - 1897

#Rev. G. K. Allen	1897 - 1905
Rev. W. L. Leisher	1907 - 1908
Rev. J. T. Fox	1909 - 1910
Rev. George D. Gross	1910 - 1912
Rev. Franz S. Shultz	1912 - 1935
Rev. Russell B. McGiffin	1936 - 1943
Rev. Glen B. Keidel	1944 - 1948
Lloyd T. Wilson (summer supply)	1952
Rev. Russell Kerns	1952 - 1953
Charles Ruby (summer supply)	1954
Rev. David E. Strasser	1955 - 1957
John Allen Roshon	1958
Rev. Gordon N. Edwards	1959 - 1968
George D. Schaetzel (supply vicar)	1977 - 1978
Rev. Paul F. Luebbe	1978 - present

* first regular pastor
^ son of the charge
# first resident pastor

Rev. Franz S. Shultz served St. John's for the longest period, from 1912 to 1935. An 1862 native of Newry (Blair County), he was confirmed in the Lutheran Church in 1877. He worked in the PRR Altoona machine shops in 1879 where he became active in YMCA and in young people's work of the First Lutheran Church.

He graduated from Missionary Institute, Selingsgrove, in 1888; Pennsylvania College, Gettysburg, 1890; and the Theological Seminary, 1893. He was licensed by the Allegheny Synod in 1892 and ordained in 1893.

Rev. Shultz served the Morrellville charge until 1909 and the next three years at Pine Grove Mills before coming to Summerhill at the age of 50.

Newspaper Accounts of Activities

Southern Cambria News, October 7, 1927 -- Rev. F. S. Schultz, pastor of Summerhill Lutheran Church, has just completed his 15th year as pastor of Summerhill, Wilmore and Jackson charges where he received 325 into the church and baptized 307 adults and children.

The Summerhill charge was established by Rev. Dr. W. J. Keedy.

Johnstown Daily Democrat, March 27, 1929 -- Evangelical Lutheran Church observes Easter (Rev. F. S. Schultz, pastor) with Sunrise prayer service at 6 o'clock.

Participants: anthem -- Beatrice Chamney, Nora Seaman, James and Willian Wilson and Fred Thomas. Junior choir under the direction of Alma Hull. Piano solo, "Dundall March" by Mercedes McGosley, 5 years old. Ruth Shettler introduces the pageant. Vocal solo, Miss Olive Myers; Mary Chamney.

Cast of characters for the pageant: Ruth Shettler, Violet Chamney, Bertha Rolla, Nora Custer, Namora Seaman, Sarah Wilson, Miles Costello, Irella Croyle, Ethel Wilson, Dorothy and Clara Jordan, Mary Robison, Helen Smay, Mary Jordan, Edward and William Wilson, Robert Matthewson, Evelyn Rolla, Margaret Nelson, Jean McWillians, Raymond Chamney, Robert Seaman, Junior Lang, John Costello, William Jordan, Dolly Mareck, Hazel Shettler and Gladys Mathewson. (all spellings as they appeared in the newspaper article.)

Cambria Dispatch, January 18, 1935 -- the regular meeting of Fidelity Girls of the Summerhill Lutheran Church was held in the home of Miss Naomi Seaman. Nora Custer is the president. Seaman and Julia Stieber were appointed hospitality committee for 1935. Elsie Maus, Hazel Shetler, Martha McGough are the visiting committee.

St. John's Lutheran Cemetery - A 1991 survey of the readable tombstones had the following surnames: Alexander, Barr, Beba, Burtnett, Cooper, Croyle, Cummins, Davis, Fern, Flenner, Ford, Gable, Gaudig, George, Gilman, Goldsworthy, Goughnour, Green , Griffith, Hammill, Hartman, Henry, Hice, Horner, Hull, Keilman, Key, Kulka, Lloyd, Luke, MacTavish, Malloy, Malonek, Mathieson, Meier, Melloy, Meyers, Myers, Nist, Noble, Novak, Patterson, Penrod, Pentek, Phillips, Pullinger, Rager, Reichelt, Reynolds, Richards, Rorabaugh, Schlosser, Seyda, Smith, Stieber, Story, Street, Thomas, Varner, Wadsworth, Weaver, Wentroth, Sherry, Williams, Wilson, Woods, Woycek and Young.

Thomas and Barbara Croyle not only donated the 2 1/4 acres for the cemetery but also gave Pennsylvania Railroad a 200-foot right-of-way.

The cemetery is bordered by Mill and Croyle Streets. Its northern boundary parallels the mainline tracks of the railroad which runs through a cut that makes the tops of engines and rolling stock level with the cemetery grounds.

A story in the **Johnstown Tribune-Democrat, May 24, 1987,** relates that "soot, belched from the engines of coal trains as they labored up the grade a few hundred feet from the cemetery, had coated the ground and covered many of the stones erected in years past."

Wallace Croyle, a fifth generation descendant of Thomas and Barbara Croyle and author of a recent family history, is quoted as saying that "the cemetery had about a foot-and-a-half of dirt from the railroad, so members of the church decided to clean it up and they took away 52 truckloads. Then they put on topsoil. Some of the headstones you could see and others had fallen over and were buried."

Wallace was unable to find headstones for Thomas Croyle and his unmarried brother, Charles. He knew they were Revolutionary War veterans and he appealed to the Veterans Affairs Office in Cambria County Courthouse for war headstones. The stones were delivered and set up by Shetler Memorials, near Davidsville, in 1987. They were furnished free of charge.

The inscriptions read:
Thomas Croyle -- Bedford Militia -- Revolutionary War -- 1760 - 1858.
Charles Croyle -- Continental Line -- Revolutionary War -- 1761 - 1836.

Other known burials of Civil War veterans include Pvt. Ephriam Bauman (1838-1920), Robert Patterson who died at the Battle of Bull Run in 1862, Pvt. John W. Griffith (1836-1910) and Samuel Varner who died in 1896.

Today, not too many headstones are left from the early burials. Some of the discernible ones for burials in the 19th century follow:

	Name	Age
James A. Patterson	1809-1847	38
Barbara Croyle	1769-1855	86
Elizabeth Patterson	1790-1855	65
Anna Elizabeth Wentroth	1798-1865	67
Sarah A. Lloyd	1838-1873	35
Maria Burtnett	1822-1873	51
Margaret Pullinger	1851-1877	26
Daniel Burtnett	1818-1881	70
Christena Schlosser	1824-1882	54
John B. Schlosser	1824-1886	58
Conrad Myers	1823-1890	67
William Story	1808-1892	84
George Wentroth Sr.	1809-1894	85
John W. Burtnett	1857-1897	40

1912 photo of St. John's Catholic Church (Credit: Lillian M. Pisarski)

Father Clement. (Credit: Lillian M. Pisarski)

St. John's Catholic Church, 1991.

St. John's Catholic Church

The number of Catholics grew rapidly in the early 1830s when Irish workers were brought to Wilmore to build and maintain the Allegheny-Portage Railroad.

St. Bartholomew's Church was built in Wilmore with stone quarried near the railroad. It was dedicated August 22, 1840.

Membership grew to 700 by 1847. The corner stone for a new church was laid in June 1852; the church was dedicated May 20, 1855.

In the early days, most parishioners walked to mass. Farmers used horses for transportation. And, since the Allegheny Portage did not operate on Sundays, a group from the Viaduct hitched a horse to one of the cars and rode to Wilmore. On the return trip, they braked on the down grade. It is most likely some Summerhill Catholics were included.

Father Thomas J. Walsh, pastor of St. Bartholomew, set up a chapel in New Germany (about 2 1/2 miles from Summerhill) in 1855 to serve the German settlers in the northwestern portion of his congregation. The chapel was named in honor of the Immaculate Conception.

The first church choir, about 1856, at Wilmore came from the New Germany settlement. Members of this choir were Barbara and Rose Kessler, Margaretta and Maggie Schrift, John Howrey, Joseph Kessler and John Hettle.

Father Walsh had jurisdiction but the chapel was served by Benedictine Fathers of St. Vincent Monastery until 1879 because Bishop O'Connor, in 1848, had transferred all the Catholic Missions in northern Cambria County to the monks of the Benedictine Order.

Father Engelbert Leist, OSB, came to New Germany to build a parochial school. The 25 by 50-foot building was to have classrooms on the lower floor and living quarters for the teaching nuns on the second floor.

The congregation couldn't support such a school. Father Leist used the second floor as a parish house. The parish couldn't even afford the services of a resident pastor. Father Leist was recalled to the abbey in 1881. The building became a church hall and was used for card parties, dinners and dances.

During the next 20 years, the abbey furnished the following priests: Fathers Isidore Feussel, Julian Kilger, Baldwin Ambrose, Augustine Minkel and Felix Fellner.

The Johnstown Weekly Tribune of May 13, 1898 had the following wedding story under the headline "Summerhill Couple Wed":

"Mr. Simon Long and Miss Annie Betts, of Summerhill were united in marriage in the German Catholic Church at New Germany, this county, at 7:30 o'clock Tuesday morning. The ceremony was performed by Rev. Father Augustine, one of the assistant priests at St. Joseph's Church, this city, and the attendants were Mr. Andrew Betts, a brother of the bride, and Miss Long, a sister of the groom.

The bride and groom and their attendants came to the city on the 9:10 train yesterday morning, the latter returning home last evening and Mr. Long and bride today."

The Catholic membership from Summerhill kept growing. A committee of J. T. Long, Anthony Werner and Michael Tully petitioned Bishop Eugene A. Garvey on August 7, 1902 for permission to build a branch chapel in Summerhill to eliminate the inconveniences and hardships of travel to New Germany.

Bishop Garvey consented with the understanding that the church cost $2,500 and that $250 be contributed from the treasury of New Germany's Church. The Bishop also ordered that Sunday services be equally divided between the two churches and that Father Felix Fellner supervise the construction.

Milton A. Sherbine sold a lot to Anthony Werner, treasurer of the new church, August 28, 1902 for $175. Another lot was purchased from George Stineman for $200.

When it came to selecting a name for the church, Joseph Long wanted to name it St. Joseph. His brother, John, preferred St. John. Each brother agreed to head a fund-raising group. John's team raised the most funds. The church was named St. John.

A building committee was organized with John T. Long as president; P. C. Yahner, secretary; and Anthony Werner, treasurer. Other members were Joseph Long, John Gallardy, James Berschneider and John M. Bodenschatz. John Long was the architect-builder and John Gallardy the mason contractor.

A month after the Bishop granted permission for the new church, Father Felix was succeeded by Father Wolfgang Kolbeck, OSB, who completed construction arrangements.

The wooden frame building, including the vestibule, measured 86 feet long and 44 feet wide. The stone and foundation work cost $335; the building and painting, $2,500.

The cornerstone was blessed by Bishop Garvey on May 24, 1903 and erected in honor of St. John the Baptist, Summerhill, Pa.

Although dedicated in honor of St. John the Baptist, a stained-glass window depicting St. John the Evangelist was installed on the front wall over the altar. One explanation was that John T. Long, the architect, donated the window and decided it should be dedicated to his patron saint. During the 1950s the main altar was changed and the window covered only to be uncovered during the 1977 renovations.

The first Mass was said on Christmas Day, 1903. There were no pews or organ. Worshippers sat on planks supported by nail kegs, empty boxes or whatever was available. By April 22, 1904, sixteen rows of pews were installed by John Long at a cost of $616.

Five months later, H. J. Engbert, undertaker and supplier of church and household furniture and builders supplies, installed the main altar for $300.

The bell was cast and installed by Van Dusen Bell Company of Cincinnati, Ohio. Weighing 800 pounds and 35 inches in diameter, it rang for Masses and daily Angelus.

August 1904, Father Clement Stratman, OSB, replaced Father Wolfgang. Father Clement was the first resident pastor.

Bishop Garvey dedicated the new church October 9, 1904 and confirmed the first class. Members of the class were: Urban, Agnes and Amelia Berschneider; Norman and Lucinda Betz; Marcellus and Firmin Beyer; Rupert, Thomas, Monica, Victoria, Leo, Edwin and Philomena Bopp; Agnes and Mary Carver; Nora Dimond; Bertha and Ethel Dugan; George Gabany; Benedict and Stella Gallardy; Anna Haberl; Anna Kick; Rose Kurtz; Francis McClaren; Albert, Patrick and Leo McGough; Rudolph, Edna, Irene and Ravinus Penatzer; James and Margaret Quinn; George, Theresa and Marcella Schmidt; Augusta, Martina and Raphael Schrift; Bernard Steger; Carl Steiger; Henry, Philomena and Mary Steinbeiser; Henry and Elva White.

The sponsors for the boys was John T. Long and his wife for the girls. The choir was made up of Alois Haberl, Mary Plummer Jones, Cecilia Dimond Askey and Wallace Hoyer of Beaverdale. Elizabeth Brown Boyer was the organist.

The parish statistics for 1904 showed 392 members from 70 families.

The first baptism was Bertha Mary Long, daughter of Simon P. and Anna M. Betz Long, on January 24, 1904. Sponsors were Peter and Frances Betz.

The first marriage was performed April 27, 1904 between Charles Kessler and Frieda Brickner. Witnesses were William Kessler and Wilhelmina Schneider.

The first convert was Charles E. Ford, baptized by Father Clement on October 11, 1905.

The first death recorded was that of Agnes M. Tully, 21, on January 1, 1905. She was buried in the Wilmore Cemetery.

Children received Holy Communion for the first time on November 26, 1905. Members of the class were: Ben and Stella Gallardy; Irvin Berschneider; Pat, Robert and Mary McGough; Hilda Kurtz; Harvey Long; Norman Betz and Frank Haberl.

Since Summerhill's church membership outgrew New Germany's, Father Clement decided it was time to build a rectory in Summerhill. Land was purchased from Henry C. and Catherine Stinebiser for $150. John T. Long was retained as architect and contractor. The total cost of the rectory and furnishings amounted to $4,130.

Soon, it became apparent that there was a need for two Masses in Summerhill and one in New Germany. So, by 1920, the new schedule was in force and help was furnished from St. Vincent for the weekends. Fathers Stanislaus Messmer, Hilary Kaib, Maximillan Duman, Vitus Kriegel, Alvin Andres, Kenneth Haines, Owen Roth, Wilfred Dumm, Anthony Burlas and Joel Lieb traveled by train from Latrobe to Summerhill.

In 1960, Father Brinstan Takach,OSB. was appointed resident assistant to Father Constantine Zech, OSB. This lasted until 1965 when the Franciscan Fathers from Loretto came to help out on weekends in place of a resident assistant.

By July 31, 1972, Father Noel Rothrauff was appointed as associate of St. John's and in charge of the New Germany Mission. He was followed by Father Innocent Farrell who served both capacities for several nonths. Father Joachim Fatora was the assistant at St. John's and in charge of the New Germany Mission from 1973 to 1976 and succeeded by Father Germain Lieb from 1976 to 1981. These dual assignments continued with Father Terence Rogan (1981-1984), Father Firmin Beyer (1984-1987) and the return of Father Germain Lieb until he was assigned as pastor in 1989. Since 1989, the former practice of weekend help from St. Vincent in Latrobe has been reinstituted.

New Organ

The church's reed organ was replaced with a $3,350 pipe organ in 1919. It was installed by Gottfried Company of Erie, Pa. Funds were raised by Organist Charles Hettle contributing fees he received for daily High Masses and the choir's sponsorship of card parties in private homes and Long's Hall and suppers supervised by Mrs. Minnie Betz at the GBU Hall.

Three more stops were added to the organ in 1953 by Kennedy Organ Company of Pittsburgh for $1,075.

Organists

The first organist was Mary Plummer who played until the end of 1908. She was succeeded by Pearl Gallardy and, then, by Charles Hettle.

Other organists have been Donald Shrift, Constance Shrift, Claudia McCall, Donna Gallardy, Tommy Connelly, Linda Long, Patricia Long and Constance Marker.

Current organists are Margie Baynham, Patty Huber and Samilda Huber. Samilda has been playing for the past 23 years.

Choirs

Charles Hettle also was noted for developing an outstanding male choir which included Albert and Bernard Seifert; Cletus and Peter Shrift; Jacob, John and Clarus Hoover; Joseph and Carl Huber; Rudy and John Penatzer along with Joseph Bodenschatz, Robert Smith, James Hettle, John McDunn, Charles Haberl, Louis Weinzierl, Hugh Brummert and Joseph Stapleton.

For the 50th anniversary celebration in 1953, Hettle directed a male choir composed of Robert Smith Sr. and Charles Costlow, first tenors; Jack Hull and Robert Smith Jr., second tenors; Rudolph Penatzer Jr. and Albert Seifert Jr., first basses; Rudolph Penatzer Sr., second bass.

Today, St. John's has a mixed choir directed by Samilda Huber. There are 10 males and 5 females: Charlie Huber, Ed Beyer Jr., Ken Thomas, Dave Ferchalk, Ray Bodenschatz, Jim Haberl, Joe Huber, Dan Penatzer, Denny Cobaugh, Lou Kitsko, Susie Thomas, Joyce Cobaugh, Dawn Ferchalk, Jan Croyle and Kathy Huber.

Basement Improvements

When the first church was constructed, there was no excavated basement except for the section which housed the furnace and a smaller area under the front of the building.

A spacious basement, with modern kitchen facilities, has evolved through the labors of volunteers. First, the portion on the rectory side was excavated and furnished with a wood floor.

In 1946, men were asked to volunteer and dig out the rest of the basement and make room for a coal bin. The appeal brought many miners who were on strike. The job was completed within two days. Within weeks, an area for a kitchen was completed and the entire basement was excavated. The wood flooring was replaced with concrete.

This basement is used for all kinds of church functions, a meeting place for parish organizations, CCD classes and weekly religious instructions.

Church Renovations

Many improvements were made during 1977. The church interior was extensively repaired with new plaster and paint. A new lighting system was installed. Heavy red brick shingling and insulation were added to the exterior. All woodwork was painted.

During the 1950s, old altars were removed. Along with new statues, a new, natural wood high altar was installed.

In 1960, the red shingling was replaced with aluminum siding.

An 18 by 29-foot addition was constructed in 1969 to provide lavatory facilities, a front entrance to the church hall that eliminated the necessity of going through the kitchen and an inside entrance and exit to the basement. L. R. Kimball and Associates of Ebensburg were the engineers and architects. Fred Knopp of Cresson was the contractor. The project cost was about $25,000.

The bell was automated by I. T. Verdin Company of Cincinnati, Ohio, at an additional cost of about $3,000.

The bell is heard daily for the 6 a.m., Noon, and 6 p.m. Angelus. It rings to alert parishioners of the 7:45 a.m. daily Masses and tolls for the dead.

Extensive interior renovations were completed in 1977. Ceiling and wall were painted, pews renewed and carpeting upgraded. The sanctuary was remodeled to meet present day liturgy requirements.

Hillegas of South Fork was contracted to paint the church interior in 1990.

Parish Activities

St. John's offers many opportunities for participation in church functions and activities.

Parishioners serve as ushers, lectors, Eucharistic ministers, choir members and members of various organizations.

The Rosary-Altar Society, the largest and most popular group, boasts up to 70 members. It started in 1932. Officers during 1991 were Margaret McCormick, president; Anna Mae Bopp, vice president; Violet Kline, secretary; and Samilda Huber, treasurer.

A Sodality, in 1950, held the first May Crowning with Mary Burns as queen; Arlene Wirfel and Florence Bodenschatz, attendants; Kitty Lou Shrift, crown bearer; Mary Jane Betz, Marian Shrift and Rosemarie Sloan, statue bearers.

A Junior Group was organized as the Children of Mary in 1951.

The Holy Name Society meets after the 10 a. m. Mass during the winter months. Dennis Cobaugh is president; Louie Rosenberger, vice president; and Clair Long, secretary-treasurer.

The Confraternity of Christian Doctrine was established in 1942. Now, Debbie Wilson is the director of religious education. Classes are held both in the church and rectory basements. Grades K through 5 meet on Saturdays; grades 6 to 12 on Sundays.

Providing catechetical instruction are 11 lay teachers: Ann Lynn Baynham and Dawn Ferchalk, kindergarten; Tammy Beyer, grade 1; Susie Pearson, grade 2; Ida Beyer, grade 3; Susan Bopp, grade 4; Jennifer Chemelewski, grade 5; Marie Gallardy, grade 6; Susan Kitsko, grades 7-8; Charles Tremel, grades 9-10; and Clair Long, grades 11-12.

Members In Religious Life

Father John A. Reichert, ordained February 20, 1931.

Father Peter Bodenschatz, son of George and Theresa Bodenschatz, ordained June 10, 1933.

Father Mario (Bernard) Seifert, T. 0. R., son of Bernard and Zita Seifert, ordained May 22, 1948.

Father Ronald (Joseph) Bodenschatz, T. 0. R., son of Edward and Bernetta Bodenschatz, ordained Febuary 10, 1949.

Father Firmin Beyer, 0. S. B., son of Firmin and Mary Beyer, ordained May 20, 1967.

Father Thomas Rosenberger, son of Thomas and Jean Rosenberger, ordained May 13, 1977.

Father Patrick Cronauer, O. S. B., son of Harold and Marian Cronauer, ordained November 17, 1984.

Sister Evanelista (Agnes) Bodenschatz, Sister of Charity, daughter of John and Margaret Bodenschatz.

Sister Andrea Kannah, daughter of Andrew and Julia Kannah.

Sister Mary Avila (Magdeline) Long, R. S. M., daughter of Joseph A. and Clara Long.

Sister Barbara (Cecilia) Yahner, O. S. B., daughter of Peter and Catherine Yahner.

Sister Hyacinth (Agnes) Yahner, O. S. B., daughter of Peter and Catherine Yahner.

Sister Helen Marie (Barbara) Shrift, C. S. J., daughter of Cletus and Frances Shrift.

Sister Carolyn Bodenschatz, C. S. J., daughter of Herbert and Olene Bodenschatz.

50th Jubilee

Father Reichert was the celebrant of the Mass for the Golden Jubilee of St. John's Catholic Church in 1953. Father Peter Bodenschatz was the Deacon; Father Ronald Bodenschatz, Subdeacon; and Father Lawrence Rogan, master of ceremonies. Father Camillus Long delivered the sermon.

Ushers were Charles, Francis and Robert Bodenschatz, James Hettle, Joseph Huber, Louis Rosenberger, Joseph Stapleton and Louis Weinzerl.

Annual Picnic

The most outstanding event of the year now is the annual parish picnic, usually held at the New Germany Grove, on the Sunday prior to Labor Day.

This event brings together former parishioners and friends from the immediate area.

St. John's Pastors

The pastors of St. John's Catholic Church have all been Benedictine Fathers. They are:

Father Felix Fellner	1900 - 1902
Father Wolfgang Kolbeck	1902 - 1904
Father Clement Stratman	1904 - 1914
Father Richard Kraus	1914 - 1918
Father Martin Singer	1918 - 1921
Father Richard Kraus	1921 - 1930
Father Peter Zupan	1930 - 1931
Father Claude Geary	1931 - 1932

Father Herman Schorer	1933 - 1945
Father Angelus King	1945 - 1947
Father Frederick Strittmatter	1947 - 1949
Father Richard Gick	1949 - 1952
Father Lawrence Rogan	1952 - 1955
Father Constantine Zech	1956 - 1965
Father Leiden Lee	1965 - 1967
Father Flavian Yelenko	1967 - 1978
Father Emmeran A. Rettger	1978 - 1989
Father Germain Lieb	1989 - present

Father Germain was born in Carrolltown, Pa., July 2, 1919, the eleventh of 13 children of Augustine and Clare Williams Lieb.

Educated in St. Benedict's Parochial School, he attended St. Vincent Prep School from 1933 to 1937. He received a bachelor of arts degree from St. Vincent's College in 1942, was ordained in 1945, and attended graduate school in Toronto, Canada, from 1944 to 1949.

Father Germain taught in the Seminary from 1949 to 1976. His parish assignments follow:

1976 -- assistant pastor to Father Flavian at St. John's in Summerhill and in charge of the New Germany Mission.

1981 -- pastor at St. Bruno's Catholic Church, South Greensburg.

1982 -- pastor at St. George's Catholic Church, Patton.

1987 -- associate pastor to Father Emmeran at Summerhill and in charge of the New Germany Mission.

1989 -- pastor of St. John's and New Germany.

St. John's Catholic Church of Summerhill now has 518 members from 161 families.

The church has no cemetery of its own. Most burials take place at St. Mary's Cemetery, New Germany.

Father Flavian wrote for the 75th anniversary that "throughout the years St. John's Church has been instrumental in bringing the savory grace of the Divine Redeemer to many, many souls. With this thought in mind therefore, we cannot fail to appreciate how God in his goodness has blessed our Christian Community, and be filled with a deep sense of gratitude.

In spite of the passing of time, the edifice has stood the test of time well. It still stands practically in its original form. It is a modern up-to-date church. It is a credit to its parishioners, past and present, and to the Benedictine Fathers who have served during all the years of its existence."

Evangelical United Brethren Church about 1926 (Credit: Elsie Mervine)

Rev. & Mrs. Fern Barner, 1944. (Credit: Elsie Mervine)

Evangelical United Brethren Church

Originally known as the United Brethren Church of Summerhill, the Evangelical United Brethren house of worship was built in 1894 and dedicated by Bishop L. F. John.

The first trustees were E. W. Hull, David Shaffer, J. S. Stull, Thomas Seaman and William Reynolds. Rev. J. C. Erb was the first pastor.

Wilmore built a United Brethren Church in 1871. Portage became part of the Wilmore charge when Rev. Erb was in Wilmore. And, when the Portage congregation purchased land on Main Street, Rev. Erb did most of the carpentry work on their first church. He walked from Wilmore to Portage every day to complete the church which was dedicated in 1897.

At the same time, Rev. Erb served as Summerhill's minister and probably walked from his Wilmore residence.

Several deeds are recorded in the Cambria County courthouse for the Summerhill congregation.

One deed was a settlement of the Dr. J. B. Green property, dated April 4, 1896, by which the Summerhill congregation secured ownership of a parcel of land for $45. Trustees listed for this transaction were Christian Shaffer, Jacob Angus, Thomas J. Seaman, Benjamin Emanuel Pringle, Joseph S. Stull, J. C. Erb (the pastor) and Isaac T. Pierce.

The other deed recorded a sale from George B. Stineman to the Church of United Brethren in Christ of Summerhill, December 23, 1896.

An 1894 date was extracted from the Women's Club history published in 1966. It is not clear why land deeds aren't recorded until 1896.

Summerhill's Brethren Church property first appears in the county assessment records in 1899 and its location is given as "Churry Street" with an assessed value of $1,200. (These county records are only available from 1895).

William McClarren, Summerhill's assessor until 1900, only listed the Lutheran Church in 1895 but had no church entries for the next three years.

Curiously enough, McClarren listed the following nontaxable properties in 1899, in adddition to the Brethren Church: the school on "Germany Street" with a value of $2,550; and the Lutheran Church and grave on Church Street with a value of $3,500.

In 1901, C. J. Berschnider assessed the Methodist Church on "Churry Street" for $800 and it wasn't until 1909 that the Methodist Church, St. John's Catholic and the school were listed on Main Street.

The Methodist Church had increased to an assessed value of $1,000 by 1909.

The Summerhill congregation was served by the pastor residing in Wilmore. Elsie Pringle recalls that her July 20, 1946 marriage to Marlin Mervine was the only wedding ceremony performed in the Summerhill Church. All other couples went to Wilmore.

When the General Conference of the Evangelical Church voted in 1946 to unite with the United Brethren, the Summerhill church became the Evangelical United Brethren and remained part of the Wilmore-Summerhill charge.

At its peak, Summerhill is reported to have 100 or more members. When the church was closed, November 1970, there were about 40 members because younger members had left the borough and many of the older members had passed away.

A newspaper article of August 18, 1949 listed Harold L. Cowher as pastor of the Evangelical United Brethren Churches in Wilmore, Dunlo and Summerhill.

The Summerhill congregation announced the following appointments:

Mrs. Calvin Engle, class leader; Mrs. Benjamin E. Pringle, assistant class leader and home department superintendent; D. L. Hull and W. E. Hull, trustees; Marlin Mervine, vice chairman of the church council and Sunday School superintendent; Mrs. D. L. (Ruth) Hull, pianist, secretary of the church council and financial secretary.

D. L. Hull was also head of the benevolent committee, church treasurer and assistant Sunday School superintendent. Mrs. C. W. Penrod was director of Christian education and cradle roll superintendent; Mrs.Elsie Mervine, director of children's work; Frank Claycomb, director of young people's work; Sewell Claycomb, director of adult work and temperance superintendent;

Ruth Hull, secretary of the Sunday School; Phyllis Claycomb, assistant secretary; and Mrs. John McConnell, missionary superintendent.

Some of the pastors who served the Summerhill congregation were: The Revs. Homer Gauntt (1940), Kelly, Fern Barner (1946), H. C. Kridland, W. R. Tyson (1953-56), Gerald Witt (1959), Merle Potter (1961), William Griffith (1961-65), Naugle (1965-70).

After World War II, the church changed to United Methodist.

Richard McCall purchased the property in 1989 from Rev. Steffey. McCall has located his optical business on the first floor and has apartments on the upper portion.

St. Paul's German Lutheran Church, 1991.

St. Paul's German Lutheran Church

St. Paul's German Lutheran Church, at the upper end of Jackson Street, became part of Summerhill on November 9, 1912. It started as a mission of the German Church in Johnstown. And, as the congregation became larger and more self-sufficient, they became a separate church of their own.

Services, at first, were strictly in the German language. Later, they changed to German and English and, finally, all English.

At its peak, membership was about 150 families from areas like Revloc, Clearfield, Ebensburg, Ehrenfeld, Devil's Hollow, Sunshine and South Fork.

There was a German Band which played for Sunday services and gave outdoor concerts in the 1930s.

Henry Malonek, son of one of the church's ministers -- William Malonek -- remembers many special programs at Christmas, the specially-decorated trees and treats for the children. There were plays, a mixed chorus and Sunday School class picnics on the church grounds. The church bell could be heard all over town.

The first pastor was Rev. Gottlieb Seyda. He served until 1932. He was succeeded by Rev. William Malonek who preached until 1960. Then, Rev. William Remick assumed the responsibility until 1974 when the church was closed because the congregation had declined to about seven families. By this time, many of the younger members had moved and a lot of the older ones had passed away.

After remaining vacant for several years, the building was purchased by Wilbur Meier of Mineral Point R. D. His intentions were to convert the building into apartments. However, in August 1991, he put up the property for sale.

Former office of Dr. Charles P. Jones.

The Sherbine Residence. Originally the home and office of Dr. John B. Green. Now, the residence of Mr. & Mrs. John Costello. (Credit: Gertrude Brummert)

Chapter 11

Is There A Doctor In Town?

Barbara Croyle was described by John McCormick in his 1906 history as "skillful in the art of curing many of the ills to which human flesh is heir by the use of herbs and simple home remedies."

It was not unusual, in the early days, to depend upon the medicinal properties of roots, barks and herbs. This use dates back to the middle ages. The early settlers brought this knowledge to America and used it to cure illness, not only their families but neighbors as well. Doctors were called upon only when the home remedies failed.

The First Doctors

The first medical doctor of record was Dr. John C. Luke (1835-1903) a native of Blacklick Township and a graduate of Western Reserve University of Cleveland, Ohio. He located in Summerhill about 1871.

After nine years, he relocated to South Fork where he pursued his profession, managed Euclid Coal Company and served as postmaster, school director and councilman.

He died in South Fork and was buried at St. John's Evangelical Lutheran cemetery in Summerhill.

It appears that Dr. J. A. Hendrick succeeded Dr. Luke in Summerhill with an office at what is now 172 Portage Lane. The 1890 Atlas shows his office between the properties of C. A. Myers and G. Gable, near the intersection of Portage Street with Main Street.

The Cambria County Medical Society listed Dr. W. A. Barnett as a Summerhill physician from 1883 to 1885.

Dr. John B. Green

Dr. John B. Green set up a Summerhill practice in 1885.

Born in 1849 near Penn's Run, Indiana County, he started as a carpenter with John Geesey of Altoona. He served his apprenticeship for three years and worked a year as journeyman.

In 1873, he went to Chest Springs as a mechancial contractor and started reading medicine with Dr. W. H. Sloan. A year later, he took a first course of lectures at Cincinnati College of Medicine and Surgery and returned to Chest Springs to practice under Dr. Sloan until July 1, 1875. He returned to Indiana County and worked a few weeks at his carpenter trade.

Green returned to medical college and graduated in the class of 1876. He formed a partnership with Dr. Sloan and on August 1, 1876 left to enter practice for himself at Dixonville, Indiana County.

After seven years at Dixonville, Dr. Green practiced two years at Carrolltown. He sold the Carrolltown practice to Dr. G. H. Sloan, son of his preceptor, and came to Summerhill.

Not only was Dr. Green one of the borough's original councilmen, he also was active in business and banking ventures.

With F. Linderman, he was a partner in the manufacture of the famous Linderman piano polish. He also was vice president of the Pennsylvania Building and Loan Association of Altoona.

Dr. Green ran into financial difficulties in 1900; his elaborate home and office were put up for sheriff sale by the building and loan he held office in.

Dr. Robert Deveraux

The Cambria County Medical Society listed Dr. Robert Deveraux as a Summerhill resident in 1892.

He was an 1867 graduate of Jefferson Medical College and practiced at the Summit and Cresson.

Dr. Charles B. Jones

Dr. Charles B. Jones (1875 - 1943) located in Summerhill in 1906.

He was born in Shade Valley, Huntingdon County, on March 27, 1875. Educated in public schools, he attended Rockhill Normal School and graduated from the Medico-Chirurgical College of Philadephia, Pa., in 1906.

He married Mary A. Plummer in 1908.

He was the physician for the Summerhill Board of Health and a member of the school board.

A serious accident at the Ehrenfeld air shaft resulted in severe electrical burns of the hands and feet which incapacitated him for a time. During this time his patients were taken care of by Dr. Healy and Dr. Girard Hickus.

Dr. Charles B. Jones resumed his Summerhill practice and continued to serve the community until his death on October 9, 1943.

There are those who remember when Dr. Jones traveled by horse and buggy. Later, his automobile was recognizable on the streets of town and surrounding highways.

Dr. Charles P. Jones

Dr. Charles Plummer Jones (1909 - 1968) continued his father's medical practice after returning home from World War II.

Born September 4, 1909, he earned a bachelor of science degree at St. Francis College, Loretto, in 1930 and a medical degree at Georgetown University Medical School in 1936.

He served as Lieutenant Commander, Marine Corp, U. S. Navy Reserve in the Atlantic Theatre of Operations during the second World War.

From 1950 to 1952, Dr. C. P. Jones was a member of the board of directors of the Cambria County Medical Society. His wife served as president of its women's auxiliary from 1951 to 1952. They made their home at South Fork R. D. 1, near Lamb's Bridge.

When Dr. C. P. Jones died December 27, 1968, the era of Summerhill doctors ended. It marked 62 years that a father and son took care of the medical needs of a community.

Today, most small towns no longer have a "town doctor". Residents travel to clinics strategically located within the area and operated by Johnstown hospitals. Others go to offices maintained by individuals or a group of doctors in larger communities like Portage, Windber and Johnstown. Some doctors are also located in shopping centers and other more visible, neighboring locations.

House calls are a thing of the past. Treatment is now paid either by health insurance and Medicare, or both. The intimate, personal attention afforded by the family doctor also is vanishing.

Other Doctors

There were other physicians who provided medical care to Summerhill residents.

It is reported that there were those who came by train from Johnstown on a scheduled basis to meet patients.

A Dr. Brunner was said to be located in Summerhill around 1900, before Dr. Green's arrival.

Coal company doctors at Ehrenfeld were known to have office hours in Summerhill. Among them were Dr. William E. Troxell (1896-1900), Dr. Arthur F. Stotts (1902-1908), Dr. Harry Myrrel Stewart (about 1900) and Dr. William C. Kessler (1915-1919).

South Fork was a close and convenient place where most Summerhillers shopped and banked in the early days. Here, they had the choice of doctors like Clyde A. Fitzgerald, Edward Pardoe, W. Raymond Hawkins, David W. Truscott, F. Orville George and others. Evidently, most dental work was performed in South Fork at the hands of Drs. John G. Broad, B. H. Dunmire, M. R. Mandelstein, John M. Maury, Samuel F. Brisini and others.

Dr. Thomas E. Seifert, M.D.

Born December 21, 1923 in Summerhill, Dr. Thomas E. Seifert graduated from South Fork High School in 1941 and the University of Pittsburgh School of Medicine in 1951.

He interned at Walter Reed Medical Center, Washington, D. C., and served at Camp Gordon, Georgia. From 1953 to 1956, he had a general practice in Johnstown.

The next three years, he returned to Pittsburgh for residency in obstetrics and gynecology. Since 1959, Dr. Seifert has specialized in obstetrics and gynecology in Johnstown.

He received board certification in 1961; was recertified in 1978. He is a fellow of the American College of Obstetrics and Gynecology and the American College of Surgeons.

From 1966 to 1976, Dr. Seifert was a member of the College of Steubenville's Board of Trustees, where he was awarded an honorary Doctor of Science degree about 1975.

During the 1960s, he was president for two years and director about 10 years of the Altoona-Johnstown Diocese Catholic Charities. He also was president, secretary and director of the Physicians and Dentists Service Bureau, Johnstown.

Dr. Seifert is a member of the Cambria County Medical Society. He served as president of Mercy Hospital Staff, Johnstown, in 1964 and 1978.

Married to the former Joan A. Houch of Washington, D. C., the Seiferts are parents of nine children, eight of whom are living, and grandparents of 11 grandchildren.

Dr. Seifert's parents, Bernard and Zita Seifert, were residents of Summerhill until his father moved to Beaverdale as a carpenter for Johnstown Coal & Coke Company in 1944.

Dr. Claude Wilfred Kirby, M. D.

Dr. Claude Wilfred Kirby practiced medicine in Cresson, Pennsylvania, for his entire medical career.

A son of William R. and Leona Kirby, he was born in Summerhill February 23, 1907.

He received a bachelor of science degree from St. Vincent College, Latrobe, Pennsylvania, in 1928. He earned his M. D. degree at Georgetown University School of Medicine in 1932.

During World War II, Dr. Kirby was a Lieutentant Colonel with the United States Army Air Force and saw duty in the Pacific Theatre from September 1942 to March 1946.

His general practice extended to Mercy Hospital, Altoona, and the courtesy staff at Johnstown's Mercy Hospital. He conducted his office practice at 617 Second Street, Cresson, until his retirement about 1988.

He makes his home in Cresson.

Forest Hills Area Ambulance Association Building, 1991.

Forest Hills Area Ambulance Service

When the Charles 0. Dimond Funeral Home of South Fork discontinued emergency ambulance services in 1975, the Forest Hills Area Ambulance Service was organized. The first ambulance was housed at Impala's Garage along Railroad Street.

Charter members of the Forest Hills Area Ambulance Association were recruited from its service area. They were: Father John J. Palko, Ray Fresch, Rick Dierling, Elio Lucci, Dominick Albertelli, Vince Beyer, Charles Dimond, Robert Oswalt, Joseph Beyer, Eugene Wilson, Robert Penatzer, Frank Kishlock, Albert Keller, Dr. John Karduck, Cindy Claycomb, Jane Gruss, Alice Gruss, Donald Koval, Allen Lutsko, Steve Partsch, Frank Rosemas, John Silvis and Butch Moss.

Family membership fees started at $12 a year; individuals at $8. The 1991 family membership is $22. The individual rate is $17 and is required for anyone age 18 or older who is not attending school and for anyone with any source of income. The family membership covers the wage earner, spouse and all dependent children up to age 18 or until out of school. Non-member fees range from $290 to $465 per call, depending upon the service.

Membership entitles participants to unlimited emergency medical services without out-of-pocket expense.

Non-emergency transportation, when medically required, is available to and from a hospital or doctor's office. Non-emergency transfers are not routinely performed. This service is provided by EAST Ambulance of Johnstown.

Participants pay fees at the Summerhill Office of Portage National Bank, South Fork Office of National Bank of the Commonwealth or the ambulance station in Summerhill.

From its area headquarters on old Route 53 in Summerhill, the association provides 24-hour advanced life support services to members in South Fork, Summerhill, Ehrenfeld, New Germany and Croyle Township.

The association is staffed with paramedics and emergency medical technicians (EMT) trained and equipped in all phases of advanced life support including cardiac monitoring and defibrillation, I V therapy, anti-shock therapy, obstetrical care, drugs and medications and trauma care.

Recently, a new ambulance was purchased at a cost of $72,000. There are now three ambulances ready for all emergencies.

In addition to cardiac monitoring and defibrillation, there also is the capability of artifical heart pacing. Special equipment for each ambulance provides "pulse oximetry", a measurement of oxygen content in the blood.

The daily staff includes a secretary, a paramedic and an EMT. During the summer of 1991, the secretary was Carole Mangus, South Fork; paramedic, Wendy Wright, Summerhill R.D. 1; EMT, Laura Penatzer, Summerhill. Daniel Penatzer of Summerhill is the manager.

Evenings and weekends are staffed by volunteers of about 8 paramedics and 20 emergency medical techicians.

The operation is funded by membership drives and municipal contributions and directed by a Board of Directors.

As of July 7, 1991, the Board of Directors consisted of Joseph Beyer, Sidman R.D. 1, president; Vincent Beyer, Sidman R.D. 1, secretary; Richard Chaney, South Fork, treasurer; Ralph Hamilton, Summerhill, vice president. Other members were Eugene Brewer, Ehrenfeld; Albert Keller, Ehrenfeld; Cindy Rosemas, South Fork; and Ted Walls, Summerhill.

Chapter 12

Do I Have-Ta Go To School?

The earliest schools in Cambria County were church-related and located in Beulah, Loretto and Ebensburg.

An academy was built and opened in Ebensburg about 1819.

John Thomas operated a subscription school at Munster in 1825. He charged $1.50 per calendar quarter.

The Ebensburg Academy had higher tuition, ranging from $2 to $5, depending upon which of the three classes of instruction was selected.

Free public schools were mandated by the Pennsylvania Legislature in 1834 but its implementation was slow.

Summerhill was represented from the onset because John McGough, who had been county commissioner in 1821 and 1822, served on the first committee which recommended the county school tax at 6 mills and established the minimum school age at 4 years.

Records also indicate that John Pringle, another former county commissioner, received Summerhill's state appropriations in these early years.

When James M. Swank, county superintendent of schools, visited 21 of the 26 school districts in 1861, he noted that George Sharretts at Summerhill School had 40 pupils present and 25 absent.

By 1877, there were 39 school districts in the county with 170 buildings and 215 teachers for an average attendance of 7,000 students.

Summerhill's first school was located along Route 53.

Early Statistical Information

The earliest information available about Summerhill's school comes from a report of J. P. Wickersham, Superintendent of Public Instruction, for the year ending June 1, 1877.

Summerhill is recorded collecting $832.46 from a 10-mill school tax, receiving a state appropriation of $152.56 and $164.09 from other sources -- a total income of $1,149.11.

The state appropriation for the school year ending June 1, 1878 was $1 million. This amount was divided as follows: normal schools, $32,000; Cornplanter Indians, $300; Philadelphia and other districts with superintendents, $297,837; and county superintendents, $77,831.

The remaining balance of $592,030 was appropriated among 2,143 school districts at the rate of 84.3¢ per taxable. Summer Hill received $114.30 which placed its taxables at 136.

Teachers Institute of 1878

December 30, 1878, a teachers institute was held in Ebensburg for 5 days and 103 county teachers. It was also attended by 12 school directors and 54 "honorary members". "The largest number of spectators present were 700; the average, 150."

The number of votes by the committee for permanent certificates totaled 85.

There were 3 instructors or lecturers. Seven essays were read.

Of the $200 given by the county treasurer and $47.50 from other sources, $175.50 was paid to instructors; $67.43, other expenses -- leaving a balance on hand of $4.57.

School Year Ending June 2, 1879

For the school year ending June 2, 1879, Cambria County was listed with 221 1/2 "schools" (defined as a body of pupils under one permanent teacher).

There were 116 male and 108 female teachers. The men teachers averaged $29.78 a month; the women, $25.50. The average school term in the county was a statistical 5.78 months.

The number of "scholars" included 5,405 boys and 4,746 girls with an average of 6,541 attending school.

Of the total income for the county's schools, $6,864.44 came from the state.

Total county expenditures amounted to $62,969.49 -- about 62% of this amount went for teachers' salaries.

The state superintendent's report showed the following tabulations furnished by the Cambria County superintendent of schools:

Grounds

Those of sufficient size -- 31
Those suitably improved -- 5

School Houses

Total number -- 173
Frame buildings -- 162
Brick or stone buildings -- 10
Log construction -- 1
Number built during the year -- 5
Number unfit for use -- 18
Number badly ventilated -- 59
Number without a suitable privy -- 7

Furniture
Schools with suitable furniture -- 61
Schools with injurious furniture -- 80
Supplied with furniture during the year -- 2

Apparatus
Schools well supplied -- 11
Schools without apparatus worth mentioning -- 199

Schools
Number of graded schools -- 66
Number graded during the year -- 2
Number of graded schools needed -- 12
Schools well classified -- 95

Cambria County, according to the report, had 42 school districts during the 1878-79 school year which employed 224 teachers for 10,151 students. The average teacher age was 26. Only 22 teachers had attended state normal schools. Teaching for the first time were 35 teachers.

Most school districts like Summerhill operated for five months but Prospect Borough had a school year of 10 months; Woodvale, 9 months; Millville, 8 1/2 months; Cambria, Conemaugh, Gallitzin and Johnstown Boroughs, 8 months; Ebensburg and Coopersdale, 7 months; and East Conemaugh, 6 months.

Johnstown Borough paid its men teachers $72 a month; women teachers, $36. Other districts with high salaries included Millville, $58 and $41.25 repectively for men and women; and Woodvale, $55 and $45.

The per pupil cost averaged 72¢ a month.

Summerhill Statistics For 1878-79

The following statistics were listed for the school year ending June 2, 1879:
Number of schools -- 6
Average number of months taught -- 5
Number of male teachers -- 1
Number of female teachers -- 5
Average salaries of male teachers per month -- $22
Average salaries of female teachers per month -- $22
Number of male scholars -- 105
Number of female scholars -- 94
Average number of scholars attending school -- 120
Average percentage of attendance -- 65%
Pupil cost per month -- 72¢

Mills levied for school purposes -- 12
Total amount of tax levied for school and building purposes -- $769.42
State appropiation -- $114.30
Receipts from taxes and all other sources except state appropriation -- $1,113.20
Total receipts -- $1,227.50
Cost of school-houses, purchasing building, renting, etc. -- $247.00
Paid for teachers' wages -- $660.00
Paid for fuel and contingencies, fees of collectors, etc., and all other expenses -- $210.75
Total expenditures -- $1,117.75
Resources -- $123.75
Liabilities -- none

Neighboring School Districts

Of the neighboring school districts for 1878-79, Croyle paid its men teachers more than women -- $22.25 a month compared to $20 a month. The township had 6 1/2 "schools" taught by three male and three female teachers. Total number of pupils were 301 compared to Summerhill's 199. Both districts employed six teachers each; the teacher/pupil ratio was 51.7 for Croyle and 33.2 for Summerhill.

Wilmore's four teachers had to accomodate 101 pupils or an average of 50.5 pupils per teacher.

South Fork, which wasn't a borough yet and was just beginning to be established, had an independent school with only one teacher and 64 students. He was paid $30 a month.

Among Croyle's early one-room schools, there were three outside of Summerhill. They were known as New Germany, Pensacola and Pringle Hill. These schools had eight grades in one room and concentrated on reading, writing, mental arithmetic, physiology, geography, spelling and grammer.

A prominent fixture was a pot belly stove which was fired by wood and coal and the responsibility of the teacher.

The **New Germany School** was primarily attended by children from the Shrift, Wess, Weinzierl, McCall and Bodenschatz families. Some of the early teachers were Monica Shrift Campbell, Magdalene Stibich, Agnes Forest, May Leahey, Ruth Bishoff, and Lena Wess Bodenschatz.

The New Germany school was destroyed by fire in the late 1940s.

Pensacola School was located along the Ebensburg-New Germany Road, about 4 miles south of Ebensburg. The original school dates back to the Civil War days. It was razed and a new building constructed in 1918.

Here could be found the families of Long, Rorabaugh, Weakland, Evans and Bumford. Teachers included Stanley Muliak, Lester Specht and Cortez Wentling.

Pensacola School was closed in 1929.

Pringle Hill's main students came from the Smith, Wirfel, Skelly and Skrout families. The first school building was located between the McGough and Zdunczyk farms. The second one was on the farm of Oscar McGough. Teachers here included Rowena Pringle, Gilbert Roberts and Jane Jones.

Pringle Hill School was closed in 1923.

Summerhill School Picture about 1931. (Credit: Stella DeLozier) Front Row (left to right): Paul Bimle, Howard Fresch, Robert Plummer, Vernon Jones, Orville Chaney, Don Betz, Edward White, Regis Wilburn, Wilfred Simendinger, James Brewer, Michael McCall, Robert Hull, Earl Hull, William Yahner. Second Row (seated): Myrtle Hull, Treva Meyers, Doris Hoover, Rita Simendinger, Stella Simendinger, Jean Jones, Margaret Nedimyer, Martha Meyers, Louise Marek, Arzella Seifert, Rose Tully, Delores Chappell, Mildred Betz, Margaret Bimle, Mary Rosenberger. Back Row: Louise Bopp, ?, Martha White, Lydia Shuman, William Hoody, Joseph Homza, Miss Short (teacher), Mary Agnes Shrift, Clifford Anderson, Rubert Kick, Melvin Geisler, Regis Kurtz, Thomas Yahner, Edward Bodenschatz, Robert Duffy, Bernard Seifert, John Figola, Junior Hill.

(Credit: Lillian M. Pisarski)

(Credit: Lillian M. Pisarski)

The teacher in this photo is Pete Betz. (Credit: Mary M. Gabany)

(Credit: Mary M. Gabany)

Teacher (center of first row) J. W. Plummer (Credit: Father Ronald Bodenschatz)

1915 First Grade Class: Stella Gallardy, teacher. (Credit: Jack Bodenschatz)

Wilmore High School Class of 1931. Seated: Charlotte Claycomb, Marcella (Mulvihill) Betz, Charles Habrel, Tory Smith, Olene (Hettle) Bodenshatz. Back Row: Francis Holsopple, Ruth Shetler, Miles Costello, Mae Bumford, William Kirby. (Credit: Jack Bodenschatz)

May Pole Dance in School Yard. Gertie Seaman's home on the left; Ross Seaman, on the right. (Credit: Anna C. Jordan)

Public School Building in the early 1910s. (Credit: Gertrude Brummert)

Summerhill School about 1984. (Credit: Charles Huber)

County Schools of 1892

The **Cambria Freeman's** edition of August 19, 1892, listed the following report about Cambria County as submitted by J. W. Leech, county superintendent of schools:
* average school term -- 6 months
* 95 male teachers averaging $36.80 per month
* 150 female teacher averaging $31.71 per month
* average monthly cost per pupil of 95¢
* 5,538 boys and 5,247 girls
* 1,121 children not in school
* state appropriation for the year ending June 1891 -- $12,913.05
* Summerhill was noted as having built a new school during the year. (During these years, a school referred to a room or grade).

County Institutes in Summerhill

The **Johnstown Weekly Tribune** of January 25, 1895, noted that the county's teachers institute would be held in Summerhill, Saturday, February 2, 1895, beginning at 9 a. m. Teachers were requested to bring their song books.

The following is the program of another county institute held at the Summerhill "schoolhouse", February 5, 1898, as published by the Johnstown Weekly Tribune of January 21, 1898:

Welcome song by school
Greeting by J. F. Long
Response by R. H. Biter
"The Recitation", A. P. Weakland
"System in Marking, Grading and Reporting Pupils Work, Charles A. Long
"Local History", J. W. McCreary
A talk on Reading, T. L. Gibson
Noon Recess
Some Phases of Mathematics, R. H. Biter
Punishment, E. T. McCall
Busy Work, J. T. Orner
Geography, W. A. McGuire
Composition Writing, Harriet Bradley

The closing feature was a spelling contest constructed of 100 words to be written. Two honors would be given to those presenting the best manuscripts.

E. J. Duffy conducted the singing.

Summerhill's Second School

The exact date of Summerhill's second school is unknown. What is known is that it was built in the upper end of town where Violette McCall and her husband, the late John W. McCall, converted into their home at 539 Main Street.

The map in the 1890 Atlas shows the school location at this Main Street location with a scattering of neighboring property owners. The rest of the area was relatively undeveloped.

The building was a two-story frame structure of four rooms.

No doubt, additions and expansions were made over the years. A courthouse deed dated June 24, 1897, records the purchase of a piece of land by the school district for $75 from S. L. Reed and Isaac Michaels, executors of George B. Wike.

The lot was described as "beginning at a rock, by Jackson Road south to the post corner of a lot of Isaac Michaels to an alley and lots laid out by William J. Nipps who deeded it to Wike August 14, 1888."

Additional deed information explains the lot was originally warranted to Benjamin Williams, deeded to James R. Cooper in 1885. It was part of Thomas Croyle's land which he sold to John Schriver in 1850.

School Terms

By 1906, Summerhill's school term had increased to 7 months and it wasn't until 1916 that students went to school 8 months.

High School Education

Summerhill never had a high school. After 8th grade graduation, students were sent to neighboring school districts which would accept them on a tuition basis. Others, at their own expense, chose to attend the Catholic High Schools in Ebensburg or Johnstown.

There was a time Summerhill students attended Wilmore High School. During another period of time, they went to South Fork and, later, to Adams Township in Sidman.

Today, all these districts have one high school -- Forest Hills.

The number of Summerhill teenagers attending high school were 18 in 1922 and 27 in 1924.

Graduation Exercises of the 1920s and 1930s

For the **1922-23 school year**, eleven eight-graders were graduated from Summerhill School: Margaret Minnie Bodenschatz, Richard Henry Costello,

Ray Claycomb, Mary Magdalene Figola, Robert Harry Horner, Charles Plummer Jones, Russell Harold McGough, Magdalene Ruth McCall, Victor Cellestine Rosenberger, Eugene Clement Shrift and George Alton Shitely.

Teachers were J. M. Baumgardner, South Fork; Clara L. Moyer, Ridgeway; Genevieve Bunton, Summerhill; Josephine Liggett, Huff; and Juanita 0. Hadley, West Middlesex.

Directors included S. S. Robine, A. L. Tully, Dr. C. B. Jones and J. I. Berschnider.

The assessed valuation of the school district was $315,250. A 12-mill tax brought $5,112.80. The state contributed $1,404.52. Total receipts were $7,552.86 which paid expenses of $6,019.30.

The school's enrollment was 208 -- 105 boys and 103 girls.

A clasic graduation program for the **1925 class** was held in Long's Hall.

Dr. Martin S. Bentz, county superintendent of schools, addressed the 14 eighth-graders.

The class began the night's exercises by singing "Heigh Ho" and ended with the song, "Life".

S. S. Robine, school board president, distributed the diplomas.

The program, conducted by the graduates, follows:

George Dopp Wonders, salutatory speech,"Under the Green Trees of the Oasis"
Bernard Arthur Tully, class poem,"The Truth"
Julia Anna Steiber, vocal solo, "Little Brown Baby"
Marvin Millroy Hull, piano solo, "Under the Lilacs"
John Francis Kick, "Tom Sawyer's Proposal"
William Storey Seaman, "Our School Library"
Kenneth Nicholas, "Story of Elaine"
George Henry Myers
William Fred Haberl
Reginald John Hettle, "The World's Greatest Violinist"
Gertrude Amelia Brummert, oration, "The Maid of Orleans"
Joseph Louis Geisler, president's address, "Ideals"
Antonia Gladys Geisler
DeLellis Rose McCall, valedictory, "Drifting on the Stream of Life"

The **1928 class** consisted of Charlotte M. Claycomb, Wallace Henry Croyle, Charles Haberl, Olene Marguerite Hettle, William Robert Kirby, Walter Kurtz, Helen Malonek, Oscar Stanton McGough, Mariella Grace Mulvehill, Mary Ellen Robertson, Mary Alberta Pringle, Clinton Peter Sipe, Harold Robert Tully, Grace Margaret Kime and John Wonders.

The school directors were S. S. Robine, A. L. Tully, Joseph Callighan, A. R. McCall and Vernon Dawson.

The teachers were Elizabeth Nangle and Mildred A. Plummer, Summerhill; Helen M. Short and Agnes S. Ryan, Lilly; and Nita Wirick, South Fork.

The school tax was 15 mills. Receipts totaled $11,702.37 and expenses were $9,726.86. The state provided $2,524.86 of the total receipts.

The **1930 graduates** were Fern Betz, Virginia Brewer, Henry Bodenschatz, Sewell Claycomb, Francis Duffy, Wilbur Geisler, Mary Kick, Walter Malonek, John McCall, Fred Mareck, Cecilia Mutchenbaugh, John Rose, Arthur Schieman, Ellis Croyle and John Rowe.

The directors were the same ones serving in 1928.

The teachers included J. W. Plummer, principal; Helena M. Short, Agnes S. Ryan, Mildred A. Plummer and Magdalene McCall.

The **1931 graduates** were Harper Claycomb, Perry Dunmire, Sophie Figola, Martha Fresch, Claire Hettle, Dorothy Kirby, Isabelle McGough, Ralph Pringle, Helen Ordie, Robert Seaman, Arthur Seaman, Dolores Tully, Henrietta Hull, Fred Seaman, Zita Seifert and Regis Hettle.

The teachers were the same as 1930 except Susan J. Keener of Johnstown had replaced Agnes S. Ryan.

The school millage jumped to 16 mills.

The **1932 graduates** were John Bishop, Donald Brewer, Mary Chaney, Kenneth Hershline, Mary Hill, Violet Hoover, Rosetta Mareck, Patrick McCall, James McCall, Martha McGough, John Mulvehill, Donald Penatzer, Josephine Tully, Raymond Chaney and Elmer Fresch.

Teaching assignments: J. W. Plummer, grades 7-8; Helena M. Short, grade 6-7; Magdalene McCall, grades 4-5; Betty A. Kohler, grade 3; and Mildred A. Plummer, grades 1-2.

School Commencement of 1947

In contrast to the graduation exercises of the 1920s, the following commencement program of 1947 was printed in the **Cambria Dispatch** of May 29, 1947:

Raymond Kirby was the guest speaker. The processional was played by the Lilly High School Orchestra. Rev.Glenn Keidel gave the invocation.

After the class song, the following class members participated: Joan Werfel, salutatorian address; Ellen J. Kearney, trombone solo, "Thoughts of Love"; Georgia Jones, class will; Patricia Smith and Betty Penrod, class prophecy; and Albert Seifert, valedictory address.

Diplomas were distributed by Robert Smith, board president.

Legion awards were presented to Agatha Weinzierl and Myron Blainer.

Benediction was offered by Rev. Angelus Klug.

The Lilly High School Orchestra concluded the program with the playing of the recessional.

Members of the graduating class were Joseph Berschneider, Ronald Bimle, Robert Bishop, Myron Blainer, Richard Davis, Glenn Hull, Albert Seibert, Paul White, Roberta Duffy, Carolyn Hoover, Georgia Jones, Florine Medimyer, Betty Penrod, Dolores Shrift, Patricia Smith, Agatha Weinzierl and Joan Werfel.

Parent-Teachers Association

The Parent-Teachers Association enjoyed many years of successful activities in Summerhill. Regular meetings were held, speakers featured, projects sponsored, programs staged and refreshments served.

Often times, the meetings spotlighted the children through exhibits of their school work and special programs for the entertainment of their parents and friends.

One such program was a special Christmas meeting reported in the **Cambria Dispatch** of December 20, 1935. Each grade had a part.

Miss Mildred Plummer directed first and second graders. A feature was "A Joke on Santa" by Ruth Hershberger.

Miss Charlotte Claycomb, grades 2 and 3, offered a poem, "When Santa Claus Comes" by James Shrift.

Miss Magdalene McCall and Helena Short directed grades 5 through 7 in an operetta entitled "Christmastide".

Joseph Plummer directed his group in a playlet.

May Day Exercises

The popularity of May Day exercises still prevailed in the 1940s.

On May 1, 1947, Summerhill students were dismissed in the afternoon to attend May Day events at the South Fork School gymnasium. Songs and dances by all grades, from first to twelfth, were featured.

Cambria County Fair Exhibits

A special attraction at county fairs in the 1920s and 1930s was the exhibits of school work from all the county's schools.

The 1927-28 school year was one of the most memorable for Summerhill because each grade placed first and second in many Class B entries.

First place awards in writing went to Arzella Seifert, grade 1; Jean Jones, grade 2; Joseph Bodenschatz, grade 3; Helen Reynolds, grade 4; Sophia Figola, grade 5; John Rowe, grade 6; and Helen Figola, grade 7.

In composition, first place awards went to Ernest Malloy, grade 2; Olive Betz, grade 3; Helen Reynolds, grade 4; Clare Hettle, grade 5; Glenn Hull, grade 6; and Oscar McGough, grade 8.

Other first place winners were Helen Figola, geography booklet; Helen Ordie, health booklet; Mary Kick, sewing; Naomi Seaman, history booklet; Virginia Brewer, nature; Hilda Penrod, sewing; Charlotte Claycomb, civics; and Marcella Mulvehill, geography.

The exhibits served to recognize students and teacher for quality work. They also brought a lot of people to the fair.

Last School Building

Summerhill Borough School District exchanged its building on Main Street, in 1934, with the Knights of St. George and built a new, red-brick school along Ebensburg Road.

The 6-room, Colonial-style building was dedicated October 26, 1934, with Dr. Martin S. Bentz, county superintendent of schools, and Attorney Charles Hasson, Ebensburg, as featured speakers.

The $20,000 project was completed with the help of the WPA (Work Projects Administration).

The first classes were held during the 1934-35 school year. Instruction was offered up through grade 8. Students continued their high school education at South Fork.

History of Jointures and Mergers

In 1952, Summerhill joined with Adams Township to form the Adams-Summerhill Joint School District. The elementary program at Summerhill was enhanced with music and art instruction and now had the services of a school nurse and a doctor. The high school years were now spent at Sidman, PA.

In 1966, Summerhill became part of Forest Hills School District which included all schools in Dunlo, Beaverdale, Sidman, South Fork, Ehrenfeld, Fifficktown, Wilmore, Salix, St. Michael, Eureka 42 and Summerhill.

Fate of the Summerhill School

The Summerhill School was used until 1976 when Forest Hills consolidated all its elementary pupils into a new elementary school at Sidman.

Summerhill Borough leased the vacant Summerhill School for several years, spent $5,000 for a new roof and provided headquarters for Mainline Police.

The borough agreed to buy the building from the Forest Hills School District for $27,800 in 1981. Council not only purchased the building but also got the entire ball field, skating rink and tennis courts.

Original plans were to trade the school for the fire company's building. The firemen were to raze the school and build a new firehall there.

A group of citizens wanted the borough to renovate the school into a community center.

After much controversy and numerous public meetings, no agreement was reached. Council advertised the school building for sale or lease in 1983.

Vandals broke many of the windows by the end of 1983.

Finally, the old school building was demolished in May 1985.

School Property Controversy

Calvin Jay Harshberger, retired IRS criminal investigator and a resident of Summerhill since 1929, researched in detail the ownership of properties sold to the borough by Forest Hills School District in 1981.

The ball field, adjacent to the Summerhill Grade School Building, consists of about 1.561 acres. Forest Hills School District acquired title by claiming adverse possession and quieting title through the heirs of the Humphries Estate and, in 1982, sold it to the borough in a package that included the unused school building.

Harshberger contended the borough could have taken the same action to acquire the ball field area because the citizens of Summerhill used this lot for recreational purposes long before the school was constructed in 1934.

Humphries purchased the ball field area in 1920 from A. J. Oaks and others who had used it as a millyard. In 1924, Humphries sold a portion to the Knights of St. George.

Humphries died intestate in January 1928 and in June of the same year the Orphans Court prepared a deed and placed the area and four other lots in a single deed in the name of his surviving widow, Katherine Humphries.

Katherine died intestate three months later with no lineal heirs. The court named an administrator who sold her personal property at auction and distributed the proceeds to approximately 40 heirs scattered as far as Minnesota. What remained in the Katherine Humphries Estate was the real estate which had been placed in her name by the Orphans Court.

The heirs named the former administrator attorney-in-fact to manage the real estate. Jay Harshberger's parents rented the property in the Spring of 1929 and when it was put up for auction, in 1934, Homer and Genevieve Harshberger were the successful bidders.

According to Jay, a deed indenture, dated November 23, 1934, contained errors such as the omissions of the citator and the ball field property description. This indenture was not recorded until 1936. Jay believes this was due to the errors of omission and probably the attorney for the Humphries heirs expected the Harshbergers to straighten out the matter.

Jay's research of deeds at the Cambria County Recorder of Deeds office revealed the exchange of properties between the Knights of St. George and Summerhill Borough School District took place in 1934 and a similar exchange between the school district and Harry Snyder were properly recorded.

No documentation was found deeding the ball field property to the Summerhill Borough School District.

The only claim Forest Hills School District had to the area, according to Jay, was by adverse possession. But, he claimed, the borough had a better adverse possession right since it used the property longer and more exclusively and borough citizens cleared the weeds and made needed improvements.

In his meeting with the borough solicitor John Taylor, council vice president Dan Penatzer, and councilman Herschel Wilson, Jay Harshberger emphasized he did this research with no intention of seeking personal gain as an heir of the Harshberger Estate but for the sole purpose of "bringing to light the details surrounding the ball field property and to prevent the taxpayers of Summerhill from being financially raped by the Forest Hills School District."

At the December 1982 borough council meeting action was taken to withhold further payment to Forest Hills pending further clarification and a letter of explanation sent to the school district.

Councilmen were told by their solicitor, at the February 1983 meeting, that he could not find any deed of record for the ground in question and that the school district was in the process of trying to get a deed by a quiet title procedure through the courts.

The Forest Hills School District's solicitor questioned what the problem was with the borough and was reported as saying that if they didn't want the property, they could give it back because Summerhill Borough knew there was a problem with the heirs.

A month later, the Summerhill council was informed that they had made an agreement to buy the property and, according to the school district solicitor, if the borough didn't make the required payment, the school district could take back the property or sue for payment.

At a special Summerhill council meeting, March 16, 1983, approval was voted to make the second payment of $6,954 which was due December 1982. Borough solicitor Jack Taylor said the agreement was entered into and approved by the courts on November 9, 1981 called for four equal installments of $6,954 payable before the 31st of December each year.

Thereupon, Summerhill council decided to honor this agreement and made the remaining payments on time.

Summerhill Faculty

There was a big turnover in the faculty in the 1910s, 1920s and 1930s. Teachers were hired by the year. In order to return a second term, the school board had to reelect the teacher and since there was no tenure, most often faculty was replaced regularily.

Local school boards were required to report the names and salaries of teachers each year to the office of the county superintendent of schools. These reports from 1910 to 1936 show that Summerhill staffed its school with 4 or 5 teachers per term. During this 27-year period, 50 different teachers were hired, many for one year and others for two or three terms.

Of these 50 teachers, 38 were women and 12 were men. The men usually were hired as principals or head of the school. They were paid the highest salary and were responsible for the administration of the school along with a full teaching schedule.

From these reports, it appears the following were hired as principals: E. V. Bearer (1910), Emerson F. Wade (1911), J. C. Gill (1912-13), John Knecht (1914), R. T. Costello (1915), Charles Bubb (1916-17), W. Clarence Weyant (1918-19), James M. Baumgardner (1920 and 1922), J. M. Baum (1921), Margaret D. Monaghan (1923-26), Elizabeth Nangle (1927), Elmer M. Luther (1928), J. W. Plummer (1929-35), Richard Costello (1936).

Note that Margaret Monaghan and Elizabeth Nangle were the only women principals during this period. However, from the 1940s and on, they dominated the position.

Teachers with more than three-year terms from 1910 to 1936 were Stella Gallardy (1910-15), Elsie Shyrock (1916-21), Helena Short (1926-36), Agnes S. Ryan (1926-29), Mildred Plummer (1927-36), Magdaline McCall (1928-36), J. W. Plummer (1929-36) and Charlotte Claycomb (1934-36).

Records were not available beyond 1936. It appears that Mildred Plummer, Helena Short and Charlotte Claycomb continued into the 1940s and longer.

Some Recent Teachers

Mary Werfel, who has been retired since 1972, taught 19 years in the Summerhill School, from 1953 to 1972. A graduate of Shippensburg Normal School in 1930, her first teaching job was at Portage. She lost this job in

1934 because it was policy that as soon as a woman teacher married she was required to submit an automatic resignation.

Mary decided to spend the next 19 years raising her family and helping her husband, Ferdinand, in the new car business.

She remembers the Summerhill School building had five rooms and an auditorium with chairs as seats.

During her teaching years, Helen Lydic of South Fork was principal and some of her colleagues included Constance Diehl, Isabel Holsopple, Helen Wess, Judith Kovach, Kathy Wagner, Claudia Urban, Magdalene McCall and Mary Smith.

When Mrs. Lydic was moved to the Forest Hills Junior High to teach mathematics, Mary Werfel served as head teacher at Summerhill.

Magdalene McCall, who was first employed in 1928, passed away about 1961.

Mary Smith was a teacher from 1944 to 1959.

Helen Wess was hired by the Summerhill School upon her graduation from Indiana State Teachers College in 1949. She married James Miller of Wilmore in 1959 and retired in 1976.

Helen also served as head teacher and recalls working with some of the aforementioned faculty besides Donna Colelli, Karen Madigan, Janice Perehinec, Sara Jane Zybura and Janice McHugh.

Helen Wess Miller was one of Summerhill's last teachers because when she retired all elementary students were consolidated into Forest Hills' new elementary school at Sidman in 1976.

Both, Mrs. Werfel and Mrs. Miller, remember the excellent work of Hilda White as school janitor. She succeeded her mother, Maggie Betz, on the job.

Mrs. Werfel also recalls the special Christmas programs she and Mrs. Miller wrote and produced for the townspeople and how they provided entertainment for many PTA meetings.

School Directors

It has been impossible to trace all the dedicated individuals who served as school directors because complete records are unavailable.

McCormick's history tells that in 1906 Elmer F. Dimond was president and P. P. Sipe was secretary of a school board comprised of George Betz, Clem Berschneider, S. S. Robine and J. F. Hoover.

County reports, executed by the presidents and secretaries, from 1910 through 1935 show the following:

Presidents -- George Betz (1910), S. S. Robine (1912-15 and 1922-33), J. F. Hoover (1916-17), Mrs. P. P. Sipe (1918-21) and Dr. C. B. Jones (1935).

Secretaries -- Charles P. Kime (1910-13), R. H. Costello (1918-24), J. H. Tully (1914-17 and 1926-33), and Dr. W. P. Jones (1934-35).

Other directors (incomplete, at best) were Alex Betz, Ray White, William Jones, Simon McCall, Joseph P. Callighan, A. L. Tully, Cletus H. Shrift, A. P. McCall, Vernon A. Dawson, Albert Seifert and J. E. Berschneider.

The 1943 school board was headed by Joseph Stapleton. Dr. W. P. Jones was the secretary. The other three members were Robert B. Smith, A. L. Tully and Hugh Brummert.

From 1954 to 1965, Joseph Stapleton and Herschel Wilson were president and secretary, respectively. The other directors during this period included Robert B. Smith (1954), Paul Bimle (1954-62), Ferdinand Werfel (1954-58), Boyd Miller (1955-56), Joseph Claycomb (1957-60), Robert Sigg (1959-63), Donald Hettle (1961-65), Arthur T. Apple (1963-65) and Raymond Penatzer (1964-65).

The newspaper obituary of Paul J. Bimle, who died in 1989 at age 71, credited him with 20 years as school director.

Herschel E. Wilson, who died in 1990 at age 64, served 14 years on the Adams-Summerhill School Board.

Joseph Stapleton, who was first elected in 1941, served as president of the Adams-Summerhill Board from 1960 through 1963.

Arthur Apple was vice president in 1964 and 1965.

Forest Hills School District

From 1952, Adams Township and Summerhill Borough operated as a joint school district, Adams-Summerhill.

In 1948, South Fork Borough and Croyle Township formed South Fork-Croyle and, in 1957, Summerhill Township became the third member of Triangle Area School District.

Pennsylvania's school district reorganization legislation of 1963 mandated all the commonwealth's school districts be reorganized by 1966. Cambria County was to reduce its 40 districts to 12.

As a result, Adams-Summerhill and Triangle Area agreed to become Forest Hills School District on July 1, 1966.

The new district's senior high school was established at Sidman in the former Adams-Summerhill High School building; the junior high school in the former Triangle Area High School building in Croyle Township. The nine elementary buildings at Beaverdale, Dunlo, Elton, Eureka 42, Salix, South Fork, St. Michael, Summerhill and Wilmore were kept in operation with periodic reshuffling of grade assignments.

David L. Smith, supervising principal of Adams-Summerhill, was named superintendent of Forest Hills. John M. Urban, supervising principal of Triangle Area, became the assistant superintendent. Paul E. Keeney, administrative assistant at Triangle Area, was named federal programs coordinator.

Joseph P. Madigan was retained as senior high school principal along with Sam Plummer as his assistant. Charles Signorino who had been assistant high school principal at Triangle Area was elected the Forest Hills junior high school principal.

Carl Sherbine was named principal of all elemetary schools and Mrs. Marian Davis, assistant principal. Other personnel assigned to serve districtwide capacities were Martin Boyer, elementary art supervisor; Mrs. Martha Kozar and Frank Leach, social workers; and Marian Kring and Dena Mitchell, elementary vocal music specialists.

The new district listed 165 professional employees.

First Forest Hills School Board

The first Forest Hills School Board consisted of William McQuillen, South Fork, president; Raymond C. Kirby, Summerhill, secretary; William Risbon, Portage R. D. 2, treasurer; James L. White, Dunlo; Raymond Wess, Portage R. D. 1; Michael Matsko, Salix; Joseph Blasic, Ehrenfeld; Louis Lentine, South Fork R. D. 1; Joseph Stapleton, Summerhill; and James T. Hughes, Wilmore.

Representation on the Forest Hills School Board is divided among three regions:

Region I -- Croyle Township (precinct 1), Summerhill Borough, Summerhill Township and Wilmore Borough.

Region II -- Adams Township (Gramlingtown precinct), Croyle Township (precincts 2, 3, & 4), Ehrenfeld Borough and South Fork Borough.

Region III -- Adams Township (precinct 1, Dunlo, Elton No. 1 and No. 2, St. Michael and precinct 7).

The voters tally for the May 1991 primary elections in Region I was to name two candidates from each party. However, both primaries candidates won and assured election in November. The results:

Democrats: Edward J. Hudak, 573; Allen M. Wilson, 473.

Republicans: Allen M. Wilson, 219; Edward J. Hudak, 191.

New Elementary School

September 7, 1976 about 2,000 kindergarten and elementary pupils of the Forest Hills School District moved into a new building at Sidman, on a 27-acre tract behind the senior high school.

Constructed with the "open classroom" concept and instructional areas known as "pods", it was hailed as one of the most luxurious, up-to-date elementary complexes in the state.

A bond issue was floated for over $12 million, to be paid over a 26-year period. The state picks up 75 to 80 percent of the payments.

All the former elementary buildings were closed and, since then, all pupils are transported by busses to Sidman for kindergarten, elementary and senior high school and to "the hill" in Croyle Township for junior high school.

The cozy, intimate neighborhood school that the "little ones" walked to from home has become a thing of the past. Now, they are bussed daily, eat in the school cafeteria and return home by busess after a whole day in Sidman.

There are those who wish we could return to the small, individually-controlled schools of the past. There are even reputable educators who now see a need for smaller schools.

Forest Hills Superintendents

In 1989, Paul J. Robinson was elected superintendent of Forest Hills School District. He is the fifth chief school administrator in the district's 25-year history. Predecessors were David L. Smith, Dr. Warren Howard, Dr. Robert L. Anderson and Alex Afton.

A South Fork native/resident and 1959 graduate of South Fork-Croyle High School, Robinson earned a bachelor's degree at Duquesne University in 1963 and a master's degree from the University of Pittsburgh in 1971. He received the principal's certificate from Duquesne in 1984 and the school superintendent's letter of eligibility from St. Bonaventure University in 1985.

Robinson began his teaching career at Windber Area High School in 1963 and taught at Forest Hills Senior High School from 1966-75. He returned to Windber as assistant high school principal in 1975.

From 1976, he has served various administrative roles at Forest Hills: federal programs coordinator, 1976-79; junior high principal, 1979-87; and assistant superintendent, 1987-88.

Paul Robinson is an active member of the U. S. Army Reserve with 28 years of service. He holds the rank of Colonel and is a graduate of the National Defense University and an honor graduate of the Command and General Staff College.

Edward Terek of South Fork is the assistant superintendent. A 1955 graduate of South Fork-Croyle High School, he was federal programs coordinator and assistant junior high school principal at Forest Hills from 1970 to 1976 and senior high principal from 1976 to 1989.

Intermediate Units

The office of county superintendent of schools was established in 1854. It was ended by legislative action on July 1, 1971.

All supervising principals positions were abolished and replaced with superintendents. School district chief administrators lost tenure and no longer were required to answer to a county superintendent.

In place of the county office, intermediate units were established with an executive director.

Cambria, Blair, Somerset and Bedford county school districts were grouped into the Appalachia Intermediate Unit 8 (IU 8) with offices in Ebensburg.

IU 8 is one of the largest of 29 intermediate units in the state. It provides special education services to the school districts and serves as a liaison between the 35 districts and the state Department of Education.

Dr. F. K. Shields was IU 8's first executive director. He was succeeded by George E. Kensinger (1974-82) and Joseph Tarris (1982-89). David Duppstadt of Meyersdale has been executive director since Joseph Tarris retired in 1989.

Forest Hills School Authority

Raymond Wess of New Germany is chairman of the Forest Hills School Authority.

Other officers named in 1991 are Robert Kranztler, vice chairman; John Kovalich, secretary; Leonard Straple of Summerhill, assistant secretary; Michael Matsko, treasurer; and Roger Layton, assistant treasurer.

Other members are Dr.Richard Frazer, Harold Walters and Dorothy Ruddek.

Attorney Mark Gregg is the solicitor and William R. McCrory is the auditor.

Vocational-Technical Education

In former years, vocational education was limited to wood and metal shop courses in some local high schools. Technical education was not available.

Conemaugh Township, Ferndale, Forest Hills, Greater Johnstown, Richland, Westmont and Windber school districts banded together to build and support a centralized vocational-technical school to provide such training to its students.

Greater Johnstown Area Vocational-Technical School was built on the former 90-acre Faustin Baumgardner farm between Schoolhouse and Elton Roads in Richland Township. The farm was purchased for $110,000. Construction costs amounted to $10.3 million and was financed with a 20-year $8.675 million bond issue sold at an average net interest rate of 4.836 percent and two federal grants totaling more than a million dollars.

The school was opened to students from the participating schools on August 31. 1970.

It is governed by a joint operating committee made up of representative school directors from the seven participating schools.

Barry Dallara has been the administrative director since 1989.

Nearly 4,000 people annually enroll in the school's evening post-secondary and adult education programs.

Currently, about 650 students are enrolled in grades 10 to 12 in vocational-technical education.

The 1991-92 operating budget is almost $8 million.

Forest Hills Demographics

Forest Hills School District encompasses an area of 94.14 square miles. It takes in four boroughs -- Summerhill, South Fork, Ehrenfeld and Wilmore -- and three townships -- Adams, Summerhill and Croyle.

It is an employer of some 200 people.

In 1972, it served a population of 14,152 as compared with the 1990 census of 14,513.

Student enrollment, however, has declined from 3,449 during the 1976-77 school term to 2,588 for 1989-90. This student population decline has been typical for the region.

The operating budget was $4.8 million for 1974-75 with a real estate tax rate of 44 mills. The 1991-92 budget projects expenditures of $13.6 million and a real estate tax of 90 mills. Other taxes include $10 per capita, $10 occupational privilege, 1% earned income and 1% realty transfer.

The 1989-90 state subsidy amounted to $6.1 million.

An Historical Note

Salix Academic Association, in 1906, formed the first high school in Adams Township. It was known as Salix Academy.

Adams Township High School was established in 1911 at Salix. It was moved to Sidman in 1923. This building currently serves as Forest Hills Senior High School.

Renovations For the 1990s

The Forest Hills School Board voted in August 1991 to proceed with a $5.27 million middle school renovation project and included a two-mill property tax hike in the 1991-92 budget to help finance the work. The state will pay about half of the costs. The rest must be financed by local taxpayers with a projected tax hike of 4.36 mills over four years.

Built in 1961 as Triangle Area Junior-Senior High School in Croyle Township, the current middle school was financed with a $2,045,000 bond issue. The exterior was constructed mostly of 8x10-foot plate glass windows which are now considered dangerous and energy inefficient. The library is too small and there is an asbestos hazard from the ceilings and floors.

Renovations are scheduled to begin in the summer of 1992 and will consist of the construction of brick curtain walls with steel studs and insulation, aluminum windows, new acoustical ceilings and floors, a handicap access to the rear of the building, expansion of the library-media center to 4,000 square feet, replacement of the two main backboards in the gymnasisum, upgrading of the boiler room and kitchen and replacement of all exterior doors.

Problems With Existing Buildings

At a public meeting September 25, 1991, taxpayers were advised that the high school building in Sidman is in need of extensive renovations, too. The estimated cost ranges from $7.64 to $10.88 million.

This building, originally built by Adams Township School District in 1922, has had two additions -- one in 1938 and the other in 1960.

The 1922 portion is deteriorated and not up to today's standards, Superintendent Paul Robinson explains. The heating, plumbing and electrical systems are antiquated. The auditorium is too small.

The 1938 wing does not meet current code requirements. The basement is subject to flooding. The library is too small. There is only one science laboratory. The wooden floors give way underfoot.

The 1960 section is in good condition but it contains asbestos which must be removed.

A proposed $10.88 million project would demolish the 1922 and 1938 sections and build six science laboratories, an auditorium, stage, library-media center, weight room, locker rooms, kitchen and cafeteria area, home economics and drafting rooms.

The lower estimate of $7.64 million covers the same specifications but eliminates a new auditorium. Under this plan, the middle school auditorium would be used.

A Future Merger?

Faced with additional tax increases in the future for these needed renovations, the Forest Hills School Board is considering another alternative -- a merger with neighboring Richland School District.

Other factors promoting this idea are the declining enrollments and escalating costs.

When Forest Hills was organized in 1966, there were 3,700 students. In September 1991, the enrollment was 2,500 -- a drop of 1,200 students (32%) in 25 years. Kindergarten enrollment is down and projections for the next ten years show a continuing decline.

Richland's current enrollment is about 1,700, from kindergarten to grade 12.

It is argued that a merger would result in a reduction of property taxes for both districts, a more diversified educational program, better utilization of physical facilities and enhanced economic benefits. It is also surmised that if the two districts would merge, there would be no need to go into Forest Hills' expensive high school renovations.

Richland currently has a 64-mill property tax compared to Forest Hills' 90 mills. The Richland budget is $10.5 million; Forest Hills is $13.6 million.

The Richland District takes in Richland Township and most of Geistown Borough and a population of about 15,000 over an area of 29.6 square miles.

Forest Hills includes Adams, Croyle and Summerhill Townships; South Fork, Ehrenfeld, Summerhill and Wilmore Boroughs; a population of about 15,000 and over 94 square miles.

The Richland School Board agreed to the idea of a feasibility study in October 1991. A comprehensive six-months study of the two districts would involve a cost of about $20,000. The two districts are exploring funding grants.

Other Area School Proposals

The problem is not only with Forest Hills. There has been a continued decline of population in Cambria County since 1940.

The city of Johnstown, once the largest school district in the county, has also taken in neighboring districts, demolished one of its junior high buildings and its senior high building, and converted the remaining two junior highs into a junior and a senior high facilities.

Now, in 1991, it is being suggested that Johnstown move its senior high school into the Greater Johnstown VocationalTechnical building in Richland Township which is only partially occupied.

The vocational-technical school, built in 1970 for 1,500 students, has a current daily enrollment of 653. This not only is due to the population losses but also, in part, with the overall decline in vocational education throughout the state.

And, as costs continue to rise and taxing limits are reached, other school districts will be forced to consider changes, too.

Chapter 13
Nothing Like An Organized Group
Knights of Golden Eagles

Summerhill had a Knights of Golden Eagles with its own club house.

The motto of the organization was "Fidelity, Valor and Honor." It was a fraternal group founded by John E. Burbage of Baltimore, Maryland, in 1872, and introduced in Philadelphia under the auspices of the Odd Fellows.

It was a popular organization during the 19th century. The early 1920s, there were 73,000 members in 26 states. A numerical decline began in the 1930s. By 1965, there were less than 15,000, with most of these in Pennsylvania. The organization is now extinct.

The Knights of Golden Eagles was a beneficiary, semi-military society whose rituals and ceremonial rites were based on the history and pageantry of the medieval crusaders. The objectives were to provide mutual relief for its members in finding employment and aiding them while unemployed.

There were three degrees, each symbolically referring to a medieval soldier. The first degree accented the pilgrim role and taught the candidate fidelity to God and man. The second degree took the medieval knight as a model and taught to revere religion, fidelity, valor, courtesy and hospitality. The third degree revolved about the symbolism of the crusader and equipped men against the evil of its enemies.

Members were required to believe in a supreme being, be white males at least 18 years of age, be free of mental or bodily handicaps, be able to write and support themselves, be a law-abiding citizen, be of sound moral character and believe in the Christian faith.

In 1885, the Legion of the Red Cross was founded by the Knights of Golden Eagles to insure its members, seek to procure employment for them and assist them in business.

Local groups were known as castles. Summerhill was identified as Golden Star Castle #81.

Courthouse deeds reveal that William Murray bought the Golden Eagle land at a sheriff sale in 1878 as a result of a judgment against John D. and Mary Ann Wentroth. Murray sold it in 1887 to Thomas Griffith of Ebensburg, John Brown of Summerhill and George B. Stineman of South Fork.

An 1895 deed records that Dr.Abner and Elizabeth Griffith, Webster and Alice Griffith, George B. and Martha Stineman, F. A. and Annie E. Lyte (Kane, Pennsylvania) sold the tract to the trustees of the Knights of Golden

Eagles for $100. The trustees were William W. Paul, Emanuel Pringle and Hiram Crum.

At the same date, in another transaction, the same trustees secured another tract of land for $17, the highest bidder at a sheriff sale of some of Dr. J. B. Green's holdings. This land was described as part of the William Murray tract #7 and also known as the Griffith-Brown-Stineman plan lot #61. It was located at the intersection of Main Street and Ebensburg Road.

An indenture executed in 1893 for this property between John Brown and Dr. Green indicates that Brown, "owing to sundry losses and misfortunes and unable to pay debts", had assigned the tract to Dr. Green for $1.

Summerhill assessors noted that a Golden Eagle Hall was located on Lot #61 of Cherry Street (now Main Street). They assessed the building at $700 for taxing purposes.

The hall is entered in the tax assessment records for the years 1896, 1897, 1898, 1899 and 1900. An entry made for 1901 was lined out and the hall failed to appear either as a taxable or nontaxable property anymore.

Knights of St. George

Another early organization in Summerhill was the Knights of St. George, Branch No. 63.

This organization was a fraternal society of Catholic men, 16 years of age and older. Headquarters were located in Pittsburgh. Insurance coverage was afforded its members.

At its peak, the Summerhill branch had about 100 members and attracted memberships from New Germany, Wilmore and other surrounding localities.

H. A. Brummert was president of the branch for many years. Hugh T. Brummert, his son, was the secretary-treasurer and one of the last officers.

The group owned property but never had a building. They met monthly in the basement of St. John's Catholic Church until the mid 1920s when membership had declined to about 25 members and the branch was dissolved.

The Knights of St. George owned three lots that began "at a post corner of the lot of William R. Kirby and Ebensburg Road to 150 feet to the corner lot of the Humphries Estate." This was the land the Knights deeded to the Summerhill Borough School District in 1934 for $1 and used to construct the borough's red brick school house along Ebensburg Road.

This land had been conveyed by A. J. and Millie Oaks to the Humphries in 1920 for $1,500 and later sold to the Knights of St. George for $800.

Originally, this tract was owned by Webster Land and Improvement Company which sold it to Thomas R. and Margaretta Marshall in 1898. The Marshalls sold it to the Summerhill Industrial Company which erected a large plank building and used it as a planing mill and furniture factory. The company did not prosper and,in 1903, A. J. Oaks had acquired the property.

Equal Suffrage Party

The Equal Suffrage Party was organized in Summerhill on August 11, 1915, by the county organizer, Mrs. George Dibert of Southmont.

Civic Club

Clarence W. Simendinger, C. K. English, Raymond Kirby and Lewis White appeared at the May 10, 1932 borough council meeting as representatives of the newly-organized Civic Club. The club was in the process of securing better fire insurance rates and council agreed to furnish them the necessary information for insurance underwriters.

Neighboring Organizations

Since Summerhill was never large enough to support many service and fraternal organizations, residents turned to those in neighboring communities.

There are those with memberships in the Masonic Orders of Johnstown, Ebensburg and Altoona; area country clubs and golf courses; and city and county historical associations.

Some belong to the Johnstown Elks; South Fork Lions; Portage Rotary; the American Legion posts at St. Michael, South Fork and Portage; Veterans of Foreign Wars at South Fork and Portage; Citizens Club of Fifficktown; South Fork Eagles; Portage Amvets and others.

Not only are Summerhill residents members but, in some instances, they have had active parts in organizational and administrative capacities.

An example is The Veterans of Foreign Wars Post #895 at Portage. It was established in 1932 with Clarence W. Simendinger of Summerhill as one of the organizers. He was elected the first commander but he never took office because he was killed on a deer hunting trip.

Another example is George Novotny. In August 1991, he was honored as one of Pennsylvania's American Legion post commanders at the annual state convention in King of Prussia. He is commander of Portage Post #340.

Eldred Jones, who lives along Portage Street, is a past commander of Portage American Legion and an active promoter and member of Portage's Amvets Band.

The late 1890s roster of the Junior Order of United American Mechanics of South Fork listed the following Summerhill residents as members: laborers William E. George, Harry Chappel and Benjamin Wess; coal miners Jacob Crum, Salaman Weeds and A. W. Zigler; carpenter John F. McGough; railroader David Plummer; merchant David A. Burtnett; and Dr. J. H. Hendricks.

The membership of this organization attracted men from a large area, including Portage, Adams Township, Elton, Richland Township, Geistown, Ebensburg, Scalp Level, Scotttown, Lilly's Station, Mineral Point, Vinco, Johnstown, Croyle Township, McKees Rock and Ehrenfeld.

Even though South Fork organized a GBU in 1911, halfway along the road between Summerhill and South Fork, the Summerhill "Deutsche Bund" outlasted the South Fork Lodge. It is still active today.

Summerhill Greater Beneficial Union

The Summerhill Lodge was chartered in 1913 as the German Beneficial Union for the purpose of "aiding and protecting the beneficiaries of deceased members. Financially aiding members by paying sick benefits to those who may become beneficiary, by reason of illness or injury from funds collected by assessment from its members. The cultivation and perpetuation of the German Language, and mutually aiding one another so far as consistent in the perpetuation of fraternalism."

GBU at the turn of the century. (Credit: Jack Bodenschatz)

GBU in 1991.

The charter reads that "the business of the corporation is to be transacted at Summerhill, Cambria County, Pennsylvania," and that the corporation "is to exist perpetually" without capital stock.

There were seven subscribers, all from Summerhill: Otto Pallarchke, Freidrich Gorba, August Hill, Adam Nowatzki, Johann Gallarch, Franz Hans and George Bodenshatz. These subscribers also were the first directors.

J. T. Long, Clarus Hoover and John Hoover witnessed the seven signatures. John H. Stephens of Johnstown served as the group's solicitor.

The intent of incorporation was published in the Johnstown Leader and the Ebensburg Mountaineer Herald.

The charter was granted on condition that "violations of the liquor laws of this Club, or any of its members, upon the premises occupied by this Club, or the sale or furnishing of liquors by it to the members of the same, or other person in their rooms in the Borough of Summerhill shall work a forfeiture of this charter."

Due to the war with Germany, an amendment of the articles of incorporation was approved September 1943 which changed the name from German Beneficial Union to the **Greater Beneficial Union of Summerhill, PA.**

This change was approved by 26 members at a July 6, 1943 meeting. Norman Betz Sr. sat as president and Fred Dierling as secretary.

Officers for 1991-92 are Walter Seder, president; Richard Shultz, vice president; Verla Mae Shultz, secretary-treasurer; Devon Mathieson, sentinel-marshall; David Wirfel, Charles (Ed) Hogue, Jr., and Leonard Straple, trustees.

Verla Mae Shultz and Francis Madison are district representatives.

Francis Madison also served as national treasurer in the parent organization from 1986 to 1990. He is now serving as the Eastern Regional vice president.

The Summerhill Lodge #291 has 587 beneficial (insured) members and over 200 social members.

Summerhill Borough Fire Company building in 1991.

Early fire company equipment from left to right: 1925, 1948 and 1973 model years. (Credit: Charles Huber)

Summerhill Borough Volunteer Fire Company

Summerhill Borough Volunteer Fire Company #1 was chartered May 19, 1952. The first officers were Arthur Apple, president; George Bodenschatz, vice president; Felix Bopp, second vice president; Cecil Bopp, secretary; and Clement Bodenschatz, treasurer.

In 1953, the company purchased a lot from Alex Betz for $600. The present fire station was built on it in 1956.

The first fire truck, a 1924 American LaFrance, was purchased from the Wilmore Fire Company.

Brownstown Volunteer Fire Company donated a Buick ambulance in 1960.

The first siren was bought for $50 from the Revloc Fire Company in 1963.

A 1952 Dodge squad truck was obtained from Portage Fire Company in 1964 for $350.

Renovations to the fire station were completed in 1965 at a cost of $1,700. The following year, a 1,000-gallon Chevrolet tanker was procured from Wilfred Kibler for $550.

The original siren was replaced by a 5-horsepower one in 1970. The new siren was purchased from Paul Miller at a cost of $650.

The following year, the first breathing apparatus was purchased.

1972 saw the addition of a kitchen and a storage area at a cost of $2,200.

A year later, the first new fire engine was delivered by John Bean. It had a price tag of $27,000.

The first radio equipment -- three mobiles and a base station -- was purchased from Dale Volunteer Fire Company in 1975.

Current 1979 American LaFrance Pumper. (Credit: Charles Huber)

Bylaws were revised the same year and the Dodge squad truck was sold to Wilmore firemen for $250 and replaced with a new Chevrolet squad truck from Stager Motors, Portage, at a cost of $5,490.

The next year, the Summerhill company bought 1,000 feet of 4" hose. They were one of the first in Cambria County to adopt this larger diameter.

A new $89,000 American LaFrance pumper was added in 1979 with the help of a $35,000 loan from the Pennsylvania Department of Community Affairs.

Additional property, adjoining the fire station, was purchased in 1983.

Fire Chief Regis Long retired in 1975 with seven years of service and, in 1980, Edward Huber completed 10 years as assistant fire chief and five subsequent years as fire chief.

Treasurer Paul Bimle retired with 29 years of service in 1981, the only member to have held this office since the company was chartered.

Joseph Claycomb retired in 1982 after 17 years as secretary.

Summerhill Volunteer Fire Company became a member of the Volunteer Firemen's Association of Cambria County and vicinity in 1959.

Annual Convention Host

In 1986, Summerhill was the host to the 65th annual convention of the association.

The joint memorial service included organ prelude and recessional by Samilda Huber. Stella DeLozier, president of Summerhill's auxiliary, served as master of ceremonies. Mayor Dennis C. Cobaugh, also a trustee of the fire company, gave the welcoming address. Presentations were made by Charles Huber, Summerhill's fire company president and president-elect of the association.

Other Summerhill participants included Rev. Emmeran A. Rettger, roll call of Summerhill's deceased firemen; Donald L. Penatzer, Summerhill fire chief, prayer; and John W. McCall II, taps.

Fire Protection

Before Summerhill had its own company, fire protection was provided by South Fork on an annual fee basis. In March of 1958, South Fork, who also was furnishing protection to Ehrenfeld and Croyle Township, realized its taxpayers were assuming too great a burden in order to service these areas.

A new plan was devised for a fairer method to underwrite operational costs. It was based on the assessed valuation of properties at 1 1/2 mills. Summerhill immediately agreed to pay about $500 a year; Ehrenfeld, $125. Croyle Township's share was to be about $1,000. Croyle's reaction was to ask for a contract including only Fifficktown, Rockville and vicinity. By October of 1958, Croyle Township signed an agreement with South Fork for $531.53 a year.

Meanwhile, Summerhill was in the process of forming its own company and, by March 1959, notified South Fork Borough Council that they would handle their own protection and since the county organization had accepted them, South Fork now would be obliged to offer free assistance, whenever needed.

Since that time, Summerhill has expanded coverage into portions of Croyle Township. And, in cases of emergencies, Summerhill is provided support by fire companies of St. Michael, South Fork, Summerhill Township and Wilmore. Other companies within the county organizations assist, when needed.

Summerhill volunteers are trained in fire fighting, equipment operations and first aid procedures. They are on call 24-hours a day to answer fire alarms or other casualties. Currently, there are 30 active volunteers.

Years ago, street carnivals were held to raise funds. In 1967, the carnivals were replaced by picnics at New Germany Grove. Fundraising continues through individual donations, and special events and functions. The Summerhill Borough Council budgets an annual amount to help the company with equipment purchases.

1991 Officers

Administrative officers for 1991 included Charles Huber, president; Dennis Long, vice president; Steven Parks, secretary; Lawrence Wilburn, treasurer; and trustees Dan Penatzer, Jeff Penatzer, Bob Gallardy, Jack Wilburn and Brian Wilson.

Line officers are Steven Parks, fire chief; Jeff Penatzer, deputy chief; Bob Gallardy, assistant chief; Joel Penatzer, captain; and Brian Wilson, lieutenant.

1966 Officers

Fifteen years earlier, there was a completely different set of officers. Jay Bimle was president; Vincent Kitchick, vice president; Paul Bimle, treasurer; Joseph Claycomb, secretary; Dean Wess, fire chief; Edward Huber, assistant fire chief.

Trustees were Charles Haberl, Charles Huber and Leon White.

New Fire Hall

In the spring of 1992, construction is expected to begin on a new $250,000 fire hall on a lot adjacent to the present location. The new building -- 62 feet by 68 feet -- will increase the available space about 3 1/2 times.

The firemen have raised about half of the construction costs and expect to finance the remainder through fundraising activities such as tickets, sub and pizza sales, casino nights, dinners and dances at New Germany Grove.

The present building will be utilized by the borough for council meetings, garage and storage purposes.

Company Services

Summerhill Volunteer Fire Company makes an average of 50 runs annually. Most calls are for automobile accidents. Others include calls for help from area companies.

Fortunately, fire calls within the borough are at a minimum.

In addition, the volunteers participate in about 15 firemen parades each year throughout Cambria County. Their meeting room displays numerous trophies won at these functions.

Firemen's Relief Association

The Summerhill Volunteer Firemen's Relief Association charter of March 19, 1959 lists the following charter members and first directors: Francis Bodenschatz, Hayden Schrift, Edward Dierling, Ronald Shrift, John McCall, Edward Kick, Clem Bodenschatz and Arthur Apple.

An Earlier Summerhill Fire Company

Jack Bodenschatz furnished this author a copy of bylaws of Summerhill Fire Company No. 1 of Summerhill, Pa., adopted July 29, 1915.

Acccording to these bylaws, Jacob Meier was the president and J. H. Tully, secretary.

The bylaws committee was made up of Jacob Meier, S. A. Brummert, C. E. Claycomb, J. C. Berschneider, T. E. Kime, S. S. Robine, C. F. Plummer and J. H. Tully.

Members listed were: T. E. Kime, Laurence Leech, A. L. Tully, Jacob Meier, C. F. Plummer, Dr. Healy, Charles Brummert, Bennet Gallardy, Edward Wicks, Joseph Callaghan, J. C. Berschneider, H. A. Brummert, C. A. Pringle, John Rose, Raymond Callagan, Raymond Crossen, Clarence Simindinger, Joseph Haberl, Paul Meier, H. G. Somerville, William Rosenberger, Irving Berschneider, John Mulvihill.

Frank Weigand, Tally Gallardy, Rudolph Peanutzer, Robert Karnes, Roy White, Edgar White, John Betz, Walter Hull, George Kirtz, Jr., John Whitely, John Simindinger, William Hampton, W. R. Kirby, Frank Haberl, C. E. Claycomb, Elmer Sellers, Cletus Schrift, Louis Haberl, Leo Sellers, Harry White, Oscar Betz, Frank Brummert, Ralph Schrift, Webster Rose, Clea Gallardy, Rudolph Bopp, William Tewart, Robert Tewart, P. J. McGough, John Rose, Isador Schrift, William Hettle, Charles Hettle, Fred Wess, Simon Robine, and J. H. Tully.

(All spellings are listed as printed in the bylaws).

In reviewing this copy, it is evident that there was a "fire building" and the equipment consisted of borough-owned fire hose and hose carriages.

Responding to a fire entailed the "drage rope" used "in drawing the apparatus".

Membership was open to "white males sixteen years of age or over; no one admitted when he is not a resident of Summerhill Borough or vicinity." Anyone under 21 years was required to submit a written consent of his parents or guardian.

Officers of the company included president, vice president, secretary, treasurer, chief, foreman, assistant foreman and five trustees.

The chief's duties were to "take command at every fire or alarm of fire, to see that apparatus is returned to the Company's building, in proper shape and keep the same in good condition." He was also charged with appointment of members "to their places and have a written list posted in the building, when at a fire, see that every member does his duty, and have the power to make a change whenever conditions require." He also was to report any members who refused to obey orders when at a fire, or when leaving a fire or drag rope without his permission.

The foreman helped the chief discharge his duties and officiate for him in his absence.

The assistant foreman acted for his superior officers during their absence.

At the first regular meeting of each year, the president appointed three fire police "whose duty shall be to arrest any person interfering with the Company in the discharge of their duties or retarding them in their work at a fire or who might be caught carrying off or destroying any property of the Company or the property of others."

An initiation fee of 50¢ was charged for new members. A committee of three investigated his character and reported at the next regular meeting where a ballot was taken. If the candidate got no more than three black balls, he was declared elected.

The president, chief and foreman made up a relief committee whose duty was to visit all sick or disabled members within 24 hours after being notified of said sickness or disability and continue their visits once a week or oftener, if necessary.

In case watchers were required, the committee appointed two members for each night in the order in which they appeared on the roll, provided "said sickness was not of a contagious nature." Any member neglecting or refusing to watch over sick members either in person or by substitute would be subject to penalties according to the bylaws.

An entire article dealt with fines. Failure to attend the regular meeting for three consecutive months incurred a fine of 50¢ if there were no reasonable excuses. Failure to attend for one year resulted in expulsion.

Any member absent at roll call after a fire was liable to a fine of 25¢, unless excused by the chief.

Violating any of the laws or rules of the Company incurred a 25¢ fine.

Any member appointed to a committee and did not perform his duty was fined 50¢.

Any member leaving the drag rope or a fire without permission was fined one dollar.

Littering the rooms of the company or spitting tobacco on the floor called for a 25¢ fine.

Bringing liquors into the building caused a member to be fined one dollar.

Making public the proceedings of a meeting was fined at one dollar for the first offense and expulsion for the second offense.

Refusing to sit up with a sick brother when properly notified was a one dollar fine.

Any officers failing to do their duty were fined 50¢ for each offense.

Any member bringing a person into the building for immoral purposes would be fined two dollars.

Fines from 10¢ to one dollar were assessed for misconduct during a meeting.

Violation of house rules incurred one dollar fines.

Summerhill Fire Company Ladies Auxiliary

The Ladies Auxiliary of the Summerhill Volunteer Fire Company was organized in August 1955.

The first officers were Mrs. Calvin Engle, president; Mrs. Edwin Wicks, vice president; Mrs. Arthur Apple, secretary; and Mrs. Charles Mulvihill, treasurer.

Past presidents are:

1958-59	Beanie Engle
1960-62	Rene Bimle
1968-74	Helen Apple
1975-76	Mary Haberl
1977-78	Louise Shope
1979-80	Samilda Huber
1981-82	Suzie Thomas
1983-84	Linda McCormick
1985-86	Stella DeLozier
1986-87	Margaret McCormick

No formal organization has existed since 1987. However, many former members serve when called upon by the firemen.

The 1986 officers who helped with the county convention in Summerhill were Stella DeLozier, president; Jean Cann, vice president; Violet Kline, secretary; and Janet "Suzie" Thomas, treasurer.

Firemen's Relief Association

The Summerhill Volunteer Firemen's Relief Association charter of March 19, 1959, lists the following charter members and first directors: Francis

Bodenschatz, Hayden Schrift, Edward Dierling, Ronald Schrift, John McCall, Edward Kick, Clem Bodenschatz and Arthur Apple.

Women's Club project in memory of Florence Seaman.

Summerhill's Veterans Memorial Park, another project of the Women's Club.

Summerhill Women's Club

The Summerhill Women's Club was organized August 19, 1959 to develop the educational, civic and social interest of the members, advance the welfare of the community and promote the progress and work of the State Federation of Pennsylvania Womens Clubs.

The first president was Mrs. Fred Montanari. Other first officers were Mrs. Joseph Lazration, vice presdient; Mrs. Stanley Seaman, secretary; and Mrs. Donald Penatzer, treasurer.

Among the charter members were Doreen Basile, Gertrude Brummert, Anna Burns, Mary Callahan, Dolores Connelly, Stella Cullen, Dorothy Hettle, Sophie Kime, Mickey Lazration, Genevieve Lenz, Gloria Montanari, Maxine Penatzer, Florence Seaman, Mary Grace Tully and Bert Wicks.

For many years, meetings were held in the fire hall. In recent years, they meet in the community room of Summerhill Office of Portage National Bank.

They have sold cook books, held card parties and sponsored a variety of fund raising activities to provide community needs.

There are about 38 members now who pay annual dues of $6, meet monthly September through May and hold a May banquet at suitable locations.

Programs are informative and entertaining and have included county attorneys, a home economist, county officers, doctors, police officials, a cosmetologist, arts and crafts experts and other professionals.

Since 1959, many of the members have held offices on the federation's county board. One time, a third of the county federation chorus were members of the Summerhill Club.

The local club has had winners in the Federation Art Festival at local, county, district and state levels. Two members placed first in poetry and third in counted cross stitch in the State.

The club also received a certificate of recognition from the state federation for the most new members for a year.

For their "fun" activities, the Summerhill women have had style shows, card parties, hat shows, international dinners, flower shows, auctions, flea markets, submarine sandwich sales, and bake sales.

They have participated in parades held by the local fire company and served dinners for them at New Germany Grove.

They sponsor trips to Pittsburgh for shows and theater productions and participated in the Good Neighbor Days at the Summerhill Branch or office of the Portage National Bank.

Annually, the club donates to many worthwhile charities, such as Cancer, Red Cross, Heart, CARE, Pennies for Art, Spina Bifida, Cystic Fibrosis, conservation, state federation projects and more. A hospital bed was purchased for use by Summerhill residents.

Summerhill Women's Club financially supports the fire company and many other community causes. They purchased pediatric trauma pants for the Forest Hills Ambulance Association, gave Christmas and skating parties for the children of the community and distributed treats and prizes to participants at Halloween parties and local parades. They have also sponsored Girl Scouts.

There are special projects each year. The list has grown into an extensive one:

For the fire company -- purchase of waterproof coats and hats, 12 card tables, 6 large formica top tables, dishes, tableware and electric stove; helped raise money to buy a new pumper; installation of a new ceiling and painting of floor in the social room; and enlargement of the Summerhill map for use at the fire hall.

For the elementary school -- purchase of several pieces of playground equipment; sponsorship of poster contests for students; distribution of tree seedlings to each student for planting at home; and arrangements for Bookmobile stops at the school.

For the community -- planting and maintenance of the Mimi-Park; erection of memorial monument; securing and flying the U. S. flag all year; contributions to the uptown park; benches around the community; street sign posts, house numbers, trash cans and street planters throughout the town; annual maintenance of the planters; national federation markers at the two entrances to Summerhill; section of bleachers at the local ball field; draperies and blinds for the community building; and a circular sliding board at the park.

For local history -- A 28-page history of Summerhill was written, duplicated and sold in 1966 by the Cultural Heritage Department of the club as a "pet project" of Mrs. Stanley Seaman's administration. The foreword contains the following appropriate paragraph:

> "While Summerhill may be only an infinitesimal speck on the crossroads of history, the heritage of our local area is of interest to our community and to its people."

Mrs. Seaman points out the dedication and tireless devotion of Miss Hilda Brummert's work on this historical project.

This history can also be considered a Women's Club project. Stella De-Lozier convinced the author to donate his services and received the support of borough council to finance the publication as part of Summerhill's centennial celebration of 1992. Sale of the book will be handled by the Women's Club.

Past Presidents

1959-1962	Gloria Montanari
1962-1964	Doris White
1964-1966	Florence Seaman
1966-1968	Naomi Costello
1968-1969	Jeanne Plummer
1969-1972	Violette McCall
1972-1974	Florence Seaman

1974-1976	Evelyn Beckman
1976-1978	Eileen Hutzell
1978-1980	Betty Penatzer
1980-1982	Catherine Hettle
1982-1984	Beatrice Cameron
1984-1986	Susan Dimond
1986-1988	Stella DeLozier
1988-1990	Violette McCall

Current Officers -- Betty Penatzer is the president for 1990-91 and is assisted by the following: Arzella Kirby, vice president; Stella DeLozier, secretary; and Naomi Costello, treasurer.

Department assignments are: Twila Claycomb, fine arts; Naomi Costello (chair), Twila Claycomb, Violette McCall, Doris Previte, Arzella Kirby and Catherine Hettle, conservation and home life; Stella Cullen, honorary chair, historian; Kathy Puruczky, education; Florine Hamilton, hospitality; Gertrude LeMay (chair), Margaret McCormick, Bonnie Novotny, Carol George and Sue Dimond, international; Sue Dimond, membership; Arzella Kirby and Doreen Basile, programs; Florine Hamilton, publicity.

Cambria County Officers -- Current county officers are Mrs. Rose Pratt, president; Mrs. Violette McCall, vice president; Mrs. Helen Greiger, secretary; and Mrs. Leona Sower, treasurer.

The county fall meeting of October 20, 1990 was held in Redwood Restaurant, Summerhill. The spring meeting, hosted by the Summerhill Club, was a luncheon at Redwood Restaurant on Saturday, May 4, 1991.

1990-91 Membership -- Summerhill's membership for 1990-91 includes Doreen Basile, Evelyn Beckman, Dorothy Brewer, Gertrude Brummert, Beatrice Cameron, Susan Cameron, Joyce Cannonie, Twila Claycomb, Naomi Costello, Stella Cullen, Stella DeLozier, Susan Dimond, Ruth Ferchalk, Carol George, Florine Hamilton, Jane Harshberger, Catherine Hettle, Arzella Kirby, Violet Kime, Mary Jane Lazration, Gertrude LeMay, Genevieve Liddle, Helen McCall, Violette McCall, Margaret McCormick, Violet Mackel, Gloria Montanari, Margaret New, Bonnie Novotny, Betty Penatzer, Sue Penrod, Pat Poling, Doris Previte, Kathleen Puruczky, Mary Robine, Jill Rosporski, Cleo Shope and Mary Grace Tully.

Membership Responsibilities -- Membership is contingent upon serving once a year on the Hostess Committee and also on one standing committee. All members are expected to give at least 24 hours service per club year by attending club meetings, participating in committee acitivites or working on special projects.

Each member is responsible for raising seven dollars each year by any means she chooses.

The executive board is required to hold regular monthly meetings. The board is made up of the officers and chairs of all standing committees.

The bylaws require that regular meetings be held on the last Monday of each month, September through May, at 7:30 p.m. The executive board meets the week prior to the regular meeting. The annual banquet meeting is held in May.

If a member is hospitalized, a remembrance is given once per fiscal year; thereafter, a card is mailed. And in case of a death of a member or a family member, a Mass or flowers is provided.

Laurel Run Rod & Gun Club

The Laurel Run Rod & Gun Club originated in 1932.

The first set of bylaws were drawn up by a committee of Stephen Wess, chairman, B. E. Pringle and W. A. Mathieson.

The first officers were I. A. Lenz, president, and C. W. Simendinger, secretary.

For the past 60 years, the club has been involved in many sportsmen's projects. As a member of the Cambria County Federation of Sportsmens Clubs, it has been a strong supporter in the building of Duman's Dam. The club was involved in raising and stocking pheasants and rabbits and there was also a dog training area.

In the mid 1950s, Laurel Run Club was pushing for a Mainline Fishing Area to be located one mile east of Summerhill. This project was dropped to support the county federation's efforts to start Glendale Lake (now Prince Gallitzin State Park). Officers during this period were Regis Shrift, president; Herbert Bodenschatz, treasuer; and Franklin H. Penrod, secretary.

Laurel Run has been affiliated with the National Rifle Association (NRA) since the mid 1930s and through the Pennsylvania Game Commission has Offered hunter safety courses for the past 20 years.

In 1985, the club helped form and run the Forest Hills Trout Co-Op, which stocks many local streams.

The Laurel Run Club is located one mile west of Summerhill on a 92-acre tract of land purchased from E. L. Jones. Through Mr. Jones' generosity, equipment and men were made available to clear 95% of the tract to date.

There is a block-brick club house, indoor rifle and pistol range, two trap fields, a skeet range and horseshoe pitching facilities.

Among the deceased members and officers who contributed in the building of the club grounds are Paul Bimle, Francis Bodenschatz, Evan Stineman, Louis White, John Andries, Joe Gideos, Karl McGough, and Dave Wess, just to name a few.

These men and many others too numerous to list have helped make the club what it is today.

Officers for 1991 are Robert McCormick, president; Roy Schrift, vice president; Eugene Wess, treasurer; and Carl Bodenschatz, secretary.

The Board of Directors include Wilber Shrift, Jay Bimle, Jeff McCall, Richard Shaffer and Ed Dierling.

Dedication of Freedom Park in 1975. (Credit: Louis Rosenberger)

Freedom Park in 1991.

Playground along Ebensburg Road in 1991.

Backstop at the playground ball field, 1991.

Freedom Park

Freedom Park is a small 0.8-acre triangular plot at Ebensburg Road and Market Street. The name was selected from those submitted by the town's youngsters.

Louis Rosenberger directed five high school boys who labored two months to complete the project under the sponsorship of the borough council.

The finished job includes a S-shaped walk, shubbery, planters, a 33-foot stainless steel flag pole and benches. For a time, there was an operating drinking fountain.

Dedicated in 1975, the park converted a potentially unsightly area into a location of beauty and tranquility.

**Above: Gene Barber of South Fork directs the drum and bugle corps at the dedication of Freedom Park.
Below: Mayor John W. McCall cuts the ribbon.
(Credit: Evelyn Beckman)**

Rev. Kester T. Sobers III applauds Brownie Girl Scout Kelley (McCall) Poborsky for winning a $25 bond for naming the park. (Credit: Evelyn Beckman)

From left to right: Louis Rosenberger, Mayor John W. McCall, Rev. Kester T. Sobers III and Councilman Herschel Wilson. (Credit: Evelyn Beckman)

Summerhill's Playground

The old mill yard along Ebensburg Road evolved into a community playground through the continued efforts of community volunteers and the cooperation of borough council. It has taken years to convert this 5.2-acre site into a multi-purpose recreational area.

There are permanent and temporary bleachers for spectators. There is a little league ball field. There are paved courts for basketball, tennis and volleyball. An area is provided for ice skating. There is a variety of play equipment for the younger children. A permanent block building is used for storage and a refreshment stand.

This is another example of how things are accomplished in Summerhill. Caring individuals and organizations pitch in, without much fanfare or publicity, and do what is needed to provide for the benefit and welfare of its people.

Other Recreational Efforts

The Summerhill Parent Teachers Association in 1934 petitioned borough council to set aside Croyle Street several nights each week for roller skating.

An item in the Cambria Dispatch of 1936 announced a dance in Long's Hall sponsored by the Summerhill Athletic Club. The music was provided by Johnny Joe's Orchestra.

Borough Council became an active partner in community recreation in 1969 when it began contributing funds each year for Little League, T-League, Cub Scouts, Girls Pony Tails, softball teams, Girl Scouts, Brownies, Pee-Wee League and Intermediate League.

Council minutes recorded the following individuals handling the activities of these groups: James Bodenschatz, Robbie Kirby, Joanne Bodenschatz, Eugene Amigh, Dan Croyle, Bob McCormick, Tom Fukas, Janet Koon, Paul Flynn, Ruth Ferchalk, Terry Miller, Rose Tripp and Karen Bantley.

A recreation commission was named by council in 1971. The members were Ray Penatzer, Betty McCall, Helen Mathieson, Bob Casti and a representative from the fire company and the Women's Club.

The same year, council granted $300 to the "Laurel Run Recreation Commission" to help with the expense of installing an ice skating rink on the school field. And, the following year, it is recorded that council authorized payment of $2,900 to Golian Brothers for"the cost of the ice skating rink."

In 1974, council gave the recreation commission $1,200 to pave the skating rink area and from $400 to $500 to buy volleyballs, nets, banking boards and baskets.

Sledding on Main Street was permitted in 1976, whenever the barricades were in place. This was also the year, borough officers sponsored Cub Scout

Pack 63 and named Bill Lawton as their representative to the scout board. Council also leased the school building and permitted the Cub Scouts, Girl Scouts and Brownies to use it for their meetings.

By 1982, councilmen Herschel Wilson, Richard Dierling and Bob Penatzer were appointed to the borough's parks and recreation committee.

Summerhill Borough Recreation Organization

The Summerhill Borough Recreation Organization was first announced in the **Portage Dispatch** of November 11, 1982.

Elwood McGough was listed as president. The other officers included Allan Berkheimer, vice chairman; Ruth Ferchalk, secretary; and Barb Bodenschatz, treasurer. Trustees were Ray Bodenschatz, Bruce Walker and Larry Lacko.

Regular meetings were held at the bank's community room.

Borough council minutes show annual appropriations of $500 to the organization since 1983. Extra amounts are recorded for playground equipment ($3,000) in 1985 and new uniforms ($750) in 1989.

The recreation organization has sponsored teams in the Adams Township Pony Tail softball league which includes New Germany, South Fork and Mt. Hope. It co-sponsors boys intermediates with New Germany.

The present program consists of girls and boys baseball: T-Ball and Middle League for two categories -- 9-10 year-olds and 11-12 year-olds.

A fishing derby which started in the 1980s is conducted in the Spring at Laurel Run Creek for children up to the age of 16.

An annual fall picnic is held at the ball field for team players, their families and organization members.

The group makes improvements to the playground, buys equipment and provides bleacher seating for spectators.

In addition to council's annual contribution, funds are raised by a yearly donut sale, sign advertisements at the field, $5 memberships from 70 to 80 individuals and proceeds from the concession stand which was built by the Seabees and the National Guard in 1984.

The 1991 officers are William Wantiez, chairman; Vivian Hogue, co-chairman; Betty McCall, secretary; Linda Tully, treasurer; and Tom Madison, trustee.

A Softball Team Reunion

A reunion at Kime Hotel was held September 30, 1989 by former members from the 1971 to 1978 Kime Hotel softball teams.

Earlier in the day, players held a golf contest at Pleasant Valley Golf Course. In the evening, a catered luncheon was served.

Rich Fisher served as the master of ceremonies and Don Blanchetti, refreshments.

A moment of prayer was observed for Joe McCall, one of the team players.

The team members in attendance were Charlie Long, Don Blanchetti, Ray Bodenschatz, Kenny Thomas, Tony Olsavsky, Larry Olsavsky, Paul McMullen, Gary Lubert, Pat Stock, Brian Basile, Lynn Jennings, Robert Wilson, Rich Fisher, Gary Fisher, John Geriak, Lou Cornell, Ray Danel, George Yokitis, Clete Wirfel, Lenny Bozic and Jude Basile, who came form San Francisco, California

The players plan to hold annual reunions.

Summerhill Junior Girl Scout Troop 952

Members of the Summerhill Junior Girl Scout Troop 952 went Christmas caroling to a Summerhill shut-in, December 1990.

Following a three-year tradition, the girls shared a homemade fruit basket.

At the troop's Christmas party, the members were entertained by Daryl Dumm and P. J. Shrift.

The troop members, at the time, were Amanda Binaut, Bridgette Tremel, Erin Haberl, Gerrica Gramling, Karissa Minor, Kelly Gruss, Keri Rosporski, Lisa Tripp, Missy Bodenschatz, Sara Binaut, Stephanie Hogue and Sonya Bantly.

Rose Tripp was the troop leader. Vivian Hogue was the assistant troop leader.

Summerhill Brownie Troop 915

A project of Summerhill Brownie Troop 915 for 1991 was the collection of food for the Portage Area Food Pantry. The troop collected 175 cans of food items in time for the pantry's Easter distribution. They started collecting the items in January as a substitute for paying dues.

Troop members included Amy Brence, Jennifer Crum, Jill Crum, Amanda Fox, Shannon Fox, Regina Gruss, Laura Haberl, Cara Harshberger, Beth Hostetler, Sara Hutsky, Kayla Leventry, Jamie McAfee, Courtney McCall, Kayla Minor, Tammy Mennecke, Christy Pearson, Kimberly Shilcosky, Allison Tripp, Sara Tully and Amanda Kornprobst.

Leaders were Karen Leventry and Kathy Gruss.

Camp Conshatawba

The Johnstown Area Girl Scouts Council (now Talus Rock Girl Scouts Council) purchased 160 acres from Ruth Crissman in January 1961 to establish Camp Conshatawba, Summerhill.

Located in Croyle Township, adjacent to Summerhill, the camp was formally dedicated August 23, 1961.

Talus Rock's service area includes all of Cambria, Blair and Indiana Counties, most of Somerset County and parts of the counties of Westmoreland, Bedford, Clearfield and Huntingdon. It serves more than 6,000 girls, ages 5 to 17, and has 2,000 volunteers.

Cookie sales and sustaining memberships make up a significant portion of the council's income along with money from other agencies and program fees.

Talus Rock Council headquarters are located in the 600 block of Locust Street, Johnstown.

In November 1990, it was announced that Camp Conshatawba would be the only camp retained because the council no longer could afford upkeep and improvements of all its properties. Three other camps were to be sold: Hidden Valley near North Fork Dam, Somerset County; Happy Trails near Tipton, Blair County; and Cherry Hill near Yellow Stone State Park, Indiana.

The Summerhill camp is geographically in the center of the Talus Rock area. It has a multi-purpose troop house, dining hall and amphitheater.

The Council plans to renovate the swimming pool, sanitary sewer and water systems and roads and bridges.

Whitestone Park 1934. (Credit: Father Ronald Bodenschatz)

Joe Bodenschatz and Violet Myers at Whitestone Park in 1936. (Credit: Father Ronald Bodenschatz)

Royale Hawaiian Orchestra at Whitestone Park in 1937. (Credit: Father Ronald Bodenschatz)

Whitestone Park's Cabin in 1934. (Credit: Father Ronald Bodenschatz)

Whitestone Park

Whitestone Park began as Joe Bodenschatz's youthful hobby in 1930 as a boys club of 15 members.

At the August 10 opening, there was a swimming pool and an entertainment platform. The rest of the 4-acres, given to Joe by his father, was a complete wilderness.

Members were "subjected to a code of rules which were strictly enforced; the infractions of which resulted in detention or expulsion." Dues were around 10¢ a year.

Annual reunions were held; the first one on August 10, 1930 and the last one exactly the same date ten years later, 1940.

Each year, improvements and additions were made. In 1931, the park was extended to a flag pole above the entertainment platform. A small log cabin was added and used as a library "housing a collection of books conducive to good reading."

The entertainment platform served as a floor for Tuesday and Saturday night dancing. It also was the stage for the Royale Hawaiian Orchestra's concerts at annual reunions.

"Say, Joe we feel great tonight; we have had both our bodily and spiritual baths" was a common saying when members danced on Saturday nights after having gone to the sacraments. Townspeople also enjoyed the music which carried into Summerhill from Joe's Park.

The following year, grounds were extended as far as a rock garden behind and above the cabin.

1933 saw more land use. The first shelter was built. Besides swimming, amusements now included swings, horse shoes, and see-saws. At the reunion, few friends were invited because the water in the pool was very low due to the year's severe drought.

Between two to three acres of woodland were thinned and landscaped in 1934. Truck loads of mountain laurel were hauled from the farm of Joe's uncle. Everywhere rambling roses were made to grow. There were rock gardens, shelters, courts for horseshoes and quoits, swings and see-saws, homemade sliding boards, fireplaces, picnic tables and park benches.

The July 22, 1934 reunion was the first year parents and friends were invited. It also was the first time for fireworks.

1935 was the first year for the island. Rustic fences were added, another see-saw, a new type of park bench, a spring, more fireplaces and a refreshment stand. The grounds were further landscaped, more woods cleared and the ice house was slabbed. At the year's reunion, musical entertainment was presented from the cabin.

By this time, it was customary to white wash all the large boulders and stones. "This created a touch not only of orderliness and cleanliness but also an attractiveness to all that mother nature had to offer", Joe explains and "of most happy memory, the living room section of a future three-room cabin was built with a terrace."

The cabin construction started in March 1934 when the frost was 3 1/2 feet in the ground and Joe recalls "what a job it was to dig the holes for the locust posts with father's long crow-bar which had a wide, flat edge."

It wasn't long that different creative styles of rustic fences were erected to separate areas, like Romance Island--the swimming pool. Rustic bridges were built to cross mountain streams. Birdhouses, stocked either in the tress or perched on poles, came into view.

The swimming pool was washed away by the flood waters of March 17, 1936 and the island was covered with debris. But, improvements were completed within three weeks and crystal, sundials and a croquet court added.

Rhododendron Island and "The Peninsula" were new in 1937, complete with sawdust trails. The bedroom, a back porch and electricity were added to the cabin, in addition to a beautiful entrance with flower boxes, more shubbery and a deeper pool.

By 1938, the 3-room cabin with two porches was complete. Joe lived there from May to October, communting between his parents' home and his daily job as lumber jack for "my most congenial, charitable and enthusiastic father." (Joe had been graduated from high school since 1936).

An ice dance was held January 1940 with dancing on the swimming pool ice and music of a night club nickeleon under colored lights, falling snow flakes and a camp fire on the ice by the rustic bridge. Sleigh and cow bells were juggled and rung at the end or beginning of every square or round dance tune.

August 10, 1940, the end came for Whitestone.

Joe entered the Franciscan monastery at Loretto in 1940.

A member of the Sacred Heart Province of the Third Order Regular, he professed his simple vows in 1942 and his solemn vows three years later. He received a bachelor of arts degree in 1945 from St. Francis College, Loretto, and completed theological studies at the seminary.

Ordained February 10, 1949, at the Shrine of the Immaculate Conception, Washington, D. C., Father Ronald J. Bodenschatz celebrated his first solemn Mass at St. John's Church, Summerhill.

He has served as superintendent of grounds and buildings, fiscal capacities and spiritual formation of brothers and clerics in Loretto; St. Francis Preparatory School, Spring Grove; College of Steubenville, Ohio. He has been a parish priest at Sacred Heart, Spring Grove and St. Annis, Geddes, South Dakota.

From 1976 to 1982, Father Bodenschatz took charge of the restoration of the former Charles M. Schwab estate, now the Mount Assisi Monastery of the Franciscan Province of Sacred Heart, in Loretto. He designed and built the shrine of the Lady of Fatima at Loretto.

Father Bodenschatz also designed and built the first national shrine in honor of St. Joseph the Workman at Loretto and , later, similar shrines at Spring Grove and Geddes, S. D.

At this writing, in semi-retirement, he is pastor at Drummond Isle, Michigan with a mission at St. Lawrence.

Whitestone's Members

Many Summerhill boys are numbered among the membership of Whitestone Park:

Joseph J. and Edward J. Bodenschatz; Paul, Lee and Jay Bimle; Donald, Gerald, Robert and Norman Betz; Leroy Dierling; James, Regis and Clyde Gallardy; Edward, Vincent, Louis, Charles and James White; Jay and Melvin Hershberger; Charles and Donald Plummer; Vernon Jones; Karl and Walter McGough; Regis and Donald Hettle; Robert, Alfred, Bernard and Thomas Seifert; Andrew Neidemyer; Wilfred and Thomas Simendinger; Raymond, Thomas, Herbert and James Shrift; James and Regis Werfel; James Maley; Thomas and Clair Rosenberger; Raymond and Orville Chaney; Donald, James, Jack and Robert Shrift; Clifford and Cletus Bopp; Michael and John McCall; Donald Penatzer; Kenneth Hildebrand; William Geisler; John Costello; Louis and Donald Wess; Joseph Claycomb; Carl Strawberry; and William Hardy.

Royale Hawaiian Orchestra

Joe Bodenschatz's Royale Hawaiian Orchestra began in 1931 and lasted to a time before 1940.

Parents invited orchestra members into their homes on Saturday evenings to practice and entertain them after weekly confessions at St. John's Catholic Church. After practices, the musicians were treated to food and refreshments.

In addition to the annual Whitestone concerts, the orchestra entertained at dances and banquets and even broadcast over Johnstown's WJAC Radio.

At its final presentation, they also had two vocalists --John Ruth and Annie Marie Burkardt.

Members of the orchestra included Joseph J. Bodenschatz, Edward J. Bodenschatz, Mary Virginia Bodenschatz, Margaret Louise Bodenschatz, Paul Bimle, Josephine Bimle, Thomas Rosenberger, Mary Margaret Rosenberger, Violet Ruth Myers, Catherine McCall and Regis Hettle.

Penn Academy of Music

Joseph J. Bodenschatz received a certificate, September 13, 1935, that certified he had completed a professional course in Hawaiian guitar music in solo, orchestra, harmony and arranging. It was issued by Professor William S. Weiser, teacher at the Penn Academy of Music of Pennsylvania.

Professor Weiser, a well-known area banjoist, came from Pittsburgh and opened a music store in Johnstown. He branched out into a music studio operation in which he combined instruction with the cost of the instrument and offered weekly lessons at over 30 locations, including Summerhill.

Weiser was instrumental in the development of many area musicians for 55 years. One of his music teachers was Leroy Dierling of Summerhill.

During the Big Band Era, Weiser directed his own 22-piece orchestra and played at the Capitol Ballroom, the Auditorium and Bachelor's Club in Johnstown; Sunnehanna and North Fork Country Clubs; and Sunset Ballroom at Carrolltown.

The fact that he stayed and made his home in the Johnstown area had a lot to do with a young woman he met and married, the former Alberta M. Wirick of South Fork.

Chapter 14
The Council Beat Goes On

As indicated in Chapter 6, there were 50 different men of the community who served as councilmen during the borough's first 20 years.

No records are available to ascertain who served from the Summer of 1911 to the Spring of 1916.

For the 25-year period from March 6, 1916 to July 11, 1940, there was less turnover in borough officers and employees compared to the first 20 years. The following topics encompass the 1916-1940 period.

Solicitors

By 1911, there had been five different solicitors. L. S. Jones and Edward J. Harkins shared the 1910-1940 period.

Council Presidents

Fourteen councilmen served as president up to 1911.

H. A. Brummert headed the council from January 1918 until his resignation January 4, 1926.

William Hettle, his successor, held the office until 1934, when Francis Bodenschatz was elected and followed by John M. Smith in 1936, R. C. Kirby in 1938 and Thomas Bopp in 1940.

Secretaries

S. S. Robine was secretary for five months in 1916. R. H. Costello handled the chores from 1916 through 1926, along with the responsibility of winding the street clock each week.

Charles Hettle served from 1926 through 1933 for $37.80 a year. He was succeeded by John G. Long, who was still listed in 1941 -- the last year of available records.

The secretary's compensation had increased to $10 per month by 1937.

Treasurers

The treasurer of Summerhill Borough was W. T. Yeckley in 1918. He represented First National Bank of Portage.

Wallace Hughes, from the Union Deposit Bank of South Fork, was proposed in 1929, but lost to Yeckley on a 3-to-2 vote. However, the following year, the voting was between Hughes and William C. Stricker of the First National Bank of South Fork. The council vote resulted in a tie. Burgess John C. Duffy voted for Wallace Hughes.

The tenure of Wallace Hughes lasted only two years; William C. Stricker became treasurer in 1932 and continued throughout the 1930s, 1940s and many years thereafter.

Police Officers

The mention of an elected police officer in the council minutes is somewhat sporadic.

H. W. Davis was elected in 1922 at $15 a month.

Sam Rose is listed from 1924, at the same rate of pay except for 1926 when it was reduced to $7.50 a month. It appears Rose continued until 1937 when a council note notified citizens to call James B. Wilson for police duty.

Wilson's regular assignment was for Fridays and Saturdays beginning at 6 p. m., if needed at $3 per night.

At this time, a fine of $5 to $10 or two days in the county jail was set for disorderly conduct.

A 1933 entry referred to a request from St. Claud Dramatic Club for a number of deputies "for social protection." Joseph Huber, John M. Sloan, James Hettle, Francis Bodenschatz and Raymond Kirby were sworn for three months, from July 17 to October 18.

Burgess

It appears Summerhill couldn't keep a burgess very long in the early years.

C. E. Claycomb was the ninth burgess by 1918.

Council minutes record that C. W. Simendinger was named January 4, 1926, but he refused to accept the appointment.

P. C. Yahner was named January 18, 1926, and he served until John C. Duffy took office on February 28, 1927. Duffy remained until 1934. Charles F. Plummer served until his resignation April 13, 1937.

It was John M. Sloan who took office in 1938 and gave the position permanency. He served until 1969 -- almost a third of a century. He completed the longest tenure of any burgess/mayor in the history of Summerhill Borough.

Street Commissioners

The first street commissioner for any length of time was C. A. Pringle, who served from 1910 through 1917. He worked for 22 1/2¢ an hour while his laborers got 20¢ an hour.

The hourly rate for a team of two horses was 47 1/2¢ while one horse cost 37 1/2¢. And, in 1917, it was noted that teams could not be hired at these rates and they were increased to 60¢ and 40¢, respectively.

When Pringle resigned in 1917, John B. Schlosser was elected. He held the job until late 1934, when he became ill. During his long tenure, he worked from a low of 37 1/2¢ to a high of 45¢ an hour. (Two-horse teams went as high as 80¢; one horse, 60¢).

Trucks were first used by the borough in 1926. Owners were paid a dollar an hour. Edward Bodenschatz and John F. Hoover were two of the first hired by the borough. Within several years, the borough also used the trucks of Glenn Claycomb, Bernard Dierling, Thomas Kirby and Miles Costello.

Thomas Bopp and Tom Kime substituted for Schlosser during his illness until Fred Wess was named in 1935.

George Dierling was street commissioner for 1936. He got the job because Burgess Charles F. Plummer broke the council's tie vote.

Summerhill Borough Real Estate Taxes
1893 - 1940

4 mills	1893-1900
5 mills	1901-1905
8 mills	1906
9 mills	1907-1910
12 mills	1911
(1912 to 1915, unavailable)	
7 mills	1916
8 mills	1917-1918
7 mills	1919-1921
10 mills	1922-1927
8 mills	1928-1929
5 mills	1930
4 mills	1931

(There was no borough tax for 1932 because "of no indebtness, no requirement for borough purposes and the existing financial depression.")

4 mills	1933
6 mills	1934
5 mills	1935-1940

Streets and Highways

It took time and money for Summerhill Borough to complete its streets and highways.

The early streets were cindered. For example, in the early Spring of 1916, council ordered 20 railroad cars of cinders for streets " with the greatest need."

The same year, council required the South Fork-Portage Railway Company to repair Portage Street with cinders so that the road would be "passable." 385 wagon loads, costing $110.33, were used. The cost was charged to the streetcar company.

This was also the year a speed limit of 15 miles-per-hour was instituted. The first violation carried a $10 fine; the second, $25.

Street signs were repainted in black and white.

The following year, council asked the county and the state to reconstruct Route 53 (Portage Street) with brick. Summerhill volunteered to pay 25% of the cost. Nothing happened for four years.

Six carloads of cinders were ordered in 1920 so that the board walks on Main Street could be removed and replaced with cinders.

Summerhill Borough Council again petitioned the county to reconstruct Route 53 in 1921 and repeated its 25% offer to help with the costs. Still no committment. However, the borough was instructed to erect "sign boards placing an arrow showing directions and miles."

(Ten more carloads of cinders were used in 1921).

An ordnance was passed in 1922 to regulate "the use of public highways by vehicles in the borough."

(Another 21 carloads of cinders were scattered).

A bond issue of $8,000 was floated in 1923 for the borough's share for Route 53 work.

In 1926, ground from Mary A. Wentroth was conveyed to the borough for Orchard Street. Ash Alley and Laurel Street were established.

Again, two carloads of cinders were used in 1927 to take care of "the worst places on the streets."

$4,000 was borrowed in 1929 to repair and improve streets and highways.

Signs -- the largest order -- was placed for: one stop sign for the corner of Main and Jackson, five school zone, 20 speed limit, and 4 end-of-speed limit.

Surface treatment of Jackson Street was tried in 1919. 24,000 gallons of tarmac at 0.166¢ per gallon was purchased from the American Tar Products Company.

First Street Pavement

April 1930, a loan of $8,000 was approved to repair and improve (1) a portion of Main Street from Route 53 to the overhead railroad bridge, (2) from Jackson to Second Avenue, (3) Croyle Street from Route 53 to the railroad bridge, and (4) Ebensburg Road from the Main Street Intersection to the borough line.

These streets were to be "repaired and improved with waterbound macadam with tar and screenings surface, the section of said streets leading to the approach of the bridge be covered with mix screenings and tar; Croyle and section of Main to the bridge to be completed first."

In June (1930), 100 tons of "amiesite" was purchased to cover the cobble stones on the approach to the overhead bridge at a cost of $8.50 per ton (f.o.b.) from Tyrone Interstate Amiesite Company, who would furnish a man, at no charge, to supervise the laying. The borough was required to furnish the labor.

In addition, 500 tons of slag were used.

Three years later (1933), the borough increased its debt another $20,000 to grade, pave and "otherwise improve" highways and construct sewers.

The following year, an application was filed with the Emergency Relief Administration for labor to grade, drain, and construct a broken base on First and Second Avenues; Main, Market, Spring, Croyle, Wentroth Streets; Ebensburg Road; and Jackson Street Extension.

The project was authorized by the Local Works Division of the State Emergency Relief Board in 1935. The council accepts the offer of Lester Penrod, Johnstown, for the use of a roller at $1.30 an hour, provided the borough furnishes the operator. Harry Hull and Edgar White are paid 50¢ each to direct traffic. A. R. Burkett was paid for grader operator. Ed Bodenschatz offered curb and base stone from his property for $25. A truck and driver were paid $1.10 an hour. Miles Costello offers to haul and tailgate 600 tons of slag from #492 siding of the Cambria-Blacklick Railroad.

In 1936, the Summerhill Council meets with Croyle Township Supervisors John Hice, Thomas Donahue and William Clark to get the road completed from Summerhill to Ehrenfeld.

Laurel Run Project

A WPA (Works Project Administration) program is approved in November 1936 to clear the debris from the 1936 flood.

Approved for employment were Roy White, general foreman; George Dierling, skilled foreman; Harry Snyder, labor foreman; Patrick McCall, timekeeper; Andy Bishop, field clerk; and John G. Long, blacksmith.

0. P. Thomas of Johnstown is the project engineer.

The borough's share of the project amounts to $6,236.

Sidewalks Project

The WPA was used in 1938 for a 4-inch surfacing of sidewalks on Summerhill streets.

Sewer and Drainage

Sewer and drainage work also took place from 1916 to 1934.

Council minutes note that in 1916 a sewer pipe would be laid to the "German Church property" to finish the line on Jackson Street.

In 1921, labor was paid 50¢ an hour to lay sewer. Continuing efforts to install and move catch basin pipes "to avoid the damming of water at corners and property owners cellars" took priority in 1923.

In 1932, the sewer line was extended to Market Street and authorization to extend it from the intersection of Main Street and Ebensburg Road to Market and from Ebensburg Road up Market to Second Avenue were approved.

A $1.50 sewer tap fee was instituted in 1933 and the system was extended on Jackson to the borough line and from Ebensburg Road to " the junction at Spring Street and Ebensburg Road." This job was paid from the delinquent light account.

0. P. Thomas was the engineer for a Civil Works Administration project to install 10 catch basins in 1934.

Other Actions of the Early 1900s

-- E. Wicks was granted permission in 1919 "to erect a gasoline tank" in front of his business. A similar approval in 1922 for Wicks also carried the following order: "and the constable not be molesting anyone driving either way when stopping at gas tanks within the borough."

-- C. W. Simendinger resigns as tax collector at the August 17, 1925 council meeting; Ben E. Pringle is named to replace him. But, at the July 13, 1926 meeting, Bernard Seifert resigns as tax collector. Once again, Ben E. Pringle is named to the position.

-- A guarantee of 50 members was made in 1927 to the South Fork Fire Company if they would provide fire protection to Summerhill Borough. Four years later, council resolved to pay South Fork Borough $100 a year for protection. South Fork responded that it wanted $50 per call and $15 per hour or fraction thereof. Summerhill Borough Council accepted.

-- An unusual item was written in the borough minutes of July 12, 1927, whereby Summerhill called in bonds held by the Loyal Order of the Moose in

Portage.

-- And, March 29, 1928, the councilmen voted to rent a safety deposit box "to keep the valuable papers, etc. of the borough in."

-- November 13, 1934, the council approved "the purchase of a picture of President Roosevelt and present it to the borough public school." The same motion authorized the borough to pay half the cost of furniture in the meeting room used in the school building.

-- By 1939, the borough funds were so low that,in July, $600 was borrowed from First National Bank of South Fork to pay current bills. An additional $1,400 was borrowed seven months later.

Council Members 1916-1940)

It is well to realize that the events described so far in this chapter took place during World War I and the Great Depression.

Those who were in office during this period include:

Joseph S. Stull	1916-1921
Henry Berschneider	1916-1918
Simon Schrift	1916-1919
E. E. Wicks	1916-1924
Thomas E. Kime	1916-1917 and 1930-1934
W. R. Kirby	1916-1926
H. A. Brummert	1916-1925
John Mulvehill	1918-1921
D. A. Sipe	1918-1921
G. W. Seaman	1920-1923
John G. Long	1922-1926 and 1928-1934
Jacob Hoover	1922-1926
Clem J. Berschneider	1922-1929
Lawrence W. Leach	1924-1927
Celestine McGough	1924-1931
Fred Wess	1926
William Hettle	1926-1934
Ed Bodenschatz	1926-1927
Charles Hettle	1926-1927
Bernard Seifert	1926-1929
Rudolph Penatzer	1928-1932
William Seaman	1930-1934
Ira A. Lenz	1932-1935
Francis Bodenschatz	1932-1935
Adolph J. Wess	1933-1935
George Bodenschatz	1934-1937
Thomas Bopp	1934-1940
John M. Smith	1934-1937

John M. Sloan	1934-1937
Herman Werfel	1936-1940
Peter Brown	1936-1940
John A. Hoover	1936-1940
Raymond C. Kirby	1937-1939
Wilbur Geisler	1938
Victor Schrift	1938-1940
Miles Costello	1938-1940

Elections (1941-1967)

Unfortunely, 27 years of Summerhill Council history is lost because minute books could not be found from January 1, 1941 to July 1968.

Fred R. Smith, supervisor of the Cambria County Election Office, was able to furnish the successful candidates for council during these years.

Elected at the November elections on odd-numbered years were:

1941 -- Miles Costello, Clarence K. English, Magnus Werfel and Francis Bodenschatz.

1943 -- John A. Hoover, John W. McCall and Peter Brown.

1945 -- Joseph F. Kirby, Joseph G. Bimle, Francis Bodenschatz and C. K. English.

1947 -- Andrew Bantley, Herbert Kime and William Yahner, Sr.

1949 -- John A. Hoover, William Weinzierl, C. L. Hoover and Francis Bodenschatz.

1951 -- John McCall, Peter Brown and John Long.

1953 -- John A. Hoover, Francis Bodenschatz, Charles Mulvehill and Regis Long.

1955 -- John McCall, Carl Huber and William Yahner.

1957 -- Earl Penatzer, Joseph F. Kirby, John A. Hoover and Hans Ruddeck.

The Democrats made a clean sweep of the **1959 elections.** The votes for three councilmen were: Harold T. Cronauer, 218; Raymond F. Penatzer, 184; Irvin Eugene Madison, 167; Tom Gallardy, 152; Francis Madison, 125; and Mike McConnell, 74.

Stella Cullen was reelected justice of the peace by defeating Karl McGough, 179 to 130. Calvin Engle (D) received 219 votes for assessor; John Figola (R), 89 votes.

Robert H. Sigg garnered 243 votes for school director and Charles Betz 257 votes for auditor.

The local election results for 1961 had a lot of candidates. The results:

Justice of Peace -- James Gallardy (R), 164; Lester C. Cullen Sr. (D), 140.

School Director (2) -- Herschel Wilson (D), 176; Donald L. Hettle (D), 172; Arthur J. Apple (R), 131; Joseph D. Claycomb (R), 114.

Constable -- Merle Mathieson (R) 201; Art Rose (D), 95.

Auditor -- Verna McDonald (D), 203; Verna McDonald (R), 83.

Tax Collector -- Amelia Hoover (D), 167; Amelia Hoover (R), 136.

Council (4) -- Lewis Brown (D), 177; Earl Penatzer (D), 166; Donald T. Bopp (R), 161; Victor L. Schrift (R), 155; Joseph V. Bimle (R), 148; John A. Hoover (D), 139; Louis Rosenberger (D), 132; Pat McCall (R), 113.

Judge of Election -- Gertrude A. Brummert (D), 235; Alberta H. Wicks (R), 73.

Inspector of Election -- Eva B. Huber (D), 172; Stella Wilburn (R), 128.

1963 -- Councilmen elected were Harold T. Cronauer, Clair Long and Stanley Seaman.

1965 -- Thomas H. Gallardy, Earl Penatzer, Victor L. Schrit and Leon White won council seats.

1967 -- Marlin B. Mervine, Francis B. Madison and Arthur J. Apple were the successful candidates.

John M. Sloan was reelected seven times during this period. In 1961, his title changed to Mayor, in compliance with new state legislation.

Council Minutes (1968-1976)

Minutes for this period show that in August 1968, Earl Penatzer, who was first elected in November 1957, became president.

Other members of council included Victor Schrift, Thomas Gallardy, Leon White, Arthur Apple, Francis Madison and Herbert Kime.

Charles Haberl, a non-member, was serving as secretary for $49.50 a month. B. G. Shrift was the street commissioner; Amelia Hoover, tax collector; Richard Frombach, policeman; and Lewis H. Ripley of Ebensburg, solicitor.

Tillie Bopp was receiving $99 a month (increased to $125 by the end of year) to collect the electric bills; John M. Sloan, $15 a month as Mayor; and councilmen, $15 per meeting.

John Hoover was being paid $3.50 an hour for the use of his truck. Clyde Gallardy read the electric meters. Laborers were being paid $1.70 an hour.

Garbage collection was contracted to Mainline Sanitation of Portage. J. E. Construction -- James C. English -- had the cable television franchise.

The Highway Department was asked to install a flashing warning light at the school. The borough ended up buying the warning signal from Ebensburg Electric Company for $1,075.

County commissioners were petitioned to supply $7,000 from the Liquid Fuels Fund to repair Pringle, West Jackson and Madison Streets.

1969 saw Charles Haberl resign as secretary because of ill health. Joe Chimelewski was named on March 12 to be the new secretary.

Council took the initiative to try and get a doctor in the borough, by contacting the Cambria County Medical Society.

A. E. Masten & Company was retained as the borough's investment brokers.

Penn Central Railroad were advised about the poor condition of the overhead bridge and the subway under the mainline tracks. The railroad answered that they planned to seal the subway because repairs were too costly -- about $22,000.

Earl Penatzer and Mayor Sloan passed away. Glenn Wilson was appointed to Penatzer's council seat; John W. McCall was appointed Mayor. Thomas Gallardy was voted president and Francis Madison, vice president.

An agreement was signed with Harris, Henry & Potter for design of a sewerage disposal plant in association with South Fork Borough Municipal Authority. Summerhill paid $8,000 of the cost.

Mayor McCall was authorized to hire a person to oversee school children crossing the overhead bridge to and from school "until the subway situation is cleared." Eva Jane Diamond and Charles W. Diamond were employed, at separate turns, to do the patrolling.

At the biennial reorganization of 1970, Thomas Gallardy and Francis Madison were reelected president and vice president, respectively. Clair Long, Herschel Wilson and Raymond Penatzer replaced Victor Schrift, Leon White and Glenn Wilson as council members.

Joe Chimelewski was approved for $150 a month for secretarial work; Lewis Ripley, $550 a year, solicitor; Tillie Bopp, $125 a month, electric bill collector ; and Richard Frombach, $2 an hour, police chief.

Herbert Wadsworth was voted treasurer and John Weld, borough engineer. Mainline Sanitation's two-year contract amounted to $9,980 for garbage collection. The Mayor had to break the council's tied vote to approve the bid.

In May (1970), Chimelewski resigned as secretary and Robert Casti was appointed. The borough auditors -- Verna McDonald, Genevieve Werfel and Olene Bodenschatz -- expressed a wish to resign, too.

Wages of the street commissioner, laborers, electricians and other employees were increased 25¢ an hour.

Attorney John Taylor, Ebensburg, was chosen as the new solicitor.

Council split on a raise of pay to $25 a month for themselves and the Mayor. Mayor John McCall, again, broke the 3-3 tie in favor of the increase.

September, the council was advertising for a street commissioner at $2.25 per hour. About a year later, Henry A. Trauger was appointed.

1971 was the year council forbid snowmobiling within borough limits and children, under the age of 16, were to be off the streets by 10 p.m., unless accompanied by a parent or guardian.

A 1972 Dodge truck was purchased from E. L. Jones for $3,506.83. The truck body was built by Costello Body Company in Fifficktown for $475.

A $6,330 contract was awarded to Golian Brothers to pave Wentroth Avenue, Croyle and Main Streets.

Reogranization in 1972 resulted in Herschel Wilson as president and Francis Madison, vice president. Richard McCall and John R. Bodenschatz replaced Apple and Kime on council.

Mainline Sanitation is voted the garbage collection contract for $9,800, over $1,000 in new street signs are purchased and borough employees receive a 25¢ hourly increase.

Richard McCall is named assistant secretary.

A donation of $8,000 is granted the fire company to help pay for a new $25,629 fire truck.

Rita Motchenbaugh is appointed special tax collector in January 1973. She resigned at the end of the year.

$825 is contributed to Mainline Police for equipment and the borough's share for the base station.

U. S. Soil & Conservation Service repairs the wall and cleans debris in Laurel Run.

Word is received that the borough's cable television system is merging with Communications Media and converting to a microwave operation. The new agreement is signed.

Residents register complaints about trailers moving into the borough.

Dust and noise from 50 trucks daily hauling coal from Ehrenfeld Mine 38 over Summerhill streets becomes a problem. Council sets a limit for operations from 7 a.m. to 10 p.m. with no Sunday runs. The trucking contractor is asked to have all trucks tarped. He is held responsible to clean any spillage and, if necessary, flush the streets. And, he must post a $15,000 performance bond.

Golian Brothers submit a $4,560 bid to repair Dibert and Market Streets and $1,400 to resurface the alley between Jackson and Main.

Thomas Gallardy and Clair Long end their terms on council and are replaced by Glenn Wilson and James Lesko in 1974.

The borough's official roster includes Herschel Wilson, president; Richard McCall, vice president; Robert Casti, secretary; John Weld, engineer; John W. Taylor, solicitor; Richard Frombach, police chief; Chester Zdunczyk, dog law enforcement officer; Tillie Bopp, electricity bill collector; Clyde Gallardy, electrician; Henry Trauger, street commissioner; Clair Long, Forest Hills Sewer Authority representative; and Samilda Huber, borough and special tax collector.

The two-year contract with Mainline Sanitation increases to $11,695.

$50 is approved to help pay for the Mainline Police radio console at the Ebensburg Courthouse.

Another $7,232 is paid to Golian Brothers to resurface streets.

Portage National Bank begins collecting electric light bills April 1, 1975 at 10¢ per collection.

The new post office opens on Route 53.

Father Flavian of St. John's Catholic Church is attempting to get a medical clinic into Summerhill.

The council announces that building permits are required for alterations or construction within the borough.

Joann Bodenschatz is appointed assessor to fill the unexpired term of Herman Werfel.

The secretary's salary is increased by $15 a month. The street commissioner's hourly rate is raised from $2.50 to $3.00 an hour.

Louis Rosenberger is hired to construct the mini-park at $3 an hour. Completion is ordered prior to the beginning of the new school year.

$8,155 is expended to resurface streets.

Approval is received for flood insurance coverage.

Council agrees to pay up to $1,500 for a new radio mobile unit for the fire company's squad truck.

A zoning commission is named: Larry Casey, 5 years; Eugene Wess, 4 years; James Gallardy, 3 years; Louis Rosenberger, 2 years; and Ray Bodenschatz, one year.

An agreement is adopted with the regional ambulance association; Richard Dierling is named Summerhill's representative.

All borough officers are reelected for 1976-77. There is no change in council members.

Chester Zdunczyk, Gerald Hancock, Dale Gilpatrick, Dick Varner, Ricky Frombach and John Fabo are approved as back-up police from the Mainline police force.

Forest Hills Ambulance Association purchases an ambulance from Richland Township for $3,000. Summerhill signs an agreement with the association and pays its $1,600 share.

For the U. S. bicentennial celebration, Summerhill sponsors a chuck wagon with food and refreshments and a street dance.

Suzie Thomas becomes secretary in June at a salary of $125 a month.

Leslie Whitaker & Son is the only bidder to pave certain designated streets. The contract is approved for $7,527.50.

Chester Zdunczyk is paid $500 to seed the area from the overhead bridge to the former subway.

The elementary school building is leased from Forest Hills School District from December 1, 1976 to November 30, 1977.

Henry Trauger is hired as full-time custodian at $3 an hour. Council meetings are moved from the fire hall. Chief Frombach and David L. Smith, police coordinator, and his secretary are given a room for Mainline Police.

During the first six months of 1977, Penelec offers to buy Summerhill's light plant. It is refused.

Summerhill sponsors the County Borough Association's Spring meeting and banquet at New Germany Grove in April.

Zdunczyk resigns as dog law enforcement officer; Jack Aslane of South Fork is hired at $30 per calendar quarter.

Summerhill Real Estate Tax	
2 1/2 mills	1968-1970
5 mills	1971-1973
7 1/2 mills	1874
10 mills	1975-1977

The Flood of 1977

The local weather forecast for July 19, 1977 called for a chance of thunder shower at night and a low near 70 degrees. The next day was to be partly cloudy, hot and humid with a 20% chance of rain. Instead, the Johnstown area was pelted with 8 to 12 inches of rain on these two days.

The National Oceanic and Atmospheric Administration (NOAA) explained that "the large-scale pattern involved a Bermuda High, which produced a flow of warm, moist air from the southwest to the northwest and pushed the westerly winds northward."

1936 flooding around Bodenschatz's Garage, Summerhill. (Credit: Jack Bodenschatz)

1936 flooding at Ehrenfeld as photographed by H. F. Snyder of Summerhill. (Credit: Mabel Duffy)

1936 flooding in Summerhill. (Credit: Anna C. Jordan)

1936 flooding along Laurel Run. (Credit: Anna C. Jordan)

Marlin B. Mervine (center), 1977 flood victim, and his family (Credit: Elsie Mervine)

1977 flood damage to Mervine home. (Credit: Elsie Mervine)

Ragin Laurel Run in 1977. (Credit: Elsie Mervine)

Another view of water damages to the Mervine basement and garage. (Credit: Elsie Mervine)

NOAA reported that a squall line had formed in the northwestern part of Pennsylvania. A small storm at 7 p. m. had dropped a half-inch of rain over Johnstown while a late afternoon storm was well to the east. The heavy squall line, they said, moved to the south-southeast during the night, but the western edge of the storm system remained nearly stationary. The western boundary "acted like a mountain, forcing the moist air that moved from about southwest to northeast to rise and produce continuously new storms over Johnstown."

The storm increased in intensity and by two or three in the morning of July 20, thousands of people were ravaged by water. Streams ran wild, water dams broke, bridges and roads were damaged, properties destroyed and lives lost.

The constant pounding of thunder resounded like an earth quake. Between the lightning and thunder, very few people got a good night's sleep. At daybreak, many were in total shock. Communities found themselves isolated without electricity or telephone services. The water was contaminated. There was no where to escape.

When the final statistics were collected, the area's losses included 77 dead -- over 3,000 dwellings ruined -- 100 miles of roads closed -- 20 bridges damaged or washed out -- 3,300 motor vehicles demolished and -- 8.2 million pounds of food lost.

Damages over an eight-county area exceeded $300 million.

Over 5,600 families were displaced and temporarily housed in mobile trailers, schools, church halls and other accomodations.

In Summerhill, Laurel Run went on a rampage and caused the evacuation of residents living between the creek and Ebensburg Road. The volunteer firemen evacuated about 50 families during the height of the flooding; some unable to return for several days. Summerhill firemen also helped evacuate residents in the neighboring Ehrenfeld area.

About 20 Summerhill properties along Laurel Run were destroyed with the total loss reaching an estimated $150,000.

A number of cars were destroyed or badly damaged. Paul Cronauer was injured when he attempted to drive his pickup truck over a privately-owned bridge to his brother's house on the other side of Laurel Run. The truck plunged into the swift waters and was washed downstream. Tom Haberl is credited with saving Paul's life by pulling him from the creek.

Marlin B. Mervine, 65, wasn't as fortunate. He was swept away as he tried to move his car from his flooded driveway. Marlin had gone to the cellar steps with his son to move the two cars, a camper and boat parked outside his garage. The waters had washed away a corner of the garage and basement. The boat had been washed away.

He directed his son to get into one of the cars and he would push from behind. Apparently not realizing the depth and velocity of the moving water, he was washed downstream. His body was found the next morning in a tree near the school.

Marlin Mervine left his widow, the former Elsie Pringle, and the following children: Marlin A., now living in Loretto; Gloria, wife of Alan Orris, Orlando, Florida; Kathy, wife of Daniel Leatherman, Baltimore, Maryland; Ginger, wife of Bob Johnson, Brockway, Pennsylvania; and David, South Fork.

Mrs. Elsie Mervine had the home repaired and continues to make her home there.

When a monument was installed in Central Park, Johnstown, commemorating area residents who died in the flood, the name of Marlin Mervine was omitted. It has been added as the only Summerhill flood victim.

A new concrete wall has been built along properties which abut Laurel Run. Rip-rap has been placed at the other locations.

Moving Into the 1980s

Eugene Gene Amigh, Eugene "Mike" Wess, Charles Tremel, Bob Penatzer and Dan Penatzer were new councilmen from 1978 to 1981.

The 1982 council was made up of Jack Bodenschatz (president), Dan Penatzer (vice president), Herschel Wilson, Mike Wess, Richard Dierling, Charles Tremel and Bob Penatzer.

Janet S. Thomas was the secretary-treasurer; Allan Berkhimer, Mayor; Jack Taylor, solicitor; Rick Chimelewski, street commissioner; Bob McCormick, electrician; and Richard Frombach, police chief.

Barbara Bodenschatz was appointed assessor.

Zoning And School Purchase Become A Big Issue

Council held a public meeting **September 25, 1982** to present a borough zoning plan. About 20 residents attended.

According to official council minutes, some residents expressed opposition. Others were concerned about the requirement limiting the number of families living in one house, only two pets per household and restrictions of building ten feet from a neighbor's property line. There were those who questioned the restriction of building more than a two-story home.

Council explained existing situations would not be affected and zoning would not create a need for higher taxes. It would help control future undesirable developments. And, variances could be granted.

A petition signed by 96 residents opposing the proposals was presented to the council.

Council's regular **October 12 meeting** was attended by more residents. They wanted to know why council couldn't vote on the zoning at this meeting.

A resident said the borough did not need a zoning ordinance since the town had not changed for many years and they could not forsee problems without zoning regulations.

The **largest public meeting in Summerhill's history** drew 100 people **November 17, 1982** to protest the proposed zoning. "NO ZONING FOR US, SUMMERHILL SAYS" was the headline of Bob Sefick's Johnstown Tribune-Democrat story. "SUMMERHILL CITIZENS STILL OPPOSE ZONING" was the Portage Dispatch's headline.

Attorney Norman Krumenacker III was hired by the residents as their spokesman but this did not prevent individual citizens speaking out.

Council members defended the zoning proposal because there was no room for growth in the borough and any expansion would have to be in the back yards. This would create overcrowding, unsale conditions and decreasing property values. Zoning would help the borough qualify for funding and regulate future development.

One resident was quoted as saying "Take a look at this room. People are here who lived all their lives in Summerhill. They created it and made it what it is, so why do you want to change it?"

A councilman said Summerhill is changing from a predominently older to a younger group. "The problem," he said, "is we don't know what will happen in the future. We have to control and protect what we have."

Another resident admonished the councilmen that they are paid servants and "why don't you present it to the citizens and find out what they want, it is their decision not yours."

This meeting was adjourned following the statement from a member of the group that "I would rather live next door to turkeys than to have them sitting on council."

Mayor Berkhimer was applauded at the **December meeting** when he told 30 residents that "I feel that overcrowding can be controlled by ordinances and is being controlled by ordinance in other communities ... I will certainly vote my veto power if the zoning ordinance comes to a vote."

Jay Hershberger questioned the borough's payment of $6,950 to the Forest Hills School District for the purchase of the **Summerhill school building.** This represented the second payment according to an earlier agreement.

Hershberger reported that his research revealed the school district never owned the ballfield and suggested the borough withhold payment. Council agreed to do so and get further clarification.

All decisions were rescinded from the December 2 council meeting because, according to Hershberger, the advertisement did not appear 24 hours in advance. Hershberger felt this was a violation of the Sunshine Act.

Council ran into trouble again in January 1983 when it had to reschedule its announced January 11 to the 18th because it failed to advertise the meeting.

Public notice under the "sunshine law" is required at least three days prior to the time of the first regularly-scheduled meeting of the new year.

There had been speculation by residents that the borough was delaying the meeting because of a controversy over zoning.

40 residents showed up for the **January 18, 1983 council meeting** at which it was decided not to act on the proposed zoning ordinance and to meet February 22 to discuss revisions.

A former councilman said he met only one supporter and judging from attendance at meetings, public opinion is strongly anti-zoning. "What the council has managed to do, by backing off," he said, "is create a division he's never seen."

Another sentiment among the residents was cynicism.

"You're gonna keep holding us off and holding us off until no one comes anymore," a resident said. "Then you'll vote it right in."

The Portage Dispatch runs a headline "SUMMERHILL WITHOUT CLEAR SCHOOL DEED" on February 16, 1983. It was reported by Solicitor John Taylor he could not find any deed of record for the ground in question and that the school district is trying to acquire a deed by a quiet title procedure through the courts.

After some discussion, council agreed to meet with the school district, its solicitor, Attorney Taylor and Jay Harshberger.

Approximately 25 residents attended the **March 8 council meeting** and learned that zoning workshops had been held and would continue to be held until the proposed zoning plan is completely understood.

Meanwhile, Cambria County Board of Elections ruled that the citizens petition to place the zoning question on the May primary ballot was rejected.

Jay Harshberger questioned council about the legality of holding an executive session during a regular council meeting. Council said it would get an opinion from the solicitor.

Larry Casey's resignation from the borough planning and zoning commission was accepted at this meeting.

At a **special meeting in March,** the second payment of $6,954 to Forest Hills School District was approved upon Solicitor John Taylor's report: the agreement between the borough and the school district was approved by the courts November 8, 1981 with four equal installments of $6,954 due before the 31st of December of each year.

Council voted to honor the agreement.

The feelings of council members at this point was perhaps best expressed by Dan Penatzer who stated that no matter what has been brought up by council, we have been having arguments about legal opinions.

Jack Bodenschatz concluded that there had been a lot of questions raised and nothing changed since the school contract was signed.

Time Out For The Television Contract

While all the controversy was going on about zoning and the school building, council rejected a proposal from TeleMedia Cable TV of Carrolltown to add ESPN at an additional cost of 35¢ a month or possibly adding ESPN and WGN Chicago for 50¢ and eliminate the educational channel.

Pennsylvania Department of Transportation wanted information on utility sites for the relocation of the new Summerhill bridge.

In addition, council was looking for a new street commissioner.

Jay Harshberger was granted permission to inspect all documents pertaining to the school building sale because he indicated there were a number of irregularities.

Council approved the addition of ESPN, a 24-hour all sports network, to the cable system at the **May 10, 1983** session. They rejected the WGN addition because WQED, the educational channel, had to be dropped. But, upon learning that South Fork and Ehrenfeld approved the WGN addition, it was decided to place petitions at various locations in Summerhill to get opinions from the subscribers.

A Spirited 1983 May Primary

The May 17 primary was somewhat unusual.

Under a claim that it was "Time For A Change", the concerned citizens endorsed Mike Cronauer, Jill Rosporski and George Bodenschatz, all Democrats, for council.

The handbill made references to "more than a year complaints regarding council have surfaced. When the complaints multiplied, the citizens began to monitor council's activities and found the complaints valid."

Listed were the waste of taxpayers dollars, abuse of powers, violation of trust and failure to respond to the wishes of the majority.

Espcially highlighted were zoning, the school building deal and council's "disregard of the letter of the law."

Voters were advised write-in stickers were available to vote these candidates on the Republican ballot.

As a rebuttal, Dan Penatzer circulated a letter, under his signature, accusing the group of "circulating petitions filled with half truths and innuendoes that deliberately misrepresent the facts. These petitions, signed by people that later admit they did not even know what they were signing, give this group the appearance of being larger than they really are."

The letter went on to mention that this concerned group criticized the borough council for purchasing the ball field, accused council of fiscal irresponsibility, charcterized their children and friends as hoodlums terrorizing the mimi-park area, had the basketball court moved, and attacked the volunteer fire department.

Concerned Group Seats Two

Two candidates supported by the citizens' group were elected in the November election. The third hopeful backed by the group lost to a write-in candidate.

Voter turnout was 93% of the registered voters!
The results:

Council (3 to be elected)
Mike Cronauer	175 (supported by citizens group)
Charles Tremel	156 (write-in and incumbent)
George C. Bodenschatz	153 (citizens group support)
John W. McCall II	142 (write-in)
Jill R. Rosporski	138 (citizens group support)
Richard Chimelewski	134 (write-in)

Assessor
Barbara Bodenschatz	241 (unopposed)

Auditor (2-Year term)
William Dipko	204 (unopposed)

Auditor (4-Year term)
Joseph R. Huber	106 (write-in elected)
Lawrence Wilburn	45 (write-in)

Auditor (6-Year term)
Lawrence Wilburn	103 (write-in elected)
Joseph Huber	40 (write-in)
Charles Treme	16 (write-in)

The 1984 Council

The newly elected council members began their two-year terms in January 1984. They replaced Jack Bodenschatz and Bob Penatzer who chose not to run for reelection.

The new council elected Dan Penatzer president; Charles Tremel, vice president; and Janet S. Thomas, secretary.

Kevin Bodenschatz retained his job as street commissioner as did John Taylor, solicitor; Robert McCormick, electrician; and Richard Frombach, part-time police chief. Rich Varner, Rick Frombach, Dale Gilpatrick and Chester Zundczyk were approved as part-time police.

Hinks and Locher were hired as borough engineers.

Mike Cronauer resigned by July of his first year. George Bodenschatz resigned in February 1985. Lawrence Wilburn was appointed to replace Bodenschatz.

Dan Penatzer resigned as president in June 1984 but remained as a councilman. Charles Tremel had advanced to president and George Bodenschatz to vice president.

August (1984) Kevin Bodenschatz gave up the street commissioner's job and is replaced by Leonard Straple.

The following month, Allan Berkhimer resigns as mayor; Dennis Cobaugh becomes mayor January 1986.

More Personnel Changes

Changes continued in 1986.

Dan Penatzer resigned his council seat in September because of his county job. Jack Bodenschatz was appointed as his replacement.

Attorney Dennis Stofko was retained as solicitor at $50 a meeting and a $300 annual retainer.

New council members in 1986 were John W. McCall II, Joe Huber and Jill Rosporski.

Charles Tremel completed his term as councilman in 1987. Ralph Hamilton became the new member.

When Joe Huber moved from the borough and resigned, in January 1989, Charles Tremel was reinstated.

The 1991 Council

There has been stability in council's membership since 1988.

The members in 1991 included Lawrence Wilburn, an accountant with L. Robert Kimball Consulting Engineers and Architects of Ebensburg, president; and Jack Bodenschatz, sales manager for Prudential Life Insurance Company in Indiana, vice president.

Other members were John W. McCall II, McCall's Jeep/Eagle; Jill Rosporski, sales representative for Reynolds Tobacco Company; Charles Tremel, customer relations department at Penelec, Johnstown; Mike Wess, employee at Universal Electric, Johnstown; and Ralph Hamilton, retired.

Samilda Huber has been borough tax collector since 1974. She collects borough real estate, per capita and earned income taxes, in addition to the residents' county and school taxes.

Dennis Cobaugh has been mayor since January 1986.

Vincent Kitchick began as street commissioner in November 1988.

Dennis Stofko was first elected borough solicitor in 1986.

Bob McCormick is the long-time electric plant electrician. Dan Penatzer, as the electric plant secretary, is responsible for billing customers. The bills are computer-generated by INFOCON of Ebensburg.

There no longer is a borough policeman. These duties are now handled by the state police.

Garbage now is collected by Croyle Township on a contracted agreement.

TCI of Carrolltown remains as the cable television provider for the borough.

Daniel L. Penatzer

Dan Penatzer has been secretary-treasurer of the borough since July 1987.

He is Cambria County's executive director of emergency services and manager of the Forest Hills Ambulance Association. He served eight years as Summerhill councilman, three of them as president.

A 1976 graduate of Forest Hills High School, he attended St. Francis College, Loretto, where he majored in chemistry.

For six years, he was a sales agent for Prudential Insurance Company, before buying his own independent agency in 1984. He is currently in the process of selling this agency.

Dan is a member and former chief of the Summerhill Volunteer Fire Company and a certified paramedic.

About 1986, he was named the county's emergency management director. He developed a hazardous-materials response team and a countywide emergency plan as well as emergency plans for public schools, industries with hazardous wastes and many municipalities. Currently, he is establishing the county's 911 emergency dispatch system.

During the 1991 primary election, he resigned his county position to run for county commissioner. He placed sixth out of a field of nine Democrats with 6,188 votes. This was his first try at a countywide elective office.

After the primaries, the commissioners rehired him as the executive director of emergency services.

Dan's father, Earl Penatzer, was a member of Summerhill Council from 1957 until his death in 1969, a time he was serving as president.

No Change In 1992 Membership

There will be no change in Summerhill's governing body for 1992.

Three incumbents -- Ralph Hamilton, Jack Bodenschatz and Lawrence Wilburn -- were nominated without opposition in the primaries. They were reelected in November 1991 by votes of 170, 175 and 165, respectively.

Dennis Cobaugh also was unopposed for another term as mayor as is Samilda Huber, tax collector.

An Associated Press writer, Cliff Hadley, in July 1991 authored an article in which he said "officials in many small towns across the nation have little to smile about these days. Experts say people in their 20s, 30s and 40s too often choose to sit on the political sidelines rather than run for the city council or school board as their parents did."

This does not hold true for Summerhill.

It is amazing when there are only some 400 registered voters that there has never been a lack of qualified candidates. Service is regarded as a civic duty and responsibility. Whenever the need arises, the citizens respond. This is an obligation that the town's predecessors accepted and passed along to their children.

This attitude appears to be strong enough to carry Summerhill into the 21st century.

Chapter 15
Providing Community Services

Under the borough form of government in Pennsylvania, it is the responsibility of a seven-member council and a mayor to provide the different services a community needs.

These include sidewalks, paved streets, waterworks, recreational areas, police and fire protection, electricity, health and sanitation regulations, snow removal, water supply, garbage collection, sewage treatment, drainage facilities, traffic control, building codes, etc.

Local laws, called ordinances, are passed to meet local needs and supplement state and federal statues. These local ordinances require the approval of the mayor whose has veto power.

Not all needs can be met immediately. Most require funding which must be raised by taxation. Summerhill depends upon taxes levied on real estate, per capita and earned income and profits generated from its own electric light plant.

Some funds are available for specific purposes from county, state and federal sources.

Electric Light Plant

The electric light plant was one of the best decisions Summerhill leaders ever made. It generates enough profit annually to keep real estate taxes at one of the lowest in the county. It also distributes the cost of government among all residents not primarily property owners.

When Summerhill was incorporated as a borough, its 1892 tax levy was 4 mills. Today, one hundred years later, it is 8.5 mills, the same rate since 1984. By constrast, neighboring South Fork Borough had a tax rate of 3 mills in 1893 but is now at 30 mills.

Historian John McCormick in his 1906 history of Summerhill claimed that the town would soon have "the modern advantages of electric lights" because Albert Oaks had recently secured a charter for a plant.

A 1907 ordinance gave Summer Hill Electric, Light, Heat and Power Company authority to establish a plant in the borough. But, in 1911, S. T. Penrose was given permission "to string electric lines of transmission and distribution of electric current."

The Summerhill Women's Club history claims electricity for the light plant was first purchased in 1913 and street lights turned on for the first time on Thanksgiving Day -- November 28, 1913. Apparently, this was the beginning of the borough-owned light plant.

Summerhill Electric Light Building. Note transformers on the poles.

Closeup view of the electric building, located on Main Street.

Minutes of the council for that year were unavailable but the meeting of August 7, 1916 mentioned the Summer Hill Municipal Light Plant and that Irwin Berchneider was hired to read meters at $4 a month and authorized to cut power when customers did not pay after a 15-day notice.

An ordinance approved in 1918 provided for the management and operation of the plant and established rates, terms and conditions of and provisions for enforcement and collection.

R. H. Costello was listed as secretary and superintendent at a salary of $75 a year.

Evidently, there was a problem in 1921 with people shooting out street lights because council offered a $5 reward for information leading to the arrest and conviction of perpetrators.

Costello's salary was increased to $300 a year by 1923.

C. W. Simendinger became superintendent of the light plant in 1924. His job was to read meters, make bills, take care of service lines, meters, etc. In addition, he was to repair all breaks caused by accident and "do everything connected with lines and plant except new work" for $25 a month. New work would be paid at 85¢ an hour.

R. H. Costello remained as secretary at $20 a year. Emma Sherbine collected bills for a 1 1/2% commission.

A notation in the December 1925 council minutes reads that Penn Central Light & Power agreed to deliver 6,600 volts to the borough substation "which is to be reduced to 2,300 volts." The power company agreed to pay the cost of installation to the borough line; the borough would pay the cost of installing an automatic oil switch.

1926 brought a change of personnel -- Charles Hettle as secretary at $10 a month; Cletus Schrift, superintendent at $30 a month; and Bertha Kurtz, collector.

The December council minutes noted the electrician's salary was $20 a month and his duties were to read meters, keep globes in street lights and keep "the clock in shape at all times." C. W. Simendinger was listed as the electrician.

The next change was noted in April 1928 with J. T. Long as superintendent of the light plant, Other employees remained the same until 1932.

In December of that year, Alfred E. Lindsey was named electrician/meter reader. He served until May 1933. Ben Gallardy began a long tenure as electrician the following month.

There was a problem with plant superintendent when John T. Long resigned in February 1933 and the position was filled by several councilmen on a month-to-month basis until John M. Sloan took it from 1934 to 1937. Afterwards, the position was abolished.

Meanwhile, in 1936, Mary Brown replaced Bertha Kurtz as bill collector and council also agreed to extend service outside the borough to Marcellus and Anna Beyer, Leroy and Lula Meyers, Charles and Dollie Gable, A. L. and

Bessie Lang, James S. and Margaret Wilson, H. E. and Annie Shetler and Emma Mathieson.

Rates were reduced in the summer of 1937.

Penn Central became Pennsylvania Edison Company.

Louise Bopp was the new bill collector in 1939.

Penelec came into being in 1946 through a merger of Penn Edison and several other companies. Penelec has supplied power ever since.

Without records available from 1940 to 1968, there is no history to report for that period. However, in August 1968, Charles Haberl was secretary; Clyde Gallardy, electrician; and Tillie Bopp, bill collector.

In September 1968, a petition was presented by residents of Croyle Township, in the area toward Triangle Area High School, to relieve them from the contract with the light plant. Council agreed.

The job of electric plant secretary was combined with that of borough secretary -- a practice which still prevails.

By 1974, borough minutes show that Clyde Gallardy was still electrician and Carl Bodenschatz, his helper. They were given an increase of 50¢ an hour which brought their compensation to $4.05 and $3.00 per hour, respectively.

Customers were given the option to pay their light bills at the bank in 1975. Meter deposits went from $20 to $50, new installations were $60 and a $2 flat fee was added each month.

In the Summer of 1976, it was noted that power from Penelec was costing the borough about $6,500 a month (a 17 1/2% increase) and the plant was operating at a loss. Therefore, a dollar was added "on the front end" and a 5% increase imposed across the board on all billings. At the same time, a contract was let to have bills computerized.

The 1980s have seen several more increases. The rates were changed from a sliding scale to a single rate for each kilowatt-hour and an initial charge of $5 a month. In 1980, the rate was 4.6¢ per kilowatt-hour. The monthly charge was advanced to $6 and the kilowatt-hour rate increased to 6.75¢ by 1986.

The cost of electrical power for Summerhill users is still lower than regular Penelec home customers who were paying an average of 8 cents per kwh during this same period. And, besides, Summerhill finances its borough services from the plant's profits and keeps the local real estate taxes far below that of other municipalities.

Today, many municipalities wish they owned their own electric plant but to do so they are now required to purchase all transmission lines and equipment which makes such a purchase a poor buy.

The borough's 1991 budget contains $150,000 for the purchase of electrical power from Penelec, $5,200 for wages and $3,000 for electrical supplies. Interest from a reserve fund built from previous profits supplements the annual income of the electric light plant operation.

Robert L. McCormick, a Penelec employee, works as Summerhill's electrician. He has handled the borough's needs on a pay-as-needed basis since the late 1970s. Carl Bodenschatz has been assistant electrician from the early 1970s.

Water Supply

A charter is recorded at the Cambria County Courthouse that Summerhill Borough Water Company was authorized to do business as of November 9, 1900. It was capitalized with 10 shares of stock at $100 a share. The original subscribers and first directors were G. W. Tappan, Summerhill, six shares; A. L. Price, Summerhill, one share; and the following Ebensburg residents with one share each: William Leckie, Philip N. Schettig and T. H. Hasson.

What happened to this company is unconfirmed but in 1905 Summerhill Council complained that the Cambria County Water Supply Company cut or broke the tops of the fire hyrants. Council authorized its solicitor to bring suit against the company.

John McCormick, in 1906, claimed that Summerhill was supplied water by the Cambria County Water Supply Company.

This company, he wrote, also supplied Ehrenfeld and that A. F. McKennon, Ehrenfeld, was the superintendent.

More confusion is evident because there was Forest Water Company which began in 1901 to supply water to Croyle Township and, in 1903, they leased all property and rights to Cambria County Water Company. But, in 1934, Summerhill council minutes recorded that Summit Water Company was to install the borough's fire hydrants.

The 1979 Summerhill Borough comprehensive plan prepared by the Cambria County Planning Commission reports that, at that time, 159 housing units were provided with water by Highland Sewer and Water Authority and 48 units depended upon individual wells.

Today, there are only a few properties in Summerhill that depend solely on well water.

Highland Sewer and Water Authority was formed in 1955 with the purchase of Geistown Borough's old water system.

The 1977 flood caused the collapse of Sandy Run Reservoir which provided 20% of Highland's water.

Customers in Summerhill and Wilmore were told to boil water July 1, 1978 because of a broken chlorinator. The notice was lifted a week later.

The installation of new water mains and a storage tank in Summerhill were completed by the authority January 25, 1980 to improve service to the St. Michael and Ehrenfeld areas.

Telephone Service

There were a number of local telephone companies providing services to Summerhill in the first two decades of the 20th century.

Summerhill had the Johnstown, Wilmore Rural and Bell Telephone Companies. There also was a time when business establishments had two phone numbers; one for Johnstown and the other for Summerhill and surrounding county areas.

Today, one company, GTE, provides local service throughout the entire area. Its operation is regulated by the Pennsylvania Public Utility Commission. Deregulation in recent years has changed the industry and offered many new service and equipment choices.

Locally, GTE Phone Marts are located at Richland Mall and its downtown Johnstown location. A variety of telephones, answering machines and other accessories can be purchased there.

Customers now may own or lease telephones. There are choices whether a consumer assumes repair responsibilities or contracts this service with the company.

Payment for monthly charges may be made by mail to a center in Indianapolis, Indiana, or at designated locations within the service area. In Summerhill, such payments may be made at Portage National Bank on Croyle Street.

Long distance guidelines which took effect in 1984 allow the telephone company to provide local and long distance services within small geographical regions called LATAs -- Local Access and Transport Areas. The company provides access to long distance companies connecting calls across LATA boundaries.

Summerhill is in a telephone area with an 814 code number and is part of the 495 exchange which also includes South Fork, Ehrenfeld, St. Michael and Wilmore.

It has become common practice to have more than one telephone within a household. Cordless models are popular because they can be used indoors and outdoors. A newer advancement is a cellular unit which can be operated from a moving automobile.

Sewer Facilities

Simply writing that "Summerhill has a pretty good sewerage system. Drainage is good", John McCormick ended his report on Summerhill's sewerage system in his 1906 history.

As implied earlier in this history, completion of the present system was achieved over a long period of time and at great expense.

Summerhill has a combined sewerage system which collects sanitary sewage from residential and commercial properties along with storm water run-off. Both are discharged into the Little Conemaugh River, running along Route 53.

According to the 1970 U. S. Housing Census, 177 housing units used this system. 24 had septic tanks or cesspools and six used wildcat collection or individual direct discharge.

In 1969, a feasibility study was completed to recommend how the borough could provide sewerage treatment service. It was suggested Summerhill use interceptor sewers and construct a sewage treatment plant on the Little Conemaugh River.

The impetus for this study was new state legislation that requires each municipality to prepare a plan or participate in or formally adopt one on a regional or county basis.

Thus, in 1970, Summerhill Borough spent $30,000 for a proposed sewerage treatment plan. Then, they tried to get a $360,720 federal grant to construct the facility. By 1971, council realized that their proposal was worthless and they would have to accept a regional plan. Council decided to become part of the Forest Hills Sewer Authority.

As of July 2, 1991, the county planning commission, of which Summerhill's John Costello is secretary, endorsed plans for developing a regional sewage-treatment system for northern Richland Township, Adams and Summerhill Townships, and Summerhill and South Fork Boroughs.

Cable Television Service

Due to the area's mountainous terrain and a limited number of regional televison stations, a cable system is required to provide a wider choice of programming. In recent years, cable television companies have prospered in areas where there is a concentration of subscribers. Usually, it is not profitable for cable companies to operate in scattered rural areas.

Summerhill Council has contracted with TCI of Carrolltown to provide borough cable services for many years. Subscribers choose the plan they want and pay the cable company on an individual basis. The borough receives a commission on monthly sales.

In 1988, Borough Council was investigating the possibility of establishing its own cable system. Mark Blaisdell, manager of Wilmore Borough Cable TV, met with Summerhill's council members to explain costs and probable income.

A decision was reached that it would be too difficult for Summerhill to compete with the larger, private companies.

Effective June 1, 1991, TCE Cable raised its basic fee from $16.65 to $17.45 a month and expanded basic service from 40¢ to $1.20 a month.

Basic service includes about 25 channels, including regular stations telecasting from Johnstown, Altoona, University Park, Pittsburgh, Nashville,

New York and special channels like Local/Meadows Racing, Discovery, Weather, Lifetime, Family, Nickleodeon, J. C. Penney and MTV.

The expanded basic service includes USA Network, American Movie Classics, ESPN, Turner (TNT) and KBL Sports.

At additional individual cost, Home Box Office, Cinemax and Showtime movie channels are available.

Garbage Collection

Weekly garbage collection is another service Summerhill Borough provides some 250 residences and 20 businesses, free of charge. A growing number of municipalities collect separate garbage fees to pay for this service.

After years under contract with Mainline Sanitation of Portage, Summerhill Council, in January 1991, voted to go with a two-year contract with Croyle Township at a cost of $24,500 the first year and $25,500 the second year.

Mainline, which was recently sold to Chambers, and Home Sanitation of Gallitzin submitted higher bids.

Fire Protection

Another important service that a borough council must provide is fire protection. This involves fire hydrants with an adequate supply of water and an organization with personnel and equipment always ready to respond to emergencies.

It appears that Summerhill had a hose-and-cart type of operation in its earliest years.

South Fork Borough began a volunteer fire company in 1908. Since it was the only company, it provided protection, at no cost, to adjoining areas. For three decades, South Fork Borough and its fire company absorbed the cost through taxes and contributions.

By 1931, overtures were made by South Fork Borough Council that neighboring areas should pay an annual contracted amount for future fire protection. But, agreements were not finalized at that time and services continued with periodic donations from the service area.

This arrangement proved unsastisfactory and, in the 1950s, South Fork Council was concerned that its taxpayers were assuming too great a share of the fire company's operating costs. An ordinance established a fee of 1 1/2 mills based on the assessed valuation of properties to be protected. Under this arrangement, Summerhill paid $125 a year, beginning in 1958. This payment ended in March 1959 when Summerhill Borough notified South Fork that their volunteer fire company had been accepted into the county firefighters association.

Each year thereafter, Summerhill Council has contributed a budgeted amount of money to its fire company. The contribution in 1991 was increased to $2,500. Other funds are raised by the volunteers through sub sales and public solicitations.

Annual Borough Budgets

The preparation of an annual budget is one of the most important exercises of a governing unit. It establishes priorities and restricts expenditures within expected income.

Every borough is required to use a standard form and file a copy with the Commonwealth. Citizens must be given an opportunity to review it before adoption. It must be balanced. There are no provisions to accumulate a deficit like the federal government. It is pay as-you-go.

Summerhill, like its counterparts, has been faced with accelerating costs but because of its profitable electric plant operation, it has not been forced to burden its property owners with high real estate taxes.

The significance of how much budgets have changed is seen by the following general fund figures:

1938	$7,040
1972	$27,350
1982	$315,150
1991	$389,430

The budget for 1992 in the amount of $484,280 is 25% higher than 1991. The increase is about $100,000. Yet, it is balanced without a tax increase and no charge for garbage collection. Besides, the $5 per capita tax is dropped for 1992!

This again points up the uniquesness of Summerhill Borough. Even though it is one of the smaller boroughs in the county and the larger ones are increasing garbage fees and real estate taxes, Summerhill has kept its real estate tax at 8 1/2 mills since 1984, without any cuts in services!

The major items of the current budget follow:

$4,800 for council and mayor salaries;
$1,700 for auditor fees;
$2,400 for tax collection commissions;
$3,600 for legal advertising;
$3,650 for fire department workmen's compensation;
$2,500 for fire department contribution;
$26,500 for garbage collection;
$8,000 for street commissioner wages;
$8,599 for laborer wages;
$2,500 for construction materials;
$3,890 for electrician wages;
$1,000 for electrical laborer wages;

$3,000 for electric supplies;
$2,160 for electric bill processing;
$150,000 for purchase of electricity;
$16,500 transfer to the centennial fund; and
$11,250 for insurance

At the same time, $29,440 is earmarked for the centennial fund budget from which the following expenditures are anticipated: book publishing, $10,000; fireworks, $5,000; parade, $3,000; entertainment, $2,000; tents, $2,000; advertisement, $4,500; and banners, $1,500.

Police Protection

Protection of person and property is another community need which has been addressed by council.

For most of Summerhill's history, the borough employed a police officer, both on a full-time and part-time basis.

From 1953, Richard W. Frombach of Croyle Township was chief of police for Summerhill Borough and Croyle Township. He was appointed chief of Ehrenfeld Borough in 1965 and Wilmore Borough in 1978 and performed policing duties for Forest Hills School District.

He was instrumental in the establishment of the Mainline Police Communications Network.

Beginning as a military policeman with the U. S. Army, he returned home and joined the Croyle Township Police Department and led efforts to unify area police departments by co-founding the Mainline Police Association. He served as the association's president from 1967 to 1987.

Chief Frombach was injured in an accident August 1988 and has been on sick leave since January 23, 1989.

Since then, Summerhill Borough has turned its police protection to the Pennsylvania State Police.

Other Community Needs

March 1990, Summerhill Borough Council adopted a flood plain ordinance to comply with federal regulations.

The ordinance requires all persons, partnerships, businesses and corporations to obtain a building permit for any construction or development; provides for the issuance of such permits; sets certain minimum requirements for new construction and development within areas of the borough subject to flooding; and establishes penalties for those who fail or refuse to comply.

The schedule of fees for building permits begins at $10 and is graduated according to the total construction costs.

The Cambria-Somerset Council of Governments (COG), with offices at 1409 Somerset Avenue, Windber, is empowered with enforcement and issuance of permits.

Even though Summerhill Borough is not required to begin recycling of garbage, discussions have been held with South Fork, Ehrenfeld and Croyle Township.

October 1990, borough council went on record to support the submission of sewage facility planning module, prepared by Mark Blaisdell, for the Summerhill Volunteer Fire Company. The project would be a septic tank, sand mound filter system with discharge into Laurel Run in preparation for the construction of a new fire building.

With all its streets, alleys and sidewalks paved and the Laurel Run wall repaired, the unfinished business of the Summerhill Borough Council is a required sewage disposal plant in partnership with other political subdivisions.

World War I Veterans. Kneeling: Rupert and Bopp. Standing: Celestine Wirfel, Frank Haberl, Marcellus Beyer, Ralph Shrift. (Credit: Louis Rosenberger)

Leon Weinzierl's early home. (Credit: Lillian M. Pisarski)

This work was painted in the 1940s by Dora Simendinger, wife of John Simendinger and daughter of William McClarren. It is now displayed in the home of Mr. and Mrs. Edward DeLozier and Mrs. Stella Cullen. Mrs. DeLozier, the former Stella Simendinger, is the painter's granddaughter.
Dora Simendinger also painted (in oils) the curtain at Long's Theatre and the stations of the cross for St. John's Catholic Church.

Agnes Bodenschatz. (Credit: Lillian M. Pisarski)

Stockade next to the GBU during the nation's bicentennial celebration. Sign reads "Woe To One Who Enter Ye Honorable BuGBU nk, Stockade Gall, Fort Summerhill, PA." (Credit: Mary M. Gabany)

A school activity: Glenn Hull, Betty Mathies, Georgia Jones, Joan Werfel, Dick Davis, Roberta Duffy. (Credit: Florine Hamilton)

Another school activity: Vera Smith, Kitty Werfel, Eleanor McGough, Miss Plummer (Teacher), Maxine Shuman, Shirley Snyder. (Credit: Florine Hamilton)

John Chappell, a Summerhill coal miner. (Credit: Anna C. Jordan)

Chapter 16

Potpourri

Potpourri, according to Webster's Dictionary, is miscellany (a collection of various kinds, especially of literary works).

This chapter is reserved for such a collection of historical tidbits not included in the preceding chapters.

Item #1
Summerhill Women's Club Directory, 1965-1966
(courtesy of Gertrude Brummert)

Club officers were Mrs. Stanley Seaman, president; Mrs. John McCall, vice president and parliamentarian; Mrs. Charles Jones, secretary; and Mrs. Lester Cullen, treasurer.

Mrs. Seaman also was first vice president of the county federation.

Department chairpersons were: Miss Hilda Brummert, bookmobile; Mrs. Samuel Basile, conservation and home life; Miss Hilda Brummert, cultural heritage; Miss Mary Grace Tully, education and fine arts; Mrs. Joseph Wess, finance; Mrs. Donald Penatzer, program; Mrs. Clair Long, hospitality and membership; Mrs. Lester Cullen, newspaper publicity; Mrs. Richard Costello, yearbook publicity; Mrs. Joseph Lazration, public affairs and community improvement; and Mrs. Charles White, international affairs.

The monthly program schedule:

September -- "Real, Artificial, Dried Flower Arrangements", Mrs. J. E. Bigan

October -- "History of Folk Music", Mrs. Hugh R. Smith, director of county chorus.

November -- "Festive Desserts", demonstration by Mrs. Eunice Tibbott, extension home economist.

December -- Christmas Party (dinner meeting at St. John's Lutheran Church Parish Hall).

January -- "New Fashion Trends for Spring and Summer", Miss Olene Shrift, buyer for Penn Traffic Company.

February -- "Teenage Drinking", panel show with Mrs. Charles Jones; moderator, Mrs. Jay Harshberger, Mrs. Donald Hull, Mrs. Eldred Jones and Mrs. Donald Penatzer -- also, creative decorating with Lenox China, film and commentary.

March -- "Illegitimacy", Attorney Fremont J. McKenrick -- and election of officers.

April -- "Tour Slides of India, Thailand and Egypt", Miss Sue Green, supervisor of social studies, Richland Township High School.

May -- Spring Banquet and installation of officers. The cultural heritage department comprised of Miss Hilda Brummert (chair), Mrs. Frank Burns, Mrs. Amelia Hoover and Mrs. John Sloan. They published the History of Summerhill 1810-1966, 28 mimeographed pages; as their project.

Charter members: Doreen Basile, Gertrude Brummert, Anna Burns, May Callahan, Dolores Connelly, Stella Cullen, Dorothy Hettle, Sophie Kime, Mickey Lazration, Genevieve Lenz, Gloria Montanari, Maxine Penatzer, Florence Seaman, Mary Grace Tully and Bert Wicks.

Meetings were held in the Summerhill Fire Hall.

Item #2
Men Who Served For Our Country
(from Golden Jubilee booklet of St. John's Catholic Church, 1903-1953)
World War I

U. S. Army -- Marcellus Beyer, Leo Bopp, Rupert J. Bopp, Simon A. Bopp, Charles Brummert, Frank Brummert, Frank Burns, Lester C. Cullen, Cletus Gallardy, Frank Habrel, Joseph Habrel, John J. Penatzer, James Quinn, Bernard Seifert, Ralph A. Shrift, Sr., Clarence W. Simendinger, George E. Smith, Charles Steiger, Frank Steiger, George Steiger, Louis Weinzerl, Roy White, Thomas P. Yahner and William J. Yahner.

U. S. Navy -- Louis White.

Killed In Action -- Frank Steiger

World War II

U. S. Army -- Andrew Bantley, Michael Bantley, Nick Bantley, Peter Bantley, Donald A. Betz, Gerald M. Betz, Norman J. Betz, Jr., Louis Betz, Leo A. Bimle, John R. Bishop, Louis L. Bishop, Ralph T. Bishop, Charles Bodenschatz, Henry Bodenschatz, Robert Bodenschatz, William Bodenschatz, Cletus M. Bopp, Clifford J. Bopp, Robert Brummert, Harold Cronauer, Joseph Duffy, Robert M. Duffy, Jr., Andrew Figola, Jr., Clyde Gallardy, Donald Gallardy, James Gallardy, Thomas Gallardy, Melvin Geisler, William Hardy, Donald Hettle, Joseph Hettle, Kenneth Hettle, Regis Hettle, Vernon A. Jones, Edward Kick, John Kime, Thomas Kime, Fred Kinley, Dr. Claude Kirby, Dr. Thomas Kirby, William Kirby, Jr., Regis Kurtz, Clair C. Long, Cletus R. Long, Joseph R. Long, Regis J. Long, Paul G. Mayers, Eugene Mathieson, Francis Mathieson, Robert Mathieson, Hilary Motchenbaugh, Charles Mulvehill, John Mulvehill, John F. McCall, Michael T. McCall, Philip McCall, Robert J. McCall, Thomas Herbert McCall, Andrew Nedimyer, Earl Penatzer, John R. Penatzer, Jr., Paul R. Penatzer, John Robine, Robert

Seifert, Thomas Seifert, Michael Sherlock, Paul Sherlock, Conrad Shrift, Donald Shrift, James A. Shrift, James J. Shrift, Ralph A. Shrift, Jr., Raymond P. Shrift, Regis R. Shrift, Richard E. Shrift, Robert E. Shrift, Robert J. Shrift, Wilbur Shrift, Rachel Simendinger, Cletus Smith, Carl Strawbridge, Robert Wallace, Gerald Weinzierl, Raymond Werfel, Robert Werfel, Arthur Wess, Joseph C. Wess, Louis Wess, Charles White, Edward White, Jr., James White, Russell White, Gerald C. Wilburn, John L. Wilburn, Regis P. Wilburn, Carl Wirfel, James Wirfel, Regis Wirfel, Leo C. Yahner, Paul A. Yahner, Thomas P. Yahner and William J. Yahner.

Killed in Action -- Fred Kinley, Philip McCall and Regis P. Wilburn.

U. S. Navy -- Edward Bodenschatz, Jr., Dr. Charles P. Jones, Kenneth A. Long, Gerald J. Penrod, John B. Penrod, John R. Shrift, Raymond L. Shrift, Wilfred L. Simendinger, William Wess and Norbert Wirfel.

Merchant Marines -- Clair Rosenberger.

Women's Army Corps. -- Margaret Kurtz.

U. S. Coast Guard Women's Reserve -- Elizabeth Robine.

Korean War

U. S. Army -- Ronald L. Bimle, Myron J. Blaner, Richard Bodenschatz, Donald T. Bopp, Lewis R. Brown, Edward Fitzsimmons, Dennis C. Jones, Camillus H. Long, Raymond C. Long, J. Lawrence Long, James J. McCall, Richard J. McCall, Edward McDunn, Charles Penatzer, Raymond F. Penatzer, Robert W. Penatzer, Albert Seifert, Jr., Clement A. Seifert, James A. Shrift, Leroy Shrift, James Wallace, David Wess, Donald Wess, Raymond Wess, Richard Wess, Leonard Weinzierl, Paul White, Raymond White, Charles Wirfel, Lawrence Wirfel, Paul Wirfel and Alfred E. Yahner.

U.S. Marine -- Robert L. Betz, Joseph V. Bimle and Ernest J. Penatzer.

U.S. Navy -- Kenneth A. Long and John B. Penrod.

Item #3
Community Shelter Plan For Cambria County
Approved by Commissioners May 15, 1968
(courtesy of Gertrude Brummert)

The plan was developed to inform people where to go and what to do in case of nuclear attack. It was prepared by the professional staff of the Cambria County Planning Commission working closely with the Cambria County Office of Civil Defense and under the supervision of the Army Corps of Engineers.

The nearest shelter areas for Summerhill were in South Fork at the Union Depot Bank Building, Siegal's Store or South Fork School.

If people could not reach public shelters in a reasonable time, they were advised to go to the best protected part of the house or building in which they found themselves.

Practice air raid drills were held during this time.

Item #4
Notes From The Burgess Record Book 1892-1919
(from Summerhill Women's Club History)

The following incidents were taken from records of the Burgess from 1892 to 1919. They provide an idea of some of problems experienced during the early years of Summerhill's history.

The first entry made October 14, 1892 was to note a license was issued to Robert McGill to sell books. Cost of the license was 50¢.

HOGS allowed to run at large in the borough brought a $4 fine in 1894.

PLAYING BALL ON SUNDAY cost violators a $2 fine and 50cents costs each in 1894. One, in default of payment, spent 10 hours in the borough jail.

KEEPING A FILTHLY STABLE too close to a dwelling drew a fine of $3, costs of $2 and constable fee of $1 in 1897. The defendant was given 24 hours to put the place in a sanitary condition.

DRUNK ON SATURDAY NIGHT was the reason for a fine of one dollar and costs. The accused was jailed and his horse taken to Patrick McCall for safe keeping. Released Sunday morning, he promised his mother-in-law would pay the fine Monday. He also was fined 50¢ extra for the condition of his cell (1897).

USING UNBECOMING LANGUAGE to a young lady cost a man $3 plus costs in 1899.

SHOOTING IN THE BOROUGH was punished by a $5 fine, costs and 48 hours in jail. The revolver was left as security for the fine and costs. It was to be redeemed within five days and $1.50 cash. The accused paid the $1.50; the revolver was sold for $1.60. This was 1899.

OBSTRUCTING THE BOROUGH ROAD WITHOUT A PERMIT was the charge brought against 11 individuals in 1901. Found guilty, each paid $3 and costs. When it became known a mistake had been made by some of the foremen, the burgess accepted a settlement of $15 and remitted the balance of the fees.

FIGHTING AND DRUNK landed this individual in jail. His brother pleaded guilty for him and paid a $2 fine in 1901.

Another incident of drunkness resulted in a CONTEMPT OF COURT charge. The defendant went into "delirium tremans or snakes" and ripped off all his clothing. Dr. Brunner was summoned. His opinion was that the person was in a "dangerous condition" and administered medicine. The policeman watched the individual all night and the next day the prisoner was taken to the Poor House in Ebensburg. Costs were paid by the borough again; the year was 1901.

For LEAVING A WAGON STAND on a public street, a man was fined $3.75 in 1906.

Multiple charges of DRUNKENNESS, DISORDERLY CONDUCT and INTERFERING WITH A RELIGIOUS AND MILITARY SERVICE got a $10 fine plus costs in 1907.

COWS TRESPASSING ON BOROUGH STREETS accounted for 14 separate arrests in 1907 and individual fines of $5 plus costs.

PRACTICING PALMISTRY in 1910 without a license, a woman was fined one dollar and costs and another dollar for the license fee.

MAINTAINING A GAMBLING HOUSE drew a $2 fine and costs in 1912.

EXCEEDING THE SPEED LIMIT, in 1918, was fined at $2 and costs.

To PUNCH ANOTHER IN THE FACE was a violation of a borough ordinance and cost the puglist one dollar in 1919.

Item #5
Lost In Woods (1853)
(from the 1896 Cyclopedia)

Lewis L. Edwards, founder of the Edwards family in Cambria County, was a native of North Wales -- came to the United States in 1842 to his brother Robert's farm, nine miles north of Ebensburg.

Lewis was a noted sheep herder.

The following incident explains the pioneer condition of the county as late as 1853:

> "he went into the woods to get a piece of timber for a sled runner, and, while seeking for a suitable stick, lost his bearings and became lost; he wandered on and on several miles before coming to a house, and did not get back to his home that night. The family becoming alarmed, aroused the neighborhood the next day, and they started out in search of him, and found him with his friends of the previous night on his way home. So delighted were they to find him that they bore him on their shoulders to his own home and family." -- (pages 188-189)

Item #6
Summerhill Keeps Pace In Popluation

The 1890 Atlas estimated Croyle Township's population at 893 with Summerhill having 343 of the total -- or 38%.

Neighboring Wilmore was listed at 310 people as part of Summerhill Township's total of 619 -- or 50%.

Over the past 100 years, Summerhill has increased about 1.8 times (1990 census of 614) and Wilmore decreased to 277 -- 66 less people than a century ago.

Compared on another basis, Wilmore reached its peak in 1940 with 410 residents. Summerhill peaked in 1960 with 863. even though twenty years earlier, it counted 861.

County-wide, the decrease, during the same period, has been from 213,459 to 163,029, or about 24%. Wilmore's drop is about 38%; Summerhill, 29%.

These statistics reflect the outmigration due to a loss of employment opportunities and the movement into rural areas. Government regulations, in many instances, have stymied new constructions in most boroughs.

Item #7
Summerhill's Future Looks Good

The first borough in Cambria County was Ebensburg in 1825. By 1890, there were Loretto, Carrolltown, Chest Springs, Wilmore, Franklin, East Conemaugh, Gallitzin, Tunnelhill, Lilly, Ashville, South Fork, Johnstown and Portage. Dale incorporated in 1891; Westmont and Summerhill in 1892.

Before the end of the century, Daisytown, Patton, Spangler, Barnesboro, Hastings, Ferndale and Scalp Level joined the parade.

Ehrenfeld became the third borough in Croyle Township in 1956.

Most of thse towns were incorporated during periods of coal, steel and railroading expansions. Today, the future is questionable for many because of declining revenues and increasing expenditures.

Franklin Borough, for all practical purposes, is bankrupt. Residents of Portage and Cassandra Boroughs and Portage Township have been considering a merger into one governing unit. Merger of numerous neighboring boroughs with the City of Johnstown periodically surfaces. Votes have constantly blocked these mergers. The mood of most people is to keep their own identity.

Summerhill has not entertained any ideas of change. Because of its electrical light plant's successful operation, it is financially stable and still able to provide the essential needs.

Item #8
Summerhill's Total Property Tax

Property taxes are based on an assessed valuation of about 35% of market value in Cambria County.

During the past two decades, Summerhill property owners have experienced a 73% increase in their combined school, borough and county taxes.

	1971	1991
School Millage	49	90
Borough Millage	5	8.5
County Millage	20	29.7
Total	74	128.2

This means that a property assessed at $8,000, paid $592 in total taxes in 1972, and, twenty years later, now pay $1,025.

Item #9
St. John's Lutheran 1928 Operational Costs
(from the church's history of 1987)

The following financial report shows that St. John's Evangelical Lutheran Church's operational costs were about $1,000 in 1928:

The receipts came from envelopes, $739; Lenten boxes, $58.14; Sunday School, $20; and chicken supper, $111.45. And, with the balance carried over from 1927 of $1.07, the parish had $929.66 to operate with.

Expenditures were: pastor's salary, $780; janitor, $12; parsonage expenses, $42.20; lights, $9.89; flowers, $6.30; envelopes and schedules, $16.75; and miscellaneous, $38.39 -- a total of $905.53.

The year ended with a balance of $24.13.

Item #10
The Lutheran Pastor's Report: 1944-1948
(from the church's history 1987)

Rev. Glen B. Keidel, pastor of St. John's Evangelical Lutheran Church, presented the following report for 1944-1948:

Pastoral calls, 2,284; private communion, 318; marriages; 12; baptists, 85; funerals, 15; new members, 61; meetings, 245; letters written, 700; and miles traveled, 40,000.

Item #11
Some Early Church Rules

Under a constitution adopted in 1874 by the new-named Zion Evangelical Lutheran Church, Summer Hill, one article read as follows: "members shall not engage in the manufacture or sale of intoxicating liquors, or become partakers of other men's sins by renting houses for this purpose, nor under any circumstances nor in any quantity use spiritous liquors except as medicine recommended by a competent person."

Another note, in the church's 1987 history, referred to November 5, 1877 when a grave for a child was not paid. The family was told to pay up or remove the corpse.

A rule for contributions was also established in 1877. Each member was required to contribute 10¢ per week. Those in arrears for two months would be notified. After non-payment for six months, the member would be suspended; expulsion would occur after non-payment for eight months.

Item #12
Mrs. Simendinger Named Justice of the Peace

An undated newspaper article announced that Mrs. Stella (Kurtz) Simendinger was appointed Justice of the Peace of Summerhill by Governor Gifford Pinchot to serve the remainder of her husband's term.

Her husband, Clarence W. Simendinger, was killed in an automobile accident along with Stella's brother, Louis J. Kurtz of Claysburg, and John Ritchey of Portage.

The news items reported that Mrs. Simendinger is a native of Brownstown and resident of Summerhill since her marriage in 1918.

Item #13
Clarence W. Simendinger

Clarence W. Simendinger was born in Summerhill August 1, 1895, the son of John and Dora (McClarren) Simendinger.

He died, at age 37, November 30, 1932 as a result of an auto accident on the William Penn Highway, near Yellow Springs, Blair County.

While employed as a fireman by the Pennsylvania Railroad, he answered the call of his country and was inducted into the U. S. Army at South Fork in June 1918. He returned from France in May 1919 and resumed his job on the railroad.

In 1921, he left the railroad and entered electrical contracting work. In 1923, he was in charge of a gang which constructed power lines throughout the county. He also served in various capacities for Summerhill Borough, as noted in other chapters of this history. In 1919, he was elected justice of the peace.

The auto accident occurred on the way to a hunting trip in Cameron County. The car, driven by John Ritchey, swerved into a tree after hitting and fatally injuring a doe which had dashed from the woods. Ritchey, a Portage wallpaper and store operator, and Simendinger were dead at the scene.

Simendinger's brother-in-law, Louis G. Kurtz, died at Altoona Mercy Hospital. He was district manager of General Refractories operations at Claysburg, Sproul and Mt. Union.

In addition to his parents, Mr. Simendinger was survived by his widow, the former Stella Kurtz, and four children: Stella and Rita, twins; Wilfred and Thomas -- all at home.

Item #14
Cambria County Motor Vehicle Registrations

Of 113,218 motor vehicles registered in 1984, Cambria County had 81,447 automobiles; 3,206 motorcycles; 609 school busses and taxis; and 26,769 trailers and trucks.

Compared to the county's population of about 130,000 old enough for a driver's license, there was one automobile for every two persons.

Today, this ratio has changed dramatically with as many as two and three cars per family.

Item #15
Summerhill Was Part of Conemaugh Township in 1809

In 1809, five years after the formation of Cambria County, Summerhill (then known as Croyle's Mill) was part of one large and extensive area named Conemaugh Township.

It was from Conemaugh Township that the townships of Croyle, Summerhill, Jackson, Taylor, Yoder and Richland and the City of Johnstown were taken.

Item #16
Summerhill Priest Dies At The Age of 33 Shortly After Receiving a Ph.D. Degree

Bernard Seifert, son of Bernard and Zita Seifert, attended Summerhill Grade School, started his high school education at Wilmore and graduated in 1937 from South Fork High School. He continued his education at St. Francis College, Loretto, and Catholic University, Washington, D. C.

He made solemn profession as a member of Sacred Heart Province of the Franciscan Fathers, July 1945, at Carmelite Monastery, Loretto. He was ordained Father Mario Seifert, T. O. R., May 22, 1948.

From 1949 to 1953, Father Seifert attended the University of Vienna and completed studies which led to a Ph. D. in languages.

After only six weeks with the Steubenville College's Language Department, he died of a heart attack, April 14, 1953, at the age of 33.

He is survived by Dr. Thomas E. Seifert whose biography can be found in Chapter 11 and a sister, Theresa Marie who is a retired laboratory techincian at Johnstown hospitals and the American Red Cross. She is the wife of Joseph Chuba, Hawthorne Street, Johnstown.

Item #17
Lumbering In Early Summerhill History

Lumbering was part of Summerhill's early history. When the railroad was completed from Pittsburgh to Philadelphia, Summerhill became a local center of population.

Farmers brought loads of logs and farm products to town and traded them for clothing, metal goods and other necessities. Lumber was used to make barrels, buckets and tubs and shipped to Philadelphia by rail.

Around 1876, cord wood brought 50¢ a cord. The chopping was done with no saws; just axes.

Railroading paid 16¢ an hour; a good wage for the time. Land sold at $1 an acre -- timber, mineral rights and all.

Much later, Edward Bodenschatz shipped hemlock bark for the tannery and paper wood for the paper mills at Roaring Springs.

Item #18
Laurel Run Wall Always A Concern

A stone wall was built along Laurel Run in the 1930s as part of WPA (Work Projects Administration).

Washed away by the 1977 Flood, the wall was replaced with one of concrete in 1978 and 1979 by federal flood recovery funds.

In 1983, Laurel Run was causing erosion beneath the wall and sinkholes on private properties.

EADS of Altoona, the engineering firm responsible for the post-flood project, claimed the erosion was due to the Department of Soil Conservation using a wire gridwork along the stream bank to stabilize the stream.

In 1984, Summerhill Borough Council awarded a $32,770 contract to Creslow Construction Company to repair the wall again.

Item #19
Summerhill Survives Many Hard Times

When Summerhill became a borough in 1892, it was right before the beginning of the Panic of 1892 which lasted until the turn of the century.

The Spanish-American War took place in 1898 and World War I in 1917.

Prohibition began in 1920 and lasted until the repeal of the 18th amendment in 1933.

There was the 1922 national coal miners strike followed by the 1929 stock market crash which triggered the Great Depression of the 1930s.

The first U. S. peacetime draft began in 1940, a year before the Japanese attack on Pearl Harbor and Congress' declaration of war on Japan, Germany and Italy.

1945, United States dropped the atomic bomb on Hiroshima and Nagaski, Japan.

United States furnished military aid to South Korea in 1950.

And, then, there was Vietnam in the 1960s, the recession of the 1980s, and the fighting in Kuwait in 1991.

Added to these events are the periods of unemployment and the decline of the coal, steel and railroading industries.

Item #20
Indians Around Summerhill?

Did Indians roam over the land of Summerhill?

There is no written evidence to indicate Indian villages existed in this area, perhaps because of the mountainous terrain, deep valleys and the cold and snows of winter.

The Women's Club history does tell about arrow heads and Indian tools found on farms near Summerhill and of a grave on McCall's farm near the top of the hill that legend claims is the location of the burial ground of an Indian brave. A stone with a carving of a snake and bird marks the spot.

Another theory expresses that Indians, by common consent or treaty, left the Summerhill area for a common hunting ground.

It is surmised that Indians who did travel through this area probably were Shawnee, Iroquois and Delaware.

Item #21
Edward W. Hull

Edward W. Hull was a contracting painter in Summerhill for 40 years. He served three terms as burgess.

He died, age 64, in January 1922 of Bright's disease. His daughter, Mary (wife of James W. Weaver), was found dead in bed the next day as a result of a heart failure. She was 29 years old.

Hull was in his third year as justice of the peace at the time of his death.

Item #22
School Officers in 1949

Ferdinand Werfel was reelected to his third term as president of the Summerhill Borough School Board; Carl Huber, vice president; Clarence Betz, secretary; and Luther Croyle, truant officer for 1949 -- (The Johnstown Tribune-Democrat, December 6, 1949).

Item #23
Life In The Early Years

Summerhill townspeople, like those typical of other towns, did extensive gardening to supplement their food supplies. Some had a cow or two for milk. And, others had chickens in their backyard coops.

Children ran barefooted during summer months. There wasn't much glass or other lacerating objects in those days. Stubbed toes were the most common ailment.

Older folks usually never dressed up except on Sundays, holidays, weddings and funerals, unless they were business people. This dressup gave rise to the term "Sunday Suit".

Mustaches and beards were common for men. Young ladies usually wore a white shirt-waist and a dark skirt. Most little girls were in pigtails, bound with bright-colored ribbons. Under no circumstances did they wear anything like jeans or masculine-looking clothes.

Boys usually wore dresses until the age of 4. Then, they were dressed in short pants and long, durable black stockings which revealed long underwear at the ankles. Long pants were unheard of until reaching the age of 16. However, long-panted overalls were common for play, work and summer wear, topped off with large multi-colored handerchiefs.

The Sunday surrey and a horse provided transportation for an outing. Men talked about horse values much like today's auto owners talk about the cost of their vehicles. Water troughs along the most traveled roads were as important as gasoline stations are today.

A penny bought a handfull of candy, like seven spearmint leaves.

Before central heating systems, the kitchen coal stove provided the heat necessary for those cold winter days and nights. It was comforting to place cold feet near the stove's firebox or in the oven.

It wasn't uncommon to allow water to run all night so it would not freeze while the fires were banked. The source of hot water was a pot or a tea kettle heated on the stove.

Most kids had daily chores and rarely said they were bored.

Many evenings were spent huddled around the radio listening to dramatic programs, Amos and Andy and other radio personalities.

The passage of an airplane brought people out to see it and follow its direction.

Neighbors visited each other for leisurely evenings on porch swings.

The ole hometowns were close-knit, comfortable communities where everyone shared their lives together.

Item #24
Summerhill Supports Local Candidates

During the 1963 elections, two local candidates were on the ballot for county offices.

Summerhill voters supported them even though they were members of opposite political parties.

The voters chose Eldred R. Jones, Summerhill Republican, over Spear Sheridan, Democrat, for county treasurer, 226 to 100; and Ferdinand Bionaz, a Portage Democrat, over Norman Krumenaker, Republican, for district attorney, 233 to 97.

Both local candidates won the elections county-wide.

Item #25
Airplane Has Forced Landing

According to a newspaper item of September 17, 1925, reported in the 1966 Women's Club history, a mail plane made an emergency landing on the Joseph Ford farm, about 1 1/2 miles from Summerhill.

The pilot was enroute from Harrisburg to Pittsburgh. He was running out of gas and decided to land in the farm field. After refueling, he took off and continued his flight.

Item #26
Summerhill-New Germany Relationships

Is New Germany an extension of Summerhill? Or, is Summerhill an extension of New Germany? This is like asking which came first, the chicken or the egg.

Comparing the April 1991 voter registration lists, here's a tally of identical family names for Summerhill Borough and Croyle Township No. 1:

	Summerhill	Croyle No. 1
Beyer	1	18
Bodenschatz	20	17
Bopp	4	13
Brown	8	1
Brummert	1	2
Cronauer	4	2
Davis	1	1
Gabany	2	4

Huber	5	1
Jones	4	3
Kirby	2	4
Leventry	2	2
Long	3	32
Madison	8	3
Makoczy	2	1
McCall	8	10
McCormick	1	2
Meier	1	7
Miller	3	2
Motchenbaugh	1	2
Penatzer	10	3
Rosenberger	2	2
Schrift	3	10
Shope	1	2
Shrift	8	7
Smay	2	2
Smith	4	12
Susko	3	2
Tully	2	4
Wess	3	31
White	2	2
Wilson	5	9

What can be concluded from these voter registrations is that Summerhill Borough is dominated by Bodenschatz, Penatzer, Gallardy, Brown, Madison, McCall and Shrift.

Croyle Township No. 1 is headed by Long, Wess, Beyer, Bodenschatz, Wirfel, Bopp, Smith, Schrift, McCall and Wilson.

Item #27
The 1918 Automobile Blue Book
(courtesy of M. J. Strittmatter, Carrolltown)

This blue book, the forerunner of today's AAA tour books, gives an insight about motoring in 1918.

One of the advertisements featured Pennsylvania Vacuum Cup Tires, guaranteed for 6,000 miles and manufactured by Pennsylvania Rubber Company, Jeannette, PA. The company also sold the Pennsylvania Auto Tube which was "Ton-Tested" and guaranteed to have tensile strength 1 1/2 tons per square inch and would not crack, check, weaken or tear.

Other tire ads were for Quaker Tempered, Hood Extra Ply and United

States.

Quite unusual was Rexall Drug Stores selling MaxImiM Red "Extra Tough" inner tubes "built of real rubber vulcanized with crimson antimony." Over 8,000 stores claimed to be the "most convenient and reliable place in every town for the motorist to secure information." These stories also were advertised as "service stations."

DuPont advertised Fabrikoid, a new Rayntite Top which was water, grease, dirt, and stain proof -- would not oxidize or turn grey and was guaranteed for one year not to crack, leak or peel. DuPont's Harrison Works manufactured VITROLAC auto finishes which were "brilliant, durable and economical."

Corning Glass Works offered Conaphore headlight glass with a range of 500 feet, no glare and piercing fog and dust.

Willard Storage Battery service stations employed experts to "look over your battery, to fill and test it, watch it for overheating and keep connections tightened up." A twice-a-week inspection was recommended when the car was on the road.

For $1.50 a Ford could be equipped with S-M-C asbestos brake lining which was unaffected by heat, oil, water or gasoline and would not crumble or glaze.

The motoring public was invited to stop at 18 New York City hotels which offered rooms from $1.50 to $6.00 a night. Club breakfasts were available for 25¢ to 35¢; luncheon, 50¢; and dinner, one dollar. Car storage was a dollar; wash and polish was a dollar; day storage cost only 50¢.

This blue book described Ebensburg as a "quaint and pretty summer resort town situated on the top of the Alleghany mountains " and mentioned that from the tower of the courthouse "a splendid view may be had of the surrounding county."

Fort Stanwix Hotel, Johnstown, solicited automobile tourist's patronage and offered the European plan with 200 rooms, 175 having tub and shower baths.

Item #28
Pennsylvania Railroad's Name Trains

The Pennsylvania Railroad was the first to place a "limited" train into service in 1876. The train ran between Jersey City and Chicago with a limited number of cars and eventually was named the Pennsylvania Limited.

This was the beginning of special names given to the PRR passengers. There was the Congressional Limited (1885) and the Broadway Limited (1912).

These trains ran through Summerhill daily. By 1952, the list included names such as The Metropolitan, The Duquesne, Manhattan Limited, Red Arrow, The Akronite, Pittsburgh Night Express, Iron City Express, Gotham Limited, The Admiral, St. Louisan, Juniata, New Englander, Philadelphia Express and The Statesman.

Many a youngster waited for his favorite train to see it speed by and watch it vanish in the distant until the last trace of smoke faded.

Item #29
Streams Were The First Public Highways

The first public highways in Cambria County were waterways. The West Branch of the Susquehanna River and the Kiskiminetas River were declared public highways by an Act of March 9, 1771.

Conemaugh River was third by an Act of March 29, 1787. While timber was rafted down rivers, the Conemaugh was never used to any considerable extent for this purpose. It was, however, part of the great western route into the Ohio, the Mississippi and the Gulf of Mexico.

In the 18th century, the Conemaugh was noted for its abundant supply of fish.

The Delaware Indians had named it "Gunamonki" or "Coughnaughmaugh" which is said to mean Otter Creek.

Item #30
History of U.S. 22

Beginning as the Huntingdon, Cambria & Indiana Turnpike in 1820, this wagon road went through Munster and Ebensburg to the west side of Laurel Hill.

Later, it was known as the Philadephia and Pittsburgh Turnpike.

Today, it is the William Penn Highway or U. S. Route 22.

Item #31
Trolley Operations

During the operation of the South Fork-Portage Railway system, it was possible for Summerhill people to travel by trolley to various points within the county.

The Summerhill trolley took passengers to the top of Maple Street in South Fork where they had to disembark, walk about a block down Grant Street and board the Southern Cambria street car on the Grant Street bridge. From here, the Southern Cambria trolleys ran into Johnstown, Nanty Glo and Ebensburg.

There were other street car operations:

Johnstown Passenger Railway Company (1882-1876) originally provided horse car service in the Johnstown area. After the 1889 flood, the line was electrified and, by 1907, there were 110 trolleys operating over 31 miles of track.

A major accident in 1907 caused a reorganization into the Johnstown Traction Company. Growth continued until 1943 when automobile use began to blossom.

Trackless trolleys and busses were placed into operation in 1960. The trolleys were discontinued in 1967 and the busses continued until 1976 under the Traction Company name.

The County Transit Authority, the current operators, purchased all assets in 1977 and the Traction Company was dissolved.

Northern Cambria Street Railway Company (1905-1926) started with trolley service between Barnesboro and Patton and, in 1907, extended its line into Carrolltown. It was sold at a foreclosure in 1918 and reorganized as Northern Cambria Railway Company.

The line quit business in 1926 because the reconstruction of U. S. Route 219 needed part of its roadway.

Southern Cambria Railway Company (1908-1928) ran from Johnstown to Nanty Glo, South Fork and Ebensburg. The dangerous terrain was the cause of many accidents. A headon collison in 1916 killed 27 and injured 80 passengers. This and the resultant financial difficulties caused the company to suspend operations December 17, 1928.

Cambria-Indiana Railroad Company (1911-1925) first began as a rail line in 1904 to haul logs from Vintondale to the northern forest lands. Passenger service began in 1911 and extended east of Colver and north of Pine Flats in Indiana County. Service to Nanty Glo and Revloc was added in 1914.

This line used only one trolley. A headon collison May 31, 1925 with a steam locomotive resulted in the end of this streetcar operation.

South Fork-Portage Railway Company (1912-1928) went through several name changes and never developed beyond South Fork and Summerhill. Derailments in South Fork, insufficient capital and the demise of the Southern Cambria sealed its fate in 1928.

Item #32
Air Travel for Summerhill
Johnstown-Cambria County Airport is located in Richland Township, southwest of Summerhill via U. S. 219 or Route 53. Excellent passenger and air freight services throughout the U.S. States is available. Commuter air service between Johnstown and Pittsburgh is provided on a regularily, scheduled basis.

A small air strip along U. S. 22, west of Ebensburg, provides charter service to residents and businesses of Cambria County. This air strip is accessible to Summerhill via U. S. 219 North.

Both airport facilities are just minutes away.

Item #33
Buckhorn Horse Thieves
Buckhorn horse thieves tried in Judge Taylor's term were a noted gang of desperados with headquarters in Summerhill. They operated throughout Cambria County in the 1860s.

Some were sent to the penitentiary.

Item #34
Casualties of Ehrenfeld Explosion of 1927
A blast which was felt in Summerhill killed three motormen and a track worker in the March 20, 1927 explosion in Mine #3 of Pennsylvania Coal & Coke Corporation, Ehrenfeld.

The motormen were Daniel McConaughy, 41; John Fesko, 29; and John Shedlock, 40. The track worker was William Connelly, 34.

Eight other miners were overcome by gas: W. T. Williams, William Brewer, Harry Marshall, David Howe, John Mulvehill, Joseph Homa, a Mr. Callahan and Fred Kalina.

Item #35
Forests Around The Little Conemaugh

The Little Conemaugh River flows swiftly from the east. Its head, near Lilly on the Allegheny Mountain, drops down a narrow, winding high-walled gorge to Johnstown, descending from 2,300 feet to 1,200 feet in less than 20 miles.

Surrounded by dense forest, this valley furnished wood for fueling iron furnaces and railroads durings the 1840s and 1850s.

During the 1870s, it was the source of timber used to make barrel shooks and staves.

By the 1880s, the original forests had disappeared causing serious runoff from spring thaws and heavy rains --(taken from Degen, **Johnstown Flood of 1889 -- The Tragedy of the Conemaugh**, 1984).

Item #36
Summerhill Advertisers in 1909

The following advertisements appeared in the Wilmore St. Bartholomew Church history of 1909:

H. A. BRUMMERT -- dealer in all kinds of meats and groceries.

CARPENTER HOUSE -- F. J. Kurtz, proprietor.

J. T. LONG -- dealer in lumber and builders' supplies, manufacturer of fine interior finish, architect, contractor and builder, planing mill and yards, builders' hardware, glass and paint, established 1872.

Item #37
Representation On School Authority

Leonard Straple of Jackson Street, Summerhill, is a member and assistant secretary of the 1991 Forest Hills School Authority. Raymond Wess, New Germany, is the chairman.

Other members include Robert Kranztler, Beaverdale, vice chairman; John Kovalich, Dunlo, secretary; Mike Matsko, Salix, treasurer; Roger Layton, Windber R. D. 2, assistant treasurer; Dr. Richard Frazer, South Fork; Harold Walters, Sidman; and Dorothy Ruddek, South Fork R. D. 1.

Attorney Mark Gregg, Johnstown, is the solicitor and William R. McCrory, Indiana, auditor.

Item #38
Charter Member of Fire Company

Oscar G. Betz, a charter member of Summerhill Volunteer Fire Company, passed away at age 91 on September 2, 1990.

He was born in Summerhill, son of George and Anna E. (Motchenbaugh) Betz.

Item #39
Fire Destroys Simendinger House

The double plank house of Mrs. Stella Simendinger, Jackson Street, was gutted by fire, according to a Cambria Dispatch story printed January 31, 1936 -- four years after the accidental death of her husband.

Caused by an overheated furnace, damages amounted to $5,000. The paper reported that fire plugs were frozen and only the sidewalk and part of the roof remained.

The story also noted that two firemen -- John McCall and Frank Penrod -- suffered from frozen ears.

Mrs. Simendinger was listed as justice of the peace, president of Portage's VFW auxiliary, officer of the Cambria County PTA and registrar of vital statistics.

Item #40
Big League Baseball Player

Joseph L. McCall, son of Thomas and Esther (Noon) McCall, played for the Detroit Tigers and Los Angeles Dodgers in minor leagues as first baseman.

Born in Summerhill, June 18, 1939, he died August 28, 1989 at his New Germany home.

At the time of his death, he owned McCall's Optical Shop in New Germany.

Item #41
The Cronauer Family

Harold and Marion Cronauer of 803 Market Street, Summerhill, are parents of 10 children -- three of whom are U. S. Naval Academy graduates.

Property of Rita Shevock.

They are Commander Harold T. Cronauer Jr., Lt. Commander Joseph T. Cronauer and Lt. Colonel Victor T. Cronauer.

Of the other seven children, there is a priest, two nurses, a sawmill employee, an artist and auto body shop man, a mechanical engineer and a homemaker.

There are 17 grandchildren, three of whom are adopted -- one from Ecuador, one from Mexico and a Mexican-American.

Harold T. Cronauer, the father, served in five major campaigns in the Pacific during World War II as a Navy radarman aboard the distroyer USS Evans. He is a retired industrial arts teacher with 29 1/2 years of teaching in the Franklin Borough and Forest Hills high schools.

Marion, the mother, is a nurse who worked mainly at Lee Hospital, Johnstown.

Item #42
From Newspaper Obituaries

Newspaper obituaries often contain historical information not found anywhere else:

ZACHARIAH T. DUNMIRE was a life-time Summerhill resident who died March 25, 1924 at age 66. He was a mechanic for Argyle Coal Company,

South Fork.

JOSEPH HABERL had a patent on a joint for rails. He died July 24, 1928 at the age of 39.

JOHN T. LONG'S obit for June 29, 1929 credited him for 50 years as Summerhill's justice of the peace and many terms as burgess. He was 81 years old when he passed away.

PAREDES J. MCGOUGH, 81, died February 20, 1929. He was born at the Half-Way House in 1848.

PATRICK J. MONAGHAN, 56, passed away March 22, 1930. He was well-known as a amateur theatrical performer for 25 years.

FATHER RICHARD KRAUS died at Johnstown Mercy Hospital in 1932.

GEORGE E. PENROD was a brakeman on the South Fork Branch of the Pennsylvania Railroad. He died at age 58 in 1934.

JOHN BODENSCHATZ was a saddler and harness maker in New Germany. His wife, the former Catherine Weinzierl, died in Wilmore in 1935 at age 84.

HENRY W. DAVIS was a stationary engineer for Pennsylvania Coal & Coke Corporation. He lived in Summerhill since 1884. He passes away in 1938, age 73.

Item #43
Notes From Various Sources

DANIEL A. McGOUGH, who was Cambria County register of wills for three terms, was born in Croyle Township in 1856. His paternal great-grandfather was James McGough who owned a lot of valuable land and was regarded as one of the pioneer settlers of the township. He was a farmer, school teacher and civil engineer. He died in 1812.

Daniel's father was Thomas McGough (1827-1870), a farmer and cooper, who married Isabella Plummer of Summerhill Township in 1855.

BENJAMIN F. SLICK operated a tannery in Summerhill from 1848 to 1861. He also served as postmaster seven years, from 1860 to 1866.

ELIAS PAUL worked for the Pennsylvania Railroad as a passenger and freight agent in Summerhill. In 1878, he and his wife, the former Maria Pringle, moved to Johnstown where he worked in merchandising and later for Cambria Iron Company. Upon retirement, in 1908, he moved to Altoona.

A son, W. H. Paul, was born in Summerhill, educated in Johnstown and, in 1920, became secretary-treasurer of Paul's Plumbing & Heating Company, Johnstown.

WILLIAM H. HESS began the Superior Steam Baking Company, Portage, in 1898. He had four trucks delivering baked goods to Lilly,

Puritan, Spring Hill, Beaverdale, Wilmore, Summerhill, South Fork and Ehrenfeld.

EDWARD SMITH, a native of Jackson Township, managed the Summerhill House five years, 1899 to 1904. He left to enter the wholesale liquor business in Nanty Glo.

A. J. OAKS (1867-1938) was a native of Somerset County. He was in the lumber business in Summerhill and used the current ball field as his mill yard. In 1907, he founded the South Fork Foundry & Machine Company which continued in business, under various ownerships, until the 1977 flood.

JOHN B. PAUL also had a lumber business in Summerhill. John Gable in his 1926 county history claims Paul built the old Union House which he managed for years and then moved to Johnstown in retirement. A son, John Frederick, worked with the postal department in Johnstown.

RAYMOND C. KIRBY was appointed chief inheritance tax appraiser and investigator for Cambria County by the State Auditor General in 1937 with an annual salary of $2,500.

FRANKLIN H. PENROD, JR. (1938-1989), son of Franklin H. and Susannah (Nelson) Penrod, was born in Summerhill, graduated from Adams High School in 1956 and was employed by SOHIO (now BP AMERICA). He served as field attest auditor during the construction and completion of the Alaskan Pipeline. At the time of his death, he was a resident of Lakewood, Ohio.

MARK D. HETTLE, son of Catherine Hettle and the late Donald Hettle, was one of 10 college and university professors in Texas named a Piper Professor for 1990 and received a $2,500 honorarium and a gold pin. He attended the U. S. Naval School of Music, Washington, D. C. and earned undergraduate and graduate degrees at the University of North Texas. He is a member of the music faculty at Mountain View College, Dallas, Texas.

P. J. SHRIFT is an entertainer who performs under the name of Patton James. He was featured on the TNN Nashville TV Network in 1990 with two of his original numbers pertaining to Johnstown steel mills, mines and railroads. He is the son of Jim and Irene Shrift of Summerhill.

Item #44
Preschool Graduation -- 1991

Summerhill Preschool graduation ceremonies were held at St. John's Catholic Church May 10, 1991. The graduates were Troy Baumgardner, Joshua Galla, Nicholas Gruss, Ronald Hostetler, Travis Hull, Ashley Keller, Jared Long, Jacob Madison, Gregory Penatzer, Ben Savlan, Monika Shrift, Emily Theys, Katie Tripp, Wayne Wess and Jessica Wolfhope. The teacher was Janet Long.

Item #45
Summerhill's Kitchen Band

Summerhill had a kitchen band in 1954-55 that performed at various events throughout the area and paraded in Summerhill.

During Cambria County's Sesquicentennial, they were part of the historical pageant, "Homeland of the Alleghenies", which gave nightly performances at the Ebensburg-Cambria Memorial Stadium, Ebensburg, August 16-24, 1954. (Participants also were S/Sgt. Ernest J. Penatzer, Pvt. Donald J. Kitchick and Pvt. Ferdinand J. Werfel, members of the 34th Special Infantry Co., United States Marine Corp Reserves).

Members of the kitchen band were Gloria Montanari, Rose Mathieson, Vern Kick, Hilda Mathieson, Marion Mulvehill, Dorothy Madison, Jennie Wirfel, Helen Apple, Cleo Shope, Marie Gallardy, Mrs. Calvin Engle, Jerry Haberl and Esther McCall.

Item #46
Liquor Licenses for 1935

The Woman's Christian Temperance Union of Cambria County issued a publication entitled "Who's Who in Cambria County" for liquor licenses issued in 1935 with the names of those who signed on their behalf.

For the German Beneficial Union, the signers were Charles F. Plummer, Louis White, J. E. Hunter, Oscar Betz, A. L. Seifert, E. F. White, C. E. Claycomb, W. R. Kirby, Bernard C. Kirby, Alex Betz, George Plummer and John Simendinger.

For Louis W. White's liquor license, the signers were Stella Simendinger, Fred C. Nelson, Homer Harshberger, Roy White, Esther R. White, R. A. Betz, Kenneth Schrift, Herman J. Werfel, Edward Werfel, C. B. Jones, Louis Rosenberger and Joseph P. Stapleton.

Listed for Ira A. Lenz's license were Stella Simendinger, H. A. Brummert, Elmer Berschneider, Joseph P. Stapleton, Victor L. Schrift, Samuel Rose, W. J. Yahner, John M. Sloan, Charles F. Plummer, Herman J. Werfel, Adolph Wess and Francis Bodenschatz.

Summerhill PTA Clash & Clatter Band of 1954-55. Beany Engle, Marie Gallardy, Dot Madison, Jerry Haberl, Jenny Werfel, Cleo Shope, Esther McCall, Rose Mathieson, Gloria Montanari, Esther Mathieson, Helen Apple, Marion Mulvihill, Hilda Mathieson.

Item #47
James D. Plummer

John McCormick wrote about James D. Plummer as a veteran postmaster in his 1906 history of Summerhill. At that time, Plummer was 74 years old and had been connected with the post office in various capacities for 36 years.

McCormick stated that Plummer was first assistant under Postmaster William Murray during President Franklin Pierce's administration (1853-1857); postmaster under President Andrew Johnson (1865-1869); assistant for J. D. Wentroth under President Benjamin Harrison (1889-1893); and made postmaster under President William McKinley (1897-1901).

According to McCormick, Plummer also carried mail for a time and during his youth was a fireman for the Old Portage Railroad but "a felon coming on one of his fingers put him off duty, and he went into the store of William Murray, his brother-in-law, as clerk."

Item #48
John M. Skelly

John McCormick also mentioned that John M. Skelly was married in 1850 and that he worked on the Old Portage Railroad and later on the Pennsylvania "under every supervisor until he retired" in 1900 at the age of 78.

Item #49
Tax Collector's Cash Book, 1922-24

C. W. Simendinger's tax collector's cash book shows 67 taxables for 1922. The number increased to 197 by 1923 and 265 for 1924.

The top ten borough taxpayers include (spelling according to the records) Emil Sheman, Homer Seaman, Alice Pringle, Harry Ruthmiller, Walter Brosch, Lawrence Leach, Joe Hettle, John Hettle, Charles Diamond Estate and Christ Kuklo. The amounts range from $18.30 to the high of $29.80.

For 1923, the following were listed for the largest school taxes: Emil Sheman ($45.95), Thomas McCall ($32), Elizabeth Myers Estate ($27); Annie Betz ($23); and John Simendinger ($20).

The combined borough and school taxes for 1924 listed the following major amounts: T. E. Kime ($91); Homer Seaman ($69); George Bodenshatz ($58.75); Lawrence Leach ($53); Lillian Kime ($50.50); and Louis Sherer ($50).

Item #50
Historian John McCormick (1847-1935)

John McCormick did a lot of historical research for the Johnstown Tribune and its editor, George T. Swank. His 1906-07 series on the communities of Cambria County are outstanding and, in many instances, the only records for the era.

Some of his unpublished papers have been preserved at the Cambria County Historical Society, Ebensburg.

In 1909, McCormick completed the history of St. Bartholomew's Catholic Church of Wilmore, another valuable reference.

He indexed the files of the Johnstown Tribune from 1853 to 1878 and served as correspondent for the Cambria Freeman, an Ebensburg weekly newspaper, and the Johnstown Tribune. He often submitted letters to the editors with the following familiar ending -- "Yours for the truth of history".

John McCormick was born January 14, 1847, on a Summerhill Township farm, a son of Patrick and Catherine McCormick (both natives of Ireland). The elder Patrick came to the United States in 1826 and migrated to Wilmore in 1832. He purchased a farm on the outskirts of Wilmore in 1839.

John McCormick was educated in the Summerhill Township and subscription schools. He was a teacher in Cambria County. His wife, Lucinda P. Kennedy, was also a teacher. She died in 1908 when they resided in Johnstown. John died November 27, 1935, age 88, at 931 Washington Avenue, Portage.

At the time of his death, he was survived by the following children: Charles P. McCormick, Wilmore; Othella and Jennie McCormick, Portage (Jennie was also a teacher); Mrs. Peter Schrift, New Germany (she was a music supervisor in Johnstown for a while); and Mrs. F. H. Leahey, a school teacher.

Item #51
New Germany Interchange

Bids for the contruction of an on-and-off ramp in the northbound lane of Route 219 in the New Germany area were opened in July 1991. Work started in October and completion is expected by late summer 1992.

The interchange will provide direct access to New Germany. The initial work of the contractor entails clearing operations between Route 219 and the intersection of State Route 2009 (New Germany Road) and township road 417, drainage, pipe installation and construction of sedimentation ponds.

Federal funds will pay for 80 percent of the construction and the state the remaining 20 percent.

The contractor is Wayne W. Knorr, Inc. of Bloomsburg, Columbia County.

Item #52
Taxables 1895-1903

William McClarren was Summerhill's assessor during 1895-1899. His reports to the county commissioners showed the following taxables:

	Individuals	Horses	Cattle
1895	140	12	34
1896		(no tabulations)	

1897	125	14	24
1898	163	14	28
1899	160	14	28

McClarren also listed 24 male dogs and two female dogs for 1897. He made no record of dogs for the other years.

However, when C. J. Berschnider (spelling according to records) became assessor in 1900, he recorded 25 male dogs along with 161 taxable persons, 19 horses and 29 cattle. He noted more horses than the previous years.

There must have been a substantial population increase in 1901 and 1902 since the individual taxables were 215 and 251, respectively. But, 1903 showed a decline to 190 taxables while the number of horses remained the same and cattle increased to 32 and male dogs increased to 34.

Item #53
Sheriff Sale in 1892

The two-story plank house and lot of J. A. Headricks, in Summerhill, was sold to T. J. Fearl, of Johnstown, for $25, and another house and lot belonging to the same party and also situated in Summerhill was sold to the same person for $5 at a sheriff's sale in Ebensburg, December 5, 1892 according to a news item in the Ebensburg Cambria Freeman of December 9, 1891.

Item #54
A Longtime Justice and Notary Public

Stella Simendinger was appointed by Governor Gifford Pinchot to serve the remainder of her husband's term as justice of the peace after his accidental death in 1932.

Stella retired as a notary public in 1985 after 53 years of such services to Summerhill and the area. She married Lester Cullen, now deceased, in the 1940s and was then known as Stella Cullen.

Another Stella -- her daughter Stella DeLozier -- has been a notary public since 1988. She and her husband, Edwin, take care of her mother who has been bedfast since 1990.

Item #55
Horse Values in 1910

Perhaps, owners of horses in 1910 commanded special notice. And, those with more than one horse were looked up to as prosperous individuals?

There were 12 men in 1910 who paid county taxes on their horses or mules.

Thomas C. Keim, a teamster, and John T. Long, lumber dealer, each had three horses valued at $50 each.

C. E. Claycomb, merchant, and J. W. Hugentogen, teamster, both owned two horses valued at $75 each. Teamster Milton A. Sherbine's two horses were valued at $50 each.

Those with only one horse, each valued at $50, were Hugh Brummert, butcher; Dr. C. B. Jones, town physician; Francis Kurtz, hotelman; and W. R. Kirby, merchant. Christ Kugla, a coal miner, had one worth $40 while another miner H. W. Davis, probably had a mule since he was assessed at $20 along with farmer Joseph Brown.

Item #56
Who Had Cows in 1910?

Cows carried an assessed value of $20 each for county tax purposes in 1910.

A total of 20 Summerhill taxpayers were listed for that year, each with one cow: Henry Berschneider, George Betz, John M. Bodenschatz, Adam Bimmel, Hugh Brummert, Joseph Brown, Zach Dunmire, Jacent Gilman, B. F. Grove, E. W. Hull Estate, Louis Habrel, John Kick, Christ Kugla, J. T. Long, William Malonek, Oscar Mervine, Adam Nowatsky, Henry Quinn, John A. Rorabugh and Samuel Rose.

(Spellings as they appeared on the records)

Item #57
Former Mayor Now District Magistrate

Allan C. Berkheimer, former Summerhill mayor of the early 1980s, is now the district magistrate with offices located in Salix which serves Adams and Croyle Townships and the boroughs of South Fork, Summerhill and Ehrenfeld.

A native of Portage and a 1972 graduate of its high school, Allan spent four years with the U. S. Army military police. He continued law enforcement work upon his return to civilian life. He attended the police academy at Greater Johnstown Vo-Tech. His employment included six years as a member of Bethlehem Steel's security force; five years, Sankertown police chief; two years, Cambria County prison; and 18 months, Penelec security. When the federal prison opened in 1984 at Loretto, he was one of the first correction officers.

Berkheimer resided in Summerhill from 1977 to 1989 and then moved to Elton.

His elected term as magistrate began January 1988. As a member of Pennsylvania's unified judical system, he is recertified annually with the completion of updated legal education at Wilson College, Chambersburg, Pa.

District justices replaced the former local justices of the peace. They have jurisdiction (except in Philadelphia) over summary, criminal and motor vehicle cases, landlord-tenant matters and civil actions not exceeding $4,000 in claims. They issue warrants, hold arraignments and preliminary hearings in criminal cases and, under certain circumstances, accept guilty pleas in misdemeanor cases of the third degree. They perform marriage ceremonies. On evenings and over weekends when the court of common pleas is closed, they may issue protection from abuse orders.

Item #58
The Centennial Committee

Charles Huber has chaired the centennial committee since its beginning. Stella DeLozier has served as secretary.

At the first meeting, October 24, 1990, the following six volunteers attended: Charles Huber, Samilda Huber, Stella DeLozier, Jim Haberl, Jill Rosporski and Larry Wilburn.

In addition, the following have been recorded as subsequent participants: Jack Bodenschatz, Anna Mae Bopp, Jean Gallardy, Tom Madison, Robert McCormick, Margaret McCormick, Bonnie Novotny, Betty Penatzer and Terry Washko.

As this book was going to press, two events were tentatively scheduled: (1) a dinner-dance May 16 at New Germany Grove and (2) centennial week activities beginning July 12. It is expected that the week's events will include a dinner at the church, food tents, craft show and fireworks.

Item #59
Other Historical Insights

A. Bofserman is recorded as minister of the Halfway House until 1868. (The Allegheny Lutheran Synod record shows that in 1845 "the church of the Halfway House in Cambria County was rereceived into the Synod.")

Pastor T. Kalie, from the German Lutheran Church of Johnstown, held communion and confirmation services in 1853 and Pastor Brant, also from the Johnstown Church, held services in April and September of 1854.

Rev. L. J. Bell preached in Summerhill (Halfway House), Burkharts School and Jefferson Mission (Wilmore) from 1856 to 1858. Rev. J. F. Kuhlman preached in Summerhill for the first time April 17, 1859 and at two-week intervals thereafter.

During the Civil War, church services and the sacraments were held at irregular intervals and by different traveling ministers.

The present church was built at a cost of $1,800 and dedicated December 24, 1871.

During 1886 when Rev. John Unruh was pastor, he was responsible for the Wilmore Charge consisting of Wilmore, Summerhill, Jackson, Portage and Lilly congregations.

The 150th anniversary publication tells about the church being heated by coal stoves and illuminated by oil lamps. Then, gas was used for lighting until 1914 when electric lights were installed. (A Summerhill Municipal Light Plant bill for a month in 1915 was 75 cents).

A new cornerstone was laid November 22, 1956. St. John was part of a merger with the South Fork congregation for nine years - 1959 to 1968. Since then, the church has been supplied with ministers from the Seminary and from other area churches.

St. John also joined the Mainline Lutheran Cluster in the 1970s and the Gallitzin Church affiliated with them. When Summerhill's German Lutheran Church closed, some of its members became part of the St. John congregation.

According to the 150th anniversary booklet, Rev. Gordon & Edwards was the last regular pastor. The congregation has been served by Vice-Pastors ever since 1968.

1992 marks the 160th anniversary of Summerhill's St. John Evangelical Lutheran Church.

View of Jackson Street in 1991.

View of Main Street in 1991.

Intersection of Route 53 and Croyle Street in 1991.

Claycomb Apartments, Main Street, 1991.

Patrick Dumm Apartments, Main Street, former location of Carpenter's Hotel and Duffy's Store.

Helicopter bringing in food and water to the Summerhill school yard in 1977. (Credit: Evelyn Beckman)

The bridge which was washed away and caused injury to Paul Cronauer as he attempted to cross Laurel Run with his truck during the 1977 flood. (Credit: Evelyn Beckman)

The winter storm in 1976 before the 1977 flood. (Credit: Evelyn Beckman)

Chapter 17
This Is Summerhill

It was first known as **Croyle's Mill,** named after the first settlers -- Thomas and Barbara Croyle -- who built a grist mill used by area farmers.

It was **Half-Way** during the days of the Old Portage Railroad because it was the midpoint between Johnstown and Cresson.

It was designated **Summer Hill** Post Office in 1840 to handle the distribution of United States mail.

The Pennsylvania Railroad Guide of 1855 described **Summerhill,** adjoining the old half-way house on the Portage Road, as a wood and water station.

Jonathan Oldbuck in the January 17, 1861 issue of **The Alleghanian** referred to **Summerhill** as a village situated near the center of Croyle Township, on the Conemaugh River "which is here crossed by the Pennsylvania Railroad on a very fine bridge. There is a Station here, also a post office, hotel and extensive shops for the manufacturing of shooks; population about 200."

Oldbuck also wrote that Frankstown Road passed through the southern part of Croyle Township and intersected a number of roads from other parts of the township. The road from Beulah to Somerset, he added, passed through "where the present village of Summerhill stands, and is one of the oldest roads in the county."

A native of Summerhill -- Father Ronald Bodenschatz, T. O. R. -- wrote the following history for his 1966 scrapbook:

"Summerhill is one of the oldest communities in Cambria County. It was formed in 1810 by two brothers, Joseph and David Somers. To build the town which today is typically German in character, curbed streets and all paved, sidewalks surfaced and homes well preserved with their attractive lawns and gardens, the people had to purchase land from families named Stineman and Griffith. The Stineman clan was in particular a guiding force in its development as well as in the areas of South Fork and Wilmore, both being akin to Summerhill.

The surveying of the land, laying out of lots and naming of streets was done by an Irishman William McConnell. The German influence was deeply felt from the Bavarian immigrants who settled in the area of New Germany, north of the village community. The village took the name of Somerhill in the beginning only later to be called Summerhill instead.

Today the Pennsylvania Railroad extends its principal tenacle, the mainline, through the borough located on State Highway 53.

Down through the years Summerhill has been primarily a coal and railroad and steel community whose wage earners have been employed by mines not too far distant, the Pennsylvania Railroad and Bethlehem Steel in Johnstown.

In earlier years industries common place to pioneer settlements sprang up in the friendly village. These industries ran their course, as happens everywhere else, and then passed out of existence. Summerhill at one time or another in the past 155 years had feed mills, saw mills, blacksmith shops, slaughter houses, hotels, a railroad company store, tannery, stone quarry, etc.

One ole time citizen who has left his mark in Summerhill because of the large homes he has built there was John T. Long. He came to settle in the village around 1872 one year after the Chicago Fire where he had been previously. In Summerhill he engaged in contracting and building. In 1877 he built a planing mill which was then operated by means of water power and on a small scale. With a prosperous business, in 1886, he enlarged the mill and changed it to a steam power plant and began the manufacture of all kinds of building material. With this improvement, his business continued to grow and expand to the extend that he had to increase his facility from time to time. In politics, this man of good judgement and strict integrity and probity of character, became the citizens choice of justice of the peace for four successive terms and also the first burgess of the borough."

The Summerhill Women's Club history, 1810-1966 used the following approach:

"If William Penn returned to see the province he founded, he would be astonished. He would perhaps see some things that would distress and sadden his Quaker heart, but he would surely approve of the political and religious freedom, and the economic plenty that his Pennsylvanians enjoy. He would be pleased that his 'Holy Experiment' succeeded so well.

Summerhill Borough, one of the oldest communities in Cambria County, was an integral part of that "Holy Experiment". It was founded in 1810 by two brothers, Joseph and David Somers. Most of the early settlers were English, German and Irish. At first the village was called Somerhill, but as time went on, the spelling was changed to Summerhill. While the town was named for the brothers, there is no recorded or hearsay evidence as to why it should have been so named. It is believed that their stay here was a short one, and that an adventuresome spirit took them to new territory to be explored."

The latest focus on Summerhill comes from the weekly "Our Neighborhood" series of the **Johnstown Tribune-Democrat**. Headlined **Summerhill described as special place to call home**, Bill Blair, staff writer, quotes several residents in his June 16, 1991 article:
Mary E. Werfel, a retired Summerhill elementary teacher, in talking about the residents, said "I'll tell you one thing, this is a very nice town."
Geoffrey McCall, a former student and now an officer of McCall's Jeep/Eagle Inc., told Blair his hometown is a "very nice town just filled with very friendly people. There's a lot of people who would like to live in this town, but there's just no more room." McCall went on to explain that it doesn't mean outsiders aren't welcome. It just means they have to be extra quick to learn about the occasional property that is for sale. Most properties, he said, are sold by word of mouth before they are advertised.
Father Lieb Germain, pastor of St. John's Catholic Church, is quoted as saying, "They're quiet, hard-working people. And, I think, for the most part, they are religious people." Father also mentioned that the community has a "lively" volunteer fire company, a focal point for many residents, especially younger ones.
Ray Penatzer of Ray's Lawn & Garden Equipment told the reporter that he grew up in Summerhill and "I think it is one of the nicest towns around. People take care of their homes, and I think it is a heck of a good place to raise a family."

Cambria County Planning Commission

The Cambria County Planning Commission's comprehensive plan for Summerhill Borough, completed in 1979, investigated the borough in five major physical areas: climatology, geology, soils, slope and watersheds.

The climatology report identifies the climate of Summerhill as a humid mesothermol (DFA) which is characterized by the four distinct seasons of spring, summer, fall and winter.

A freeze-free period of 140-150 days occurs between early May and early October.

Precipitation is usually adequate, despendable and well distributed throughout the year, the report states. The average annual precipitation is about 52 inches but short periodic dry spells are not uncommon during the hot summer months.

Temperatures range from 0 degrees to 90 degrees Farenheit.

Summerhill is subjected to highly changable weather because of contrasting air masses and severe frontal activity. This is due because Summerhill is located in climate between the polar continental air masses to the north and the maritime continential tropical air masses to the south and southeast.

The area is characterized by large amounts of spring rains and temperatures around 32 degrees F during the winter months.

The geology report states that a subsurface rock structure formation of Summerhill was formed in the Pennsylvania geological period. The Conemaugh series covers the entire subsurface of the borough and is made up of sandstone, shale, clay, thin coals and thin beds of limestone. The thickness of this series in Summerhill varies from 300 to 500 feet.

Within the borough, there are primarily four coal beds of significance -- Upper and Lower Freeport, Upper and Lower Kittaning.

There are 11 basic types of soils in Summerhill Borough, classified and mapped by the U. S. Department of Agriculture Soil Conservation Service.

Elevations within the borough range from a low of 1,500 feet to a high of 1,760 feet above sea level.

"The northern portion of the Borough is accented by two distinct belts of steep slopes while the central and southern areas gradually slope away and level out around the Conemaugh River."

According to this report, 17.7% or 67.8 acres of the land area in the borough has slopes over 16%. These areas are restricted from most development. A total of 64.8 acres, or 26.5%, of the undeveloped land area makes development possible but on a scattered and limited basis.

Summerhill is part of the Little Conemaugh River watershed/ drainage basin. The town's drainage patterns help to form the headwaters of the Little Conemaugh on its flow towards South Fork and into Johnstown.

Much of the southern part of the borough was inundated or affected by the July 1977 flood waters which caused damages in excess of $285,000.

Another part of the commission's report dealt with land use. The study pointed out that developed land comprised of 122.07 acres, or 49.8% of the total. Undeveloped land, like woodlands, vacant areas and water areas, made up 50.2% or 122.87 acres. Most of the undeveloped category is vacant land and woodlands which either are too steeply sloped or too close to stream or river channels.

The use of land, at this time, was tabulated at 60 acres residential; 47 acres, transportation; 11.16 acres, commercial; and 4.18 acres, public or semi-public (firehall, school and two churches).

About half of the borough's land area was classified as undeveloped.

Population

The planning commission reported the average number of persons per Summerhill household in 1970 was 3.4 persons and 3.5 in 1977.

In 1960, the report said, Summerhill had an average of 3.55 persons per acre. This dropped to 2.96 people per acre in 1970 because of a population decrease. (The population declined from 870 in 1960 to 726 in 1970).

Occupational Data

Summerhill can be characterized as a working class community.

1978 statistics show 46% of the working force belonged to the laborer group; 30% to the service category; 5%, craftsmen; and 18%, professional.

The laborer group included miners, steelworkers, railroad employees. The service category counted business proprietors, policemen, waitresses, clerks, beauticians and the like. Craftsmen were the industrial workers who possess specialized skills like carpenters, electricians, plumbers, etc. Professional workers included ministers, nurses, teachers and all others who obtained academically-oriented skills by additional years of formal education.

Housing Study

Using the 1970 census of housing, Summerhill was credited with 207 housing units -- 152 owner-occupied; 45, renter-occupied; and 10, vacant but available.

Of the 197 occupied homes, 44% were one-and-two-person households; 16%, three-person; 13%, four-person; 10%, fiveperson; and 17%, six-or-more-persons.

The average household size was 3.6 persons compared to a county average of 2.9; 2.7, state; and 2.7, nation.

The most predominant housing units were four, five and six rooms. This made up 71% of the town's home uses.

The peak years of housing construction took place before 1939. The period produced 170 homes. Only 37 houses were constructed from 1940 to 1979.

The 1970 census also sampled 76% of the owner-occupied homes in Summerhill and placed the value of 50 homes at $5,000 or less; 26, from $5,000 to $7,499; and 31, between $7,500 and $14,999. Only nine homes were valued over $15,000.

The planning commission classified 183 properties in 1979 as standard (structures with complete plumbing facilities). 24 homes lacked some or all plumbing facilities.

Less than 1% were externally substandard. This, the report pointed out, indicates that property standards are high in the community. Compared to other areas, it said, the number of substandard housing units in Summerhill was rather low.

COMPARISON OF POPULATION GROUPS		
	1960	**1970**
Male	427	356
Female	443	380
Total	870	726
Under 5	116	63
5-14	175	163
15-24	121	113
25-34	106	70
35-44	110	75
45-54	84	85
55-64	75	73
65 & over	83	84

The 1980 census counted 348 males and 377 females. Summerhill's median age was 28.8 compared to 31.8 for Cambria County. 28% of the population (220 people) were under 18 years of age. Only 12% (89 people) were 65 years old or over.

Demographic Data For 1984

-- The average Summerhill per capita income rose to $6,774 in 1983 compared to $5,207 in 1977.

-- Summerhill's per capita income in 1983 was second highest of its three neighbors. Wilmore was first with $6,850; South Fork, third, $6,429; and Ehrenfeld, fourth, $6,140.

--The number of housing units in these four boroughs were: South Fork, 522; Summerhill, 252; Ehrenfeld, 125; and Wilmore, 107.

-- 71.3% of Summerhill's population were high school graduates and 7.5% were college graduates.

-- Only one housing unit in Summerhill lacked complete plumbing. Five were considered as overcrowded (1.01 or more persons per room).

-- The median value of an owner-occupied Summerhill home was $32,600.

-- The median rent was $165 a month.

The Summerhill of 1992

Summerhill is a clean, neat, well-kept, peaceful residential community of some 600 people.

The homes, mostly owner-occupied, have generally been renovated to modern architectural designs, both internally and externally. There are practically no signs of deterioration or abandonment. The scars evidenced in other communities which once prospered and now have lost their former pride are not visible in Summerhill.

To a large extent, Summerhill's pride of owner is due to the stability of family occupancies and that it was never an industrial town.

There is no crime problem. The most serious complaints involve noise and disturbances from teenagers.

There are two churches, both named St. John's -- one Lutheran and the other Catholic. Their steeples dominate the air over the town and are visible from many directions. A smaller church, now vacant, once served German Lutherans and still stands in the northern sector.

Conrail and Amtrak maintain an east-west right-of-way through the middle of Summerhill. The three-track mainline conveys passengers and freight but never stop. The thumping sounds and belching smoke of the steam locomotives have been replaced by quieter and cleaner diesel power. Their movements are the only major disruption of the quiet, peaceful atmosphere. But, residences, even those adjoining the tracks, are unaware of any disturbance.

The upper part of the borough was taken over in the 1960s for the construction of a new limited access, four-lane Route 219. It passes above houses in the northern section with an elevated roadway that forms a underpass on upper Jackson Street. This, also, does not disturb the town's tranquility.

On the positive side, the new highway provides Summerhill residents quick and easy access to shopping areas, places of employment and professional services. Medical and emergency services are available from the Forest Hills Ambulance Association housed within the borough. Most other needs are minutes away.

The business district has moved to the lower part of town, along Route 53. Just off the Route 219 interchange, the post office and eight businesses serve community and out-of-town customers.

The Jeep/Eagle new car dealer, two taverns and a convenience store are the only survivors of the former Main Street Railroad Station business area. The GBU and the firehall have located nearby.

Except for employment in local businesses, wage earners commute to jobs and positions in Johnstown, Ebensburg and neighboring areas.

The elementary school building is gone. Most students are bussed to the Forest Hills Schools in Sidman or at the top of the hill in Croyle Township.

The annual projects of a very active Women's Club are visible throughout the community.

A recreation organization conducts youth activities at the playground maintained by the borough on Ebensburg Road (the site of the former school building).

Summerhill is predominatly a Catholic community.

Voter registration favors Democrats, 226 to 92, over Republicans.

As one of 33 boroughs in Cambria County, Summerhill stands as one of the most attractive and financially sound. Its smallness and concentrated area makes coordination and agreement more feasible.

Summerhill has shown that it can prosper without an industrial tax base and offer an attractive place for comfortable living.